Teaching Philosophy

Teaching Philosophy

Theoretical Reflections and Practical Suggestions

EDITED BY TZIPORAH KASACHKOFF

ROWMAN & LITTLEFIELD PUBLISHERS, INC.
Lanham • Boulder • New York • Toronto • Oxford

Teaching Philosophy is an expanded edition of *In the Socratic Tradition*, edited by Tziporah Kasachkoff, copyright 1998 by Rowman & Littlefield Publishers. In addition to new chapters, text material has been updated throughout.

ROWMAN & LITTLEFIELD PUBLISHERS, INC.

Published in the United States of America
by Rowman & Littlefield Publishers, Inc.
A wholly owned subsidary of The Rowman & Littlefield Publishing Group, Inc.
4501 Forbes Boulevard, Suite 200, Lanham, Maryland 20706
www.rowmanlittlefield.com

PO Box 317, Oxford, OX2 9RU, UK

Chapters 7, 10, 23, 24, 26 Copyright © 2004 by Rowman & Littlefield Publishers, Inc.
Copyright © 1998 by Rowman & Littlefield Publishers, Inc.

British Library Cataloguing in Publication Information Available

Library of Congress Cataloging-in-Publication Data

Teaching philosophy : theoretical reflections and practical suggestions / edited by Tziporah Kasachkoff.
    p. cm.
  Expanded ed. of: In the Socratic tradition. c1998.
  Includes bibliographical references.
  ISBN 0-7425-1448-X (hardcover : alk. paper) — ISBN 0-7425-1449-8 (pbk. : alk. paper)
  1. Philosophy—Study and teaching. I. Kasachkoff, Tziporah, 1942– II. Kasachkoff, Tziporah, 1942– In the Socratic tradition.
  B52.I56 2004
  107'.1—dc22   2004003354

Printed in the United States of America
♾ The paper used in this publication meets the minimum requirements of American National Standard for Information Sciences—Permanence of Paper for Printed Library Materials, ANSI/NISO Z39.48-1992.

Contents

    Cahn describes four curriculum-defined approaches to
    introductory philosophy: the topical approach, the great
    texts approach, the historical approach, and the secondary
    source approach. He examines the disadvantages of each
    and makes recommendations as to how best to construct
    an introduction to philosophy course.

    Garver agrees with Cahn about the shortcomings of each
    of the four approaches to teaching introductory philoso-
    phy discussed in chapter 1, but has doubts about Cahn's
    suggested correctives. Garver suggests abandoning all
    four of the traditional approaches that Cahn describes and
    recommends the use of biographies as working texts for
    introductory philosophy courses. Garver describes how he
    uses such texts and makes bibliographical suggestions.

Responding to Cahn's and Garver's suggestions (chapters 1 and 2) about how best to construct an introduction to philosophy course, the authors argue for an introductory course that is structured around the analysis of a single philosophical topic.

Part II. Helping Our Students Improve

Cahn focuses on three common mistakes to which instructors, and especially beginning teachers, are prone and he makes practical suggestions for their remedy.

Adler offers guidelines to help introductory philosophy students learn to read a classic text so that they can grasp what the author is saying and come to see what makes the author's claims plausible.

Eflin suggests an exercise to help students write better philosophy papers despite large classes which often make personal commentary on each paper impossible. She describes the exercise, her grading criteria, her classroom procedure, the advantages afforded by the exercise, and some of the problems that can arise.

Figdor describes a method for helping students write better and learn more through a process of writing essay examinations in stages, with each stage open to revision and improvement.

Part III. Teaching Applied Ethics

Callahan discusses the content, focus, and goals for professional ethics courses and offers strategies for successfully engaging students in professional ethics study. She stresses the desirability of establishing a particular emotional tone in the classroom and suggests methods to structure class discussion.

Missner describes a game that clarifies for students the notion of self-interested action in the context of cooperative ventures. He explains how it helps students see what is involved in making the right decision in free-rider situations and remarks on some possible difficulties and drawbacks of using the exercise.

Part IV. Teaching Philosophy with Computers

Hinman describes how computers can be used in the classroom as an aid to teaching philosophy. He describes various software programs that he uses for this purpose and he indicates both the advantages and the pitfalls of each.

Part V. Teaching Aesthetics

Moore describes his use of the "case method" in teaching aesthetics and argues for its effectiveness in engaging student interest in, and encouraging discussion of, aesthetics problems. He presents sample cases and suggests questions concerning each that help to focus discussion on aesthetics issues.

Part VI. Teaching Philosophy of Religion

Pojman suggests eight topics that, he claims, cover the domain of philosophy of religion. These may be covered either in a semester-long course, or as part of a general introductory philosophy course. Pojman discusses methodology and materials for teaching these topics, and provides annotated bibliographical suggestions.

Martin comments on three different courses in philosophy and religion: an introductory course designed to acquaint students with philosophical issues connected with the Judeo-Christian tradition; a graduate-level seminar on philosophical issues connected with Christianity; and a middle-level seminar on religious epistemology.

Part VII. Teaching Critical Thinking

Moore suggests using egregious examples of pseudo-science to teach techniques of critical thinking. She explains the rationale for using such examples, supplies a summary of the course plan, and details a sample class exercise. She also offers readers advice on resources.

Gracyk describes the "portfolio" that he requires of his students—a compilation of twelve distinct items drawn from the student's own everyday reading matter, along with his or her reasoned assessment of each item. The portfolio helps students in critical thinking courses learn to apply critical thinking skills beyond the classroom.

Part VIII. Teaching Philosophy through History

McDermott argues not merely for the importance, but for the indispensability, of taking historical context into account when teaching philosophy (or any other subject, for that matter). He offers the reader a detailed illustration of the philosophical pedagogy for which he argues.

Part IX. Teaching Kant/Teaching Hegel

Westphal describes how he brings home to students, via understandable analogies, Kant's view of how a priori

synthetic propositions are possible, and what it means to
say that the forms and categories are conditions of possible experience.

Cadello suggests, as a visual aid for students, a chart that
helps them grasp the outline of Kant's system as he presents it in the *Critique* and *Prolegomena*. By use of examples, Cadello shows how to use the chart to clarify terminological distinctions made by Kant, and to identify
different levels of analysis.

McCumber reviews some of the difficulties in teaching Hegel and some of the reasons Hegel is profitably
taught nonetheless. He offers suggestions as to how to
present Hegel to students and includes useful bibliographical references.

Westphal describes two "strategic" moves he uses in
teaching Hegel's *Philosophy of Right*. He explains the way
in which these moves illuminate Hegel's views and the
advantages of presenting Hegel's political philosophy in
this way.

**Part X. Teaching Existentialism/
Teaching Continental Philosophy**

Kelly details four ways to approach the teaching of existentialism. He suggests both rationales and sources for

these various approaches. Kelly notes the difficulty of teaching existentialism in a way that truly conveys its spirit, and offers suggestions as to how instrutors might deal with this difficulty.

Daniel reports on a course that he has developed in current Continental Philosophy. He argues for including various writers often left out of such courses and for stressing certain particular themes. In addition, he provides bibliographical suggestions for both primary and secondary sources and describes how he structures the course within the framework of one semester.

Part XI. Teaching Philosophical Explanation

Martens describes a method for teaching students how to recognize, construct, and evaluate philosophical inferences to the best explanation—a method that is adaptable for various sorts of philosophy courses. Martins offers readers concrete examples that illustrate the method.

Part XII. Teaching Philosophy of Gender

Wolf-Devine describes a course designed to acquaint students with the philosophical issues concerning gender differences. She describes the goals of the course, how she structures her own course on the topic, and the problems one is likely to encounter in such a course and how one might deal with them. She also offers specific and detailed

pedagogical techniques that help to encourage and structure classroom discussion of gender issues. Throughout,
Wolf-Devine gives detailed suggestions for readings relevant to each topic covered in the course.

XIII. Looking at What We Do in the Classroom

Weston describes a philosophy of education course that he
teaches for upper-level undergraduates. The chief aim of
the course is to have students draw out and examine the
presuppositions of specific forms of pedagogy as well as
of education in general.

Benjamin details his seminar on how to teach students to
become better teachers of philosophy. He includes his
seminar syllabus, the writing assignments, and complete
bibliographical information.

Acknowledgments

Below is the issue in which each article (or version thereof) appeared in the *American Philosophical Association Newsletter on Teaching Philosophy.*

- Chapter 1, "Teaching Introductory Philosophy," by Steven M. Cahn: fall 1986.
- Chapter 2, "Introducing Philosophy," by Newton Garver: January 1988.
- Chapter 3, "Teaching Introductory Philosophy—A Topical Approach," by Alan White and Jo A. Chern (under the title "Thinking, Writing, and Introductory Philosophy—A Topical Approach"): winter 1991.
- Chapter 4, "How To Improve Your Teaching," by Steven M. Cahn: June 1988.
- Chapter 5, "Reading and Interpretation: A Heuristic for Improving Students' Comprehension of Philosophy Texts," by Jonathan Adler (under the title "Reading and Interpretation"): fall 1994.
- Chapter 6, "Improving Student Papers in 'Introduction to Philosophy' Courses," by Juli Eflin: spring 1994.
- Chapter 7, "Using Essay Exams to Teach and Not Merely to Assess," by Carrie Figdor (under the title "Essay Exams as a Process, not Merely a Product"): spring 2003 (vol. 02, no. 2).
- Chapter 8, "From the 'Applied' to the Practical: Teaching Ethics for Use," by Joan Callahan: fall 1990.
- Chapter 9, "A Social Dilemma Game for an Ethics Class," by Marshall Missner: spring 1994.
- Chapter 10, "Teaching With a Screen," by Lawrence M. Hinman: spring 2003 (vol. 02, no. 2).
- Chapter 11, "The Case Method Approach to Teaching Aesthetics," by Ronald Moore: November 1987.
- Chapter 12, "Teaching Philosophy of Religion (either as a course in its own right or as part of an 'Introduction to Philosophy')," by

Louis Pojman (under the title "Teaching Philosophy of Religion"): spring 1990.
- Chapter 13, "Three Courses in Philosophy and Religion," by Michael Martin: fall 1997.
- Chapter 14, "Using Pseudoscience in a Critical Thinking Class," by Kathleen Dean Moore: summer 1987.
- Chapter 15, "A Critical Thinking Portfolio," by Theodore A. Gracyk: fall 1991.
- Chapter 16, "The Teaching of Philosophy—Historically," by John J. McDermott: fall 1988.
- Chapter 17, "A User-Friendly Copernican Revolution," by Merold Westphal: fall 1993 (92, no. 2).
- Chapter 18, "Charting Kant," by James Cadello: fall 1993 (92, no. 2).
- Chapter 19, "Teaching Hegel: Problems and Possibilities," by John McCumber: fall 1993 (92, no. 2).
- Chapter 20 "Hegel and Family Values," by Merold Westphal: fall 1993 (92, no. 2).
- Chapter 21, "Teaching Existentialism," by Eugene Kelly (under the title "The Existentialist in the Classroom"): spring 1993.
- Chapter 22, "Teaching Recent Continental Philosophy," by Stephen H. Daniel (under the title "Current Continental Philosophy: A Comprehensive Approach"): spring 1993.
- Chapter 23, "Teaching 'Inference to the Best Philosophical Explanation," by David Martens: fall 2003 (vol. 03, no. 1).
- Chapter 24, "Teaching Gender Issues Philosophically," by Celia Wolf-Devine: spring 2004 (vol. 03, no. 2).
- Chapter 25, "Uncovering the 'Hidden Curriculum': A Laboratory Course in Philosophy of Education," by Anthony Weston: winter 1991.
- Chapter 26, "A Graduate Seminar on Teaching Philosophy," by Martin Benjamin: fall 2003 (vol. 03, no. 1).

Note of Gratitude:
This book is dedicated to Richard Hogan, whose talents as a philosopher and as a philosophy teacher have been an inspiring model for me. I am also indebted to Steven M. Cahn for his good advice on this (as on other) projects.

Introduction

Tziporah Kasachkoff

Philosophy continues as an academic discipline because philosophers earn their living, for the most part, by being teachers of philosophy. And yet the nature of what we do in the classroom has, until recently, rarely been perceived as an issue worthy of philosophical discussion. Even today, philosophers are much more willing to share their philosophical views and have others read their philosophical papers than they are either to talk about how they teach philosophy or have others observe them teach.

In the first edition of this book (titled *In the Socratic Tradition: Essays on Teaching Philosophy*) I attributed our reticence to talk about our classroom performance to the low status accorded philosophers working in "applied philosophy." I noted that as late as only three decades ago many philosophers saw engagement in applied philosophy as a departure—indeed, an illegitimate departure—from the only task that some in our recent philosophic past saw as an appropriate philosophical task, namely, "pure" analysis, with only issues abstracted from culture and time deemed worthy of philosophical reflection. On this view, the point of philosophical reflection was only intellectual clarification, not normative elucidation, the analysis of concepts and not the giving of normative answers. Philosophy could, of course, concern itself with the elucidation of what it *means* for something to be a normative rule, but, so it was argued, it was not within its province to determine and specify the norms we ought to endorse.

We have seen enormous changes over the past few years. One has only to note the appearance of the myriad articles and the proliferation of courses in such subjects as bioethics, legal ethics, police ethics, the ethics of journalism, environmental ethics, the ethics of computer use, and feminist ethics, to realize just how far academic philosophy has come in conferring legitimacy to topics that were hitherto considered beyond its purview. This has, of course, been good for discussions concerning the teaching of philosophy, for teaching philosophy and discussions about how to teach philosophy are unabashedly *not* value-free enterprises: how we teach what we teach, the range of issues we deem appropriate to include in our syllabi and to emphasize, the pedagogic methods we adopt, the notion we have of what constitutes progress and sophistication in philosophy, and our view of how best to foster and to test for these—all reflect our notion of what philosophy itself is and so manifest a normative perspective concerning the nature of philosophy. Our believing that certain ways of teaching philosophy would not be to teach philosophy at all reflects our view that teachers of philosophy are not value-neutral pedagogic technicians trying to impart predesigned packages of information and skills but shapers of an educational process and representatives of certain values (not all of them intellectual). We have come to recognize that in helping to set the goals of philosophical education, as well as in having a hand in implementing them, we do not merely carry out programs that cater to interests already present. Rather, we take it as our task to *create* interests and to fulfill (what we believe to be) laudable aims. There is thus an undeniable normative dimension to our teaching, our pedagogic choices reflecting our view of the character of philosophy and being those we believe necessary for that character to be preserved. Thus, in talking about the teaching of philosophy, no less than when we do applied philosophy, we are not engaged in the value-free reasoning that, according to some philosophers, should set our work apart from—some might even say "above"—the messy affair of making actual practical choices.

Furthermore, just as the writing about, and teaching of, applied philosophy has now gained popularity despite the once loudly-voiced objection that since we do not all "do" applied philosophy against the background of the same theoretical framework, the field is devoid of the theoretical credentials that could confer upon it philosophical respectability, so too, writing about and discussing the teaching of philosophy has gained popularity despite the fact that there is no single—and perhaps not even any—educational or pedagogic theory from which all of our views about how best to teach our subject invariably emanate.

But one source of resistance to viewing discussions concerning the teaching of philosophy as not worth philosophers' attention is unique to it and has not abated with philosophical acceptance of applied philosophy as worthy of philosophical reflection. Though almost all of us teach our subject, it is only "doing" philosophy for which our university education and training prepares us. As a result, our expertise (and confidence) as philosophers does not signify our talent and ease as teachers of the subject. Notwithstanding the fact that some of our best-known philosophers—Socrates, Plato, and Kant, for example—were also good teachers of their subject and had much to say about good teaching, good philosophy and good philosophy teaching are not natural corollaries. It was precisely the recognition of this fact that, early on, led Michael Scriven, Steven M. Cahn, Terrell Ward Bynum, and Martin Benjamin to begin exhorting their teaching colleagues to find ways to make particular philosophical issues comprehensible and interesting to our students, to construct good philosophy exams, and to improve our course syllabi. This recognition also led the American Philosophical Association, in the early 1970s, to begin to give emphasis to two-year-college teaching in philosophy; to include a session titled "Workshop on the Teaching of Philosophy" in its annual divisional meetings; to begin publication in 1974 of the *Newsletter on Teaching Philosophy;* and to establish in 1977 a standing Committee on the Teaching of Philosophy. It also led (in 1971) to the regular inclusion in *Metaphilosophy* of a section titled "The Philosopher as Teacher"; to the founding (in 1972) of *Aitia,* a magazine devoted in part to articles on the teaching of philosophy; to the establishment (in 1975) of the journal *Teaching Philosophy;* and to the publication (in 1979) of *Thinking,* a journal devoted to articles on the teaching of philosophy to children. All of these developments served to spur the growing interest in the promotion and improvement of teaching philosophy that in the late 1970s spawned the American Association of Philosophy Teachers, an organization devoted exclusively to the advancement and improvement of philosophy teaching.[1]

This history makes clear that, despite the reluctance of many philosophers to publicly address their role as teachers of philosophy, there has been a growing recognition both that the teaching of philosophy requires separate attention and that the problems of teaching philosophy are an appropriate concern for philosophers themselves. This recognition is reflected in the fact that there are at present two universities that require their doctoral students in philosophy to take a course or seminar in teaching philosophy and some other universities that offer a course in teaching philosophy as a recommended option for students who are planning a career in teaching the subject. (The syllabus for one such course, offered by Martin Benjamin, is included in this volume.)

In the present collection of papers—six of which are new additions to the anthology—the reader will find suggestions for good teaching that are distilled from the practical and personal experience of their authors. They include: how to teach and what to cover regarding specific philosophical topics (such as continental philosophy, existentialism, Kant's critique of pure reason, Aesthetics, and Hegel); methods to help students hone their ability to think critically; advice on both what to cover and what *not* to convey in a professional ethics course; how to structure and the topics best covered in a Philosophy of Religion course; how to use specific examples and exercises to help students come to understand and evaluate 'inference to the best philosophical explanation' arguments; suggestions concerning the various ways in which one might construct an introductory course in philosophy; advice on how to sequence and what bibliographical sources to use in a course on the history of philosophy; pedagogical strategies one might use and bibliographical sources one might draw upon for a course on philosophy of gender; the ways in which one might use the computer as an aid to teaching and the computer software programs that might be especially helpful in the teaching of logic and of ethics, exercises one might use to guide students in their reading of original philosophical texts; ways in which one might use essay examinations to help students learn more and write better; a writing assignment that can be used despite the inability of the instructor to comment personally on each student's paper; and finally, suggestions for encouraging students to reflect on both teaching in general and teaching philosophy in particular.

With one exception, each of the chapters in this volume began as an informal paper, contributed to the *APA Newsletter on Teaching Philosophy*, for the purpose of sharing with like-minded colleagues ways to better the teaching of our subject. Most have been revised (some quite extensively) for this volume. The spirit in which they are offered here remains the same—as an invitation and, perhaps, as an incentive to help us become better teachers of philosophy and our students better learners of the subject.

NOTES

1. For a detailed summary of the development of interest in the teaching of philosophy in America between 1965 and 1985, see Terrell Ward Bynum's two-part article, "The Renewal of Interest in Philosophy Teaching in America: Developments from 1965 to 1985," *APA Newsletter on Teaching Philosophy* (fall 1986) and *APA Newsletter on Teaching Philosophy* 88, no. 2 (March 1989).

PART I
Introducing Students to Philosophy

Chapter 1

Teaching Introductory Philosophy

Steven M. Cahn

Instructors usually structure introductory philosophy courses in one of four ways. The first uses readings grouped by topic and drawn from historical and contemporary sources. Students thereby become acquainted with major problems of philosophy, read important historical and contemporary writings on each subject, and are encouraged to think through issues for themselves. Historical philosophers are given a word but not the last word; contemporary philosophers are seen as innovators but not creators ex nihilo.

This approach, however, has its pitfalls. As students shift quickly from Aristotle to Locke to Rawls, they are tempted to treat these authors as contemporaries. Students can also lose hold of the threads that are supposed to connect the selections. Furthermore, excerpts taken out of context can be difficult to understand. Most important, the approach may do a disservice to major historical figures, since reading a few pages from a philosophical classic is somewhat akin to listening to a few measures from a great symphony—the overall effect is typically disappointing.

An alternative curriculum consists of studying several major historical works in their totality. An immediate advantage is that most students are more easily motivated to read a classic by a renowned thinker rather than an article by a recent scholar unfamiliar to them. Most great works of the past, unlike contemporary journal articles, were not intended only for specialists. They embody a breadth of vision that has inspired generations, and reading these works in their entirety is intellectually satisfying.

This approach, however, also has its disadvantages. It suggests that philosophy is mainly the contemplation of works written long ago. Students may be led to suppose that their sole obligation is to grasp what others have said, not to think critically. This problem is magnified by the need to spend much time and effort struggling with unfamiliar terminology and trying to understand the concerns that motivated our intellectual forebearers. Philosophy can thus be turned into a passive tour of the past rather than an active inquiry of present importance. One further difficulty is that in jumping from one classic to another a student hurdles centuries and is in danger of losing historical perspective. On the reading list Hobbes's *Leviathan* may follow Plato's *Republic,* but in history two millennia intervened, and students unacquainted with what occurred during that period, even if only in philosophical thought, are apt to have a distorted view of how these works relate. Furthermore, the fewer works read in such a course, the greater the danger of student boredom. An instructor may delight in spending fifteen weeks studying Descartes's *Meditations,* but for the uninitiated the experience may be excruciating.

A third format offers a systematic study of the history of philosophy with emphasis on historical perspective. Students are apt to be excited by the array of great books and ideas. But beginners may not appreciate that philosophy is an ongoing enterprise and that its practitioners do not primarily pore over ancient texts but read contemporary journals and analyze contemporary issues. Philosophy, after all, is not just the history of philosophy.

A fourth format uses a single-authored textbook written with a student audience in mind. The obvious difficulty, however, is that, unlike physics or chemistry, philosophy does not consist of a body of accepted truths and one author can hardly do justice to all competing viewpoints. Why should students be reading a textbook when they could be reading original materials? Granted, philosophy may be difficult to understand and a textbook can ease the strain, but philosophical disagreement is best grasped by confronting various authors of diverse styles and opinions, not by reading homogenized textbooks. And one designed to avoid giving the impression of uniformity is apt to confuse students, leading them to wonder why the author appears indecisive.

In the face of these difficulties inherent in any introductory course, how should a teacher proceed? The key is to be aware of the pitfalls inherent in whichever approach is chosen.

If instructors prefer a problem-oriented format, they should recognize the need to supply historical perspective and links between articles. Students can be reminded that the great philosophers wrote books, not five-page excerpts, and can also be told something about the books from which the selections are chosen.

If instructors prefer a classics format, they should recognize the need to make clear that philosophical inquiry did not cease centuries ago, that philosophers continue to work on issues that concerned Leibniz or Hume, that we read these authors not to venerate them, but to help ourselves think more clearly about issues facing us today. Students also need to be reminded that the authors chosen lived at different historical times and were influenced by them.

If instructors prefer a historical format, students should be encouraged to approach the material with a critical attitude. And they need to be alerted to contemporary discussions of traditional issues as found in recent books and journals.

If instructors choose a single-authored textbook, students ought to be reminded of the availability of perspectives other than that provided by one author. And an attempt should be made to stress the importance of historical writings in helping us think about today's problems.

Whichever format is chosen, a teacher should explain the available options and indicate the reasons behind a curricular decision. Students will then be less likely to identify philosophy with one particular approach. And this insight itself will provide increased understanding of the complex subject to which they are being introduced.

Chapter 2

Introducing Philosophy

Newton Garver

I have taught all four courses that Steven M. Cahn describes in "Teaching Introductory Philosophy," and I have felt the shortcomings he correctly attributes to each. He may be right that the key to successful teaching of these courses is "to be aware of the pitfalls inherent in whatever approach is chosen." In my own classes, however, I have found it easier to be aware of the pitfalls than to find effective corrective measures.

In my experience, the pitfalls Cahn describes have been exacerbated by the inadequate preparation with which students arrive at the halls of higher education. Our university entrants have normally had no previous study of philosophical texts, no teachers who have even informally exposed them to philosophical thinking, no sense of a difference between philosophy and ideology, and no inkling of a kind of study and discipline that does not consist in the accumulation and marshaling of facts. But these inadequacies have been givens for decades, and the reason we need to introduce philosophy at an introductory level is precisely to overcome these traditional gaps. A further problem I encountered in the 1970s and early 1980s was decreasing student competence in reading and writing. Contributing to this are a restricted and pampered vocabulary, a reluctance to use a dictionary, befuddlement (almost never fascination or playfulness) with double negatives and other elementary logical transformations of everyday speech, limited attention span, and no patience for working through difficult texts. In addition, there is an expectation of being entertained, atrocious spelling, ignorance of the principles of punctuation (with a dozen errors not uncommon on a page of typescript), and almost no sense of paragraphs as units of thought and expression (although in very short papers this is somewhat mitigated by the well-learned lesson that an essay needs an introduction, a body, and a conclusion). It is my experience that these serious deficiencies make the pitfalls of the four traditional approaches described by Cahn increasingly difficult to overcome.

I have found that the key to devising a course under these conditions is to recognize two things. First, philosophy is not a body of doctrine, nor even a body of texts, but rather a kind of activity, namely a way of approaching doctrines or texts. Second, because this sort of activity requires certain language skills, introducing students to philosophy requires that the students receive some substantial training in the relevant language skills. This recognition has led me gradually to abandon all four traditional approaches that Cahn describes. In particular, I have abandoned not only all pretension to being comprehensive or systematic in the introductory course—most of us abandoned that long ago—but also the idea that there is any particular material or problems or texts that constitute the proper foundation for the study of philosophy. So the books I assign need not even be "philosophy" books—and they are not.

The principal book assigned has been Blanshard's *Four Reasonable Men*,[1] of which Blanshard himself says in the preface, "This book is not philosophy, but biography." I will not be so bold as to dispute Blanshard's characterization of his own work. I must add, however, that it is biography with a philosophical flavor. The four "reasonable" men about whom Blanshard writes are Marcus Aurelius, Ernest Renan, John Stuart Mill, and Henry Sidgwick—whom Blanshard characterizes as follows: "an emperor of the civilized world, a poverty-stricken son of a Breton fisherman, an intellectual boy-wonder who barely survived his Draconian education, and a modest Cambridge professor of the Victorian era." As can be imagined, in Blanshard's biographical sketches of these men there is quite enough philosophical meat to introduce students to philosophy.

There is, of course, the danger that some students will pay more attention to biographical than to philosophical details, and I confess to being dismayed by the repeated attempts to make something profound out of Marcus's reaction to the treachery of Avidius or out of Mill's relations with Harriet Taylor. I sympathize with colleagues who wish to avoid diluting their courses with such details. My own judgment is that biographies help both to attract attention to concepts and abstract truths and to show philosophizing as a human activity. Confining the exams and assigned papers to philosophical issues can minimize the dangers of distraction.

Apart from its theme, *Four Reasonable Men* has three important merits in this context. The first is that it is well written. The second merit is that Blanshard is clearly not proselytizing. He is, of course, in favor of being reasonable, and does not pretend to hide his commitment on that score. The point is rather that he chooses as examples of reasonable men thinkers against whose substantive views he would argue, and has argued, in a more philosophical work. He rejects the disdain of feelings in Marcus Aurelius and his doctrine of determinism, the empiricism and utilitarianism of Mill, the hedonism and the intuitionism that Sidgwick embraces. So there is little danger that being reasonable will be confused with subscribing to a certain philosophical theory or to a narrow set of principles. Finally, perhaps the greatest merit is the interweaving of the lives and the thoughts of these men, so that there is constantly a concrete person, a biography, to enliven each abstract idea. Even Plato mixed personalities and ideas, but it is particularly important to do so, I have found, when dealing with students who lack patience for sustained argument and easy engagement with abstract ideas.

Fortunately *Four Reasonable Men* is as appropriate in its theme and content as in its style. A consideration of what it means for these men to be reasonable leads naturally into traditional philosophical questions. Marcus Aurelius, for example, is a determinist, but at the same time articulating a profound ethical view. How can one be a determinist and also have any sense of what *ought* to be done? Part of the answer lies in his belief that moral behavior has more to do with resignation (to whatever fate brings) than with action—but this position raises new questions about whether such resignation is a satisfactory moral view, or whether it is even a moral rather than a religious view. What is the difference between religion and morality?

Discussion of the nature of morality and religion, which arises in connection with the Stoicism of Marcus, comes up again in connection with Henry Sidgwick. Sidgwick considered the problem of ethical egoism central to moral philosophy; but although he believed it to be incompatible with sound morality as well as with Christianity, he was unable to find any convincing arguments against ethical egoism. Blanshard reports that he therefore avoided discussions with his nephew while the nephew was a student at Cambridge, lest the discussions undermine his nephew's Christian faith or his good character, or both. So one question to discuss in this connection is whether, if one rejects egoism, that rejection must be based on religious or nonrational grounds rather than on rational or philosophical arguments. Sidgwick's consideration of ethical egoism also provides a context for class discussion of various related issues, such as the plausibility of psychological hedonism (which Bentham endorsed and Mill seems to have rejected), the contrast between psychological and ethical egoism, and the contrast between ethical hedonism and the brand of utilitarianism that John Stuart Mill advocated.

Other philosophical questions to which the question of what it means to be reasonable are raised by Blanshard's account of Renan, who rejected miracles as supernatural events—a view that, incorporated into the naturalistic account of the origins of Christianity in his immensely popular *Life of Jesus*, cost Renan his prestigious appointment at the Collège de France. Here discussion may focus on whether it is reasonable to believe in purely random events or, alternatively, in events that are not the result of natural causes but rather of supernatural powers.

Clearly, the theme of reasonableness set in the context of biography is rich enough not only to fill the hours of the course but also to allow wide variation among instructors and from semester to semester.

Blanshard's book makes a good text for six to ten weeks, depending on how closely one looks at the issues and whether one includes (as I have not) the book's final chapter on prejudice. I believe that any slower reading of the book would exceed the average limits of student patience and attention span. After eight weeks, furthermore, turning to a new text serves as a new beginning, and can thereby help to regain any flagging attention. I see quite a range of possibilities, each providing a natural sequel. One might, for example, choose one of Sissela Bok's books, such as *Lying*[2] or *Strategy for Peace*,[3] or one of Mary Midgley's, such as *Beast and Man*[4] or *Wickedness*,[5] or a minor classic, such as one of the shorter works of Leibniz (say, *Monadology* or *Principles of Nature and Grace*) or Rousseau (perhaps *Essay on the Origin of Language*) or Berkeley (one of the *Three Dialogues*, or perhaps the *Essay Towards a New Theory of Vision*)—not books that would ordinarily seem to be textbooks but which have meat enough for a more focused discussion of what it means to think reasonably. In making the choice of text here, I believe that an engaging and accessible style is as important as meaty matter. I began rather timidly using Elmer Sprague's *What Is Philosophy?*[6] as a supplement, since it seemed usefully pedestrian, systematic, cautiously technical, and consciously written for students. But the students found it less accessible than Blanshard or Midgley, and that has put me off "pedagogic" material. I now choose something I would not hesitate to recommend to a friend or colleague as a good book to read and think about.

Although my own particular choices are less important (and more variable) than the criterion just presented, the story would be incomplete without them. One of them is somewhat dramatic: the story of Franz Jägerstätter. Franz Jägerstätter was an Austrian peasant from St. Radegund in the diocese of Linz, married and father of three small children, who became both devoutly Christian and passionately anti-Nazi in the late 1930s, and was beheaded for refusing military service in 1943.[7] I arrange for my students to see excerpts from the ninety-minute award-winning Austrian TV docudrama,[8] based on Zahn's biography, that tells the story from Jägerstätter's refusal to serve in the Nazi army to his execution, with contemporary comments from his widow and others who knew him. The case is interesting for two reasons. For one thing, it extends the discussion of conscience, and of the relation of conscience and reason—introduced in Blanshard's book by a consideration of the way in which both Renan and Sidgwick lost appointments because of forthright and unconventional stands they took. Jägerstätter lost his head, which is more dramatic, but the issue remains pretty much the same. The issue—which seems to me perennial and recurring rather than soluble—is how conformity, accommodation, deviance, per-sonal responsibility, and sanity are connected with being reasonable. These are all matters of interest to undergraduates, as well as matters that lend themselves to philosophical discussion that is both rich and solid. I find it an advantage for purposes of such a course that Jägerstätter had, among other considerations, a simple unsophisti-cated argument for his refusal, which is apparently reasonable, because of its combination of logical validity and plausible premises. It can be represented as follows:

> It is impermissible knowingly to kill harmless and innocent people.
> Fighting in a war for an unjust cause involves doing just that;
> The Nazi cause is unjust;
> *So* it is impermissible [for me] to fight for the Nazi cause.

While there are problems about how one's personal knowledge and awareness bear upon one's moral duties,[9] this argument is a splendid example of practical reasoning. The first premise, a Roman Catholic dogma with special authority for Jägerstätter (a devout believer), has independent appeal to most students—and at the very least is worth discussing. The second premise derives from the view that in a war of unprovoked aggression (that is, an unjust war)—which was how Jägerstätter (rightly) perceived Hitler's war—the people being at-tacked (even the soldiers) are innocent, and would have been harmless if it had not been for their taking measures to defend themselves against the aggression. The just war doctrine is, of course, worth dis-cussing among students. From all accounts, Jägerstätter as a *person* was apparently rational; but since he clearly understood that steadfast refusal to "adjust" to his community and his times would cost him his life, it can be argued that he was not being entirely "reasonable."[10] I have found it worth discussing whether, although conscience draws most attention in instances of deviance, every rational person must act in conformity with his or her conscience, and, conversely, whether everyone who acts on the basis of con-science thereby acts rationally. Dramatizing the discussion of these questions with the cases of Renan, Sidgwick, and Jägerstätter helps to bring home to my students the moral importance and human interest of these philosophical questions.

Another text I often use is Robert Axelrod's *The Evolution of Cooperation*.[11] The book is a full-length treatment of an extension of the two-person variable-sum game called "Prisoner's Dilemma," so named because of a story about two prisoners. In that story two men are arrested and charged with a felony, although the district attorney has enough evidence to convict them of only a misdemeanor, leaving the felony unresolved. The district attorney therefore holds the men in separate cells and interviews them separately, proposing to each that he can expect a lighter sentence (or none) if he rats on the other. Here is the deal, with A's payoffs listed first:

	A is silent	A rats on B
B is silent	6 mo./6 mo.	Free/5 yr.
B rats on A	5 yr./Free	2 yr./2 yr.

Inspection of the payoff matrix shows that A does better by ratting on B (only two years instead of five years, or going free instead of six months), and B similarly does better by ratting on A. *But*, if *either* of them rats on the other, the total time spent in prison by the pair is vastly increased—from one year total (six months plus six months) to four years or five years. The fact that the total time in prison is not fixed in advance, but varies depending on the choices made, makes this a *variable-sum* rather than a fixed-sum or zero-sum game. Variable-sum games reflect the fact that our lives often depend not only on our own choices but also, to some extent, on the choices of others. The Prisoner's Dilemma, in the classical form represented in the story, is a variable-sum game that casts a gloomy light on cooperation: it suggests that in some circumstances it is rational for individuals to betray their comrades, even though cooperation would produce better results for the group as a whole.

One of the advantages of the story is that plea bargaining is a familiar and controversial topic, and the story does illustrate the dilemma about individual choice and social benefits. But there are several factors that make the story less than ideal for scholarly purposes: (1) the Prisoner's Dilemma is one of a large number of two-person games that scholars compare, but here there is a third person (the district attorney) whose decisions can also alter the payoffs; (2) the payoffs here have to do with penalties, whereas we more often think of payoffs in positive terms; (3) there is a legendary "honor among thieves" that adds very heavy penalties, which are not built into the matrix, for ratting on a fellow gang member; (4) "ratting" and "betrayal" are emotionally loaded terms, apt to cloud a purely utilitarian consideration of the dilemma; and (5) ideological views about plea bargaining can similarly divert attention from the dilemma itself. Scholarly discussions therefore proceed in terms of an abstract matrix that represents the positive payoffs of A and B either cooperating or defecting, with A's payoffs again listed first:

	A cooperates	A defects
B cooperates	3/3	5/0
B defects	0/5	1/1

Inspection of the matrix again paints a gloomy picture, in this case that A and B each does better by "defecting" rather than co-operating. The results seem devastating to ordinary morality, for they seem to demonstrate that cooperators always lose—that "Nice guys finish last," to put it in the words of a famous football coach—and that social life without artificial penalties and constraints is apt to be, as Hobbes put it, "solitary, poor, nasty, brutish, and short."[12]

Axelrod's study begins by noting that, in the original formulation, the dilemma is divorced from past and future, since each player chooses to defect or cooperate on just one occasion. The extension considered by Axelrod, called the "Iterated Prisoner's Dilemma," eschews the focus on a single action and examines instead the consequences of each player choosing a *strategy* designed to win the most points *in the long run*. In the Iterated Prisoner's Dilemma, it is not possible to determine the best strategy just by examining the payoff matrix—nor by any simple calculation. Axelrod therefore organized a tournament, inviting specialists in policy studies and game theory to submit strategies that they thought might win the tournament. Taking into account prior moves of its adversary, each strategy played a "match" against each other strategy, a match consisting of about 200 "games" (where a "game" consists of one simultaneous choice by each player). The "winner" of the tournament would not be the strategy that won most matches but the one that accumulated most *points* over the whole tournament, so it was theoretically possible (though most contestants did not think it likely) that a strategy could win the tournament without winning many matches.

The winning strategy in the tournament had the rather nasty name of "Tit for Tat," but it was really more nice than mean. It is a very simple strategy: cooperate in the first game; in each subsequent game, do whatever the other player did in the immediately previous game. It was submitted by Anatol Rapoport, whose underlying idea about rationality is that there are many circumstances in which it is unreasonable (counterproductive, you might say) for an ambitious egoist to try to achieve a better result than another ambitious egoist—notably ongoing variable-sum games in which there is every reason to think that you and your adversary are equally matched. In such circumstances it is rational to *help* your adversary to achieve as good a result as is compatible with your also doing well. In the Iterated Prisoner's Dilemma tournament, this conception of reasonableness implies not trying to exploit the other strategy and avoiding being exploited oneself, thereby keeping the scores as much as possible in the upper left-hand cell of the matrix. To avoid exploiting the other, Tit for Tat always cooperated in the first game and never started a round of defecting. To avoid being exploited, Tit for Tat always retaliated in the very next game, whenever its adversary defected. The ideal result for Tit for Tat would be a tie, with each getting 600 points (3 points for each of 200 games); the worst result would be that Tit for Tat would lose by 5 points, through the other player defecting and then continuing to defect, with Tit for Tat getting 199 points and its adversary getting 204. Thus Tit for Tat could tie or lose a match, but *never win* one; yet it won the tournament by garnering *more points* than any other entry.

These results raise interesting questions—ones that intrigue students because of the way variable-sum games make it possible to win tournaments without ever winning "matches." Are there social structures analogous to the structure of the Iterated Prisoner's Dilemma? How can one recognize them? What is the nature of trust and loyalty, and when are they appropriate? Is "defecting" a kind of betrayal, or just good sense? What should be the balance between concern for security (not being exploited) and loyalty to others (cooperation)? How might we decide when distrust, which might procure security in the short run, will be self-defeating in the long run? When does cooperation become an act of conspiracy or restraint of trade, or even treason? Under what conditions would cooperation be morally bad even though profitable?

One merit of Axelrod's book is that it deals with problems of political philosophy and social organization, topics that, in Blanshard's book, are treated less frequently than problems of metaphysics, epistemology, and ethics. It also introduces students to the difference between fixed-sum and variable-sum games, and it makes students appreciate that there are different sorts of social structures, about which different things have to be said. This is a lesson they will be able to make use of throughout their education and into their adult lives. That the winner turns out to be a cooperative strategy that *never* wins a match is well worth pondering, for it has implications about what it can mean to be reasonable in social situations. Moreover, questions about the apparent conflict between cooperation (altruism) and self-interest (egoism) are of intrinsic as well as practical interest.

The other two texts I use are selections from Martin Luther King and Simone Weil, which return us to the combination of ideas and biography. In the case of King, "Letter from Birmingham Jail" is an obvious choice because it both recounts a prominent event in King's life and conveys a passionate defense of civil disobedience.[13] The question raised by civil disobedience extends the discussion of conscience and provides a stimulating context for testing how one understands what it means to be reasonable. In the case of Weil,[14] I alternate between her two essays "The *Iliad*, Poem of Force" and "Human Personality."[15] The first essay not only acquaints students with one of the classics of world literature but also serves to deepen their consideration of the difference between a zero-sum activity (war) and cooperative activity (home life in civil society), a contrast that Weil emphasizes. The second essay probes vexing issues about the competing values of collectivities and individual personality, raising questions about what it is reasonable for society to demand of us. The use of these texts helps to deepen the discussion of what it means to be reasonable, as well as to broaden the range of philosophic writing with which students may become acquainted.

In his article, Cahn does not discuss written requirements, but it is certainly not a matter that can be taken for granted. The written requirements for the introductory course in philosophy have proved as difficult for me as for my students. Teachers are expected to require the equivalent of ten pages of typescript from each student each semester (toward which essay exams may contribute a fraction). At first I required one paper eight to ten pages long but, with no practice in writing philosophy and in some cases no practice in writing essays at all, students were unable to produce satisfactory results. So I revised the requirement, first to two shorter papers, then to five exegetic papers of one to two pages each, and finally to three two-page papers with specific assigned topics. I do not record credit for any paper that contains significant errors of spelling, punctuation, grammar, paragraphing, or relevance—which means, of course, that a majority of the papers are rewritten at least once. So

Philosophy 101 has become more and more like a writing course, with added emphasis on coherence and relevance.

My quizzes and exams have two parts, one part requiring exposition and the other part requiring conceptual explanation. In the first part I expect students to be able to write a coherent expository essay on topics that have come up in texts and class discussions. This expectation is standard and my experience with it is unremarkable. In the other part I expect students to be able to explain clearly and effectively the concepts that figure in the texts and lectures. In detailed instructions and in class practice, I try to make clear that such explanation should be concise (not encyclopedic) and contain three complementary components: a straightforward definition, a contrast or polar opposite of the concept or idea being defined, and an example that illustrates the concept. For example, I expect something like the following as explanations of ethical egoism and determinism:

Ethical egoism is the philosophical theory that I ought to act to maximize my own ends. It contrasts with psychological egoism (or: with utilitarianism or altruism). Hedonism and self-realization are forms of ethical egoism. Determinism is the philosophical theory that whatever happens *has* to happen. Both rational choice and randomness contrast with determinism. Marcus Aurelius was a determinist. My object is that students be able to say *what* it is that we have been talking about, without rambling and without material that belongs in an essay, such as discussion of the truth or falsity of doctrines or conclusions associated with the concepts. I have found that explaining concepts is much more difficult for students than writing expository essays. I have considered whether it might be an unreasonable requirement to make students give concise explanations of the sort described above. But I remain unrepentant. Philosophers are perhaps more sensitive to the meaning of words than other scholars, but it hardly seems an idiosyncratic or narrowly professional concern, nor one appropriate only for philosophy majors. On the contrary, developing more sensitivity to meaning, and nurturing the skills to explain meaning, has been a contribution of philosophy to society since the days of Socrates. So this requirement will remain in the course, frustrating both me and the students until I find a better way to teach the requisite skills.

In suggesting that the course I have described here provides a useful introduction to philosophy even though it makes minimal use of philosophical texts, I do not mean to denigrate those texts—especially not the classical ones. Nor do I wish to deny that some beginning philosophy students are ready to read those texts, or that other philosophers can teach them directly to freshmen more effectively than I. No doubt the four sorts of introductory courses described by Cahn will continue to dominate the field. My purpose in this essay is to show another valid approach, not the "best" approach. Emphasis on biography and language skills may never become popular. But they can serve as an introduction to philosophy, and students of mine do go on to take other philosophy courses, in which the texts and the syllabi are more conventional.

NOTES

1. Brand Blanshard, *Four Reasonable Men* (Middletown, CT: Wesleyan University Press, 1984).

2. Sissela Bok, *Lying* (New York: Pantheon, 1978).

3. Sissela Bok, *Strategy for Peace* (New York: Pantheon, 1987).

4. Mary Midgley, *Beast and Man* (London and New York: Routledge & Kegan Paul, 1995).

5. Mary Midgley, *Wickedness* (London and Boston: Routledge & Kegan Paul, 1984).

6. Elmer Sprague, *What is Philosophy?* (New York: Oxford University Press, 1961.

7. I first learned of him through Alan Donagan's book, *The Theory of Morality* (Chicago: University of Chicago Press, 1977), and subsequently read Gordon Zahn's biography, *In Solitary Witness: the Life and Death of Franz Jägerstätter* (New York: Holt, Rinehart and Winston, 1961). More recently, Zahn has condensed the story into a 20-page pamphlet (*Franz Jägerstätter: Martyr for Conscience*, Erie, PA: Benet Press, n.d.), which I assign to my class in addition to the video.

8. *Die Verweigerung* [*The Refusal*], available through the Pax Christi Center in Boston.

9. Jägerstätter held that he, being aware, had duties that others who had doubts did not have.

10. A large number of my students, to my dismay, have been ready to call him insane.

11. Robert Axelrod, *The Evolution of Cooperation* (New York: Basic Books), 1984.

12. Thomas Hobbes, *Leviathan*, chap. 13.

13. An alternative choice might be two or three of the sermons in *Strength to Love* (New York: Harper & Row, 1963), where King considers different kinds of love and different kinds of humility.

14. Weil died in the same month as Jägerstätter. Like Jägerstätter, she was still in her thirties when she died and was done in by the strictness of her conscience in those agonizing years of WWII. In her case she began, in WWI, by refusing to eat more than the rations of soldiers at the front. In 1943 she refused to eat more than peasants in occupied France, and was consequently too weak to recover from tuberculosis she had contracted in London. Here again the biography stimulates useful discussion.

15. Both are contained in George A. Panichas, ed., *The Simone Weil Reader* (New York: David McKay, 1977). They are also available from Pendle Hill Publications (Wallingford, PA), respectively as pamphlet #91 (1956, rev. 1973) and pamphlet #240, "Two Moral Essays" (1981). An excellent alternative would be Weil's discussion of "needs of the soul," which takes up about thirty pages at the beginning of *The Need for Roots* (New York and London: Routledge, 1978).

Chapter 3

Teaching Introductory Philosophy: A Restricted Topical Approach

V. Alan White and Jo A. Chern

Steven Cahn and Newton Garver describe and endorse quite distinct approaches to teaching introductory philosophy.[1] In response to some criticisms that Garver makes of Cahn's rather classic offerings, we offer yet another approach that not only synthesizes some of Cahn and Garver's main concerns, but also proposes a fundamental rethinking of the goals of introductory philosophy.

Cahn describes four curriculum-defined approaches to introductory philosophy that are currently popular with instructors: the topical approach, the "great texts" approach, the historical approach, and the secondary-source approach. Cahn briefly sketches the strengths and weaknesses of each of these approaches, and recommends overall that as teachers of philosophy we should strive to balance the presentation of material so that the slant of a given approach does not give students a distorted impression of philosophy.

Garver suggests that, in his experience, all of the approaches that Cahn describes may fail because each presupposes a level of communication and reasoning skill that many students who are new to philosophy lack. Because of this, Garver submits, philosophy is perhaps better presented to beginning, underprepared students as "a way of approaching [philosophical] doctrines or texts." Consequently, Garver recommends a nontraditional course that attempts to inculcate in his students the requisite language and thinking skills for understanding and engaging in philosophical discourse.

It is a mistake, we think, to conclude from Cahn and Garver's exchange that either introductory courses must be "properly philosophical" *surveys* (as assumed by Cahn's four approaches) or that they must be exercises in critical thinking remediation (Garver's point). We propose an approach—hereafter referred to as the restricted topical or "single-issue" approach—that explicitly lays claim to a middle ground between the desire for a traditional curriculum and the practical need to improve students' thinking and writing skills: an entire Introduction to Philosophy course organized around a single philosophical topic.

The "Restricted Topical Approach" wasn't created in one fell swoop, but evolved over the years as a result of many adaptive influences. Its forebear was in fact a traditional topical survey course very much like the one Cahn describes. That course, taught by one of the authors largely in a fashion imitative of his own undergraduate experiences, was framed around a primary-source anthology and attempted to cover the entire book. Classes therefore proceeded in a strictly scheduled fashion and in a familiar lecture/exam format.

From early on, most of the same disturbing shortcomings that Garver reports in his own experience with traditional approaches arose in that course. Many students found the readings impenetrable, and the sheer number of them daunting. Evaluations of student work revealed a shocking lack of collegiate-level language and analytical skills. Clearly, changes in the course were needed.

The first major change involved merely slowing down. More time was devoted to in-depth exposition, and since this was done within the framework of a topic-oriented course, the number of topical areas covered in the course was reduced (from five or six down to two and the number of articles from over thirty to about fifteen).[2]

Benefits from putting on the brakes were almost immediately apparent.[3] Significantly more students understood more of what they read (and reread, now that they had time to do so). Class participation increased. Insights on philosophical positions and articles began to pop up in student discussion and essays as never before. At this point the course resembled Garver's in many respects.

However, not all problems were solved; indeed, new ones arose. Though students undoubtedly attained somewhat better comprehension within the reduced number of areas of philosophy that they studied, that understanding was still in many ways flawed and inadequate. In particular, many students still could not construct coherent arguments in critical discussion of philosophical positions, and the overall quality of their writing remained unsatisfactory. In addition, the more deliberate pace of the course seemed to leave some bright, eager students bored. Moreover, since the course at this point essentially involved only intensive exposition of texts, it seemed to reinforce in many student's minds the sense that philosophy was merely an academic exercise with little bearing on real life.

It was at this juncture that the first purposeful design of the restricted topical approach began to take shape. Since a more focused topical approach was suggested by the fact that students' general comprehension of philosophical problems improved with more intense study, we decided to preserve conceptual continuity throughout the course and make only one topic the theme of the entire course. As the course was developed over several years, various topics were tried out to see which worked best. Among those tried were the ethics and metaphysics of abortion, the existence of God, personal and object identity, and free will. Since the latter topic of free will has been the focus of the most recent (and overall most successful) versions of the course, we will use that topic to illustrate features of the restricted topical approach as it developed over the years in all its incarnations.

First, we needed both (i) to enable students to see how the chosen topic surfaces in real life contexts and (ii) to begin to equip students to handle the topic philosophically. To introduce the free-will issue, students were provided with excerpts of accounts of the trial of John Hinckley.[4] These were used as a basis for discussing the commonsense notions of moral responsibility, reason, and freedom of choice. As the complexity of these issues emerged, it became necessary to introduce fundamental concepts of analysis, such as the nature of deductive and inductive inferences, standards of evidence, analogical reasoning, the nature of knowledge and belief, and the ways in which various claims may be compatible or incompatible. Trial and error revealed that these stalwarts of inquiry are best introduced as development of the topic demanded, and thus discussions of them were scattered across the semester. (For example, after reading about Hinckley's successful use of the insanity defense early on in the course, we introduced, as a plausible account of Hinckley's lack of moral responsibility, an explanation of mental illness based on a deterministic interpretation of mental disease. By drawing an analogy between the causal inevitability of symptoms of physical diseases and a causal account of mental states arising from mental illness, we set the stage for students' understanding both of incompatibilism and of the use of thought experiments in the exploration of concepts and their implications.)

Next, a comprehensive overview of the free-will problem was provided in the form of a sketch of compatibilism and incompatibilism, using a variation of William James's dilemma of determinism as a means of doing so.[5] The dilemma, which serves double duty as a model of deductive reasoning (an explanation of which is also introduced at this time), pits the students' intuitions in favor of a metaphysically "open" future against their simultaneous intuition that free will must involve control of any given choice: determinism threatens the first; random-chance indeterminism threatens the second. Since the only way to dissolve the dilemma is either to redefine free will so that it does not conflict with determinism, yielding compatibilism, or to attempt to refine indeterminism so as to encompass control, yielding libertarianism, we attempt to draw the student into an exploration of all the classic stances on free will by starting with an analysis of the dilemma. About 20 to 25 percent of a semester (three to four weeks of three one-hour classes per week) are devoted to this part of the course.

The second section of the course looks at primary sources

for a detailed understanding of various positions on free will. In several instantiations of the course, students began with Schopenhauer's rather difficult but rewarding *Essay on Freedom of the Will*,[6] which, in addition to offering a simple but ingenious destructive analysis of introspective evidence for free will, also includes a sweeping, inductive argument for the determinism of human nature. (This reading introduces the contrast—to which we refer throughout the course—between scientific and more traditional metaphysical conceptions of human nature.) Students then read John Hospers's classic argument for psychological determinism,[7] followed by Hume's compatibilism from the *Inquiry*[8] and Walter Stace's wonderful "ordinary language" defense of (Hobbesian) compatibilism.[9] We end with libertarian pieces by Richard Taylor[10] and C. A. Campbell.[11] We always intentionally assign the readings on libertarians last so that more unorthodox ideas have a better chance against students' culturally ingrained bias for a libertarian-like position.

In keeping with the tenor of a single-issue philosophy course, the class read, discussed, and analyzed assigned articles slowly and carefully over a period of many weeks. For example, to enable students to better appreciate Hume's argument for the determinism of human nature in the *Inquiry*, a class session was devoted to examining Hume's conception of causality, which serves as the foundation for that argument. Students were thus able to have greater appreciation of the inductive ground of causal knowledge and so were better able to appreciate the force of Hume's marshaling of commonplace observations of constantly conjoined behaviors in support of the ascription of causality to human nature. By the end of this part of the class (which took up half the semester), the students were conversant with the differences in the way that free will is conceived of by compatibilists on the one hand and incompatibilists on the other, and among compatibilists, the differences to be found between classic Hobbesian models and more recent internalist, psychological versions, such as that of Harry G. Frankfurt.[12] Additionally, we explored how various incompatibilist positions differ among themselves over the truth and nature of indeterminism (for example, hard determinist reactions to the distinction between libertarianism and "simple" indeterminism).

The purpose of the third phase of the course was to show how the philosophical positions one holds may have implications for that person's other positions. For example, drawing upon assigned readings in the area of the philosophy of religion, students were introduced to the problem of evil, the possibility of a freewill solution to that problem, and the logical consequences of determinism and indeterminism for a theological picture of God's relation to humankind. This section of the course is meant to bring home to students how the demand for consistency of truth and meaning places constraints on the sort of positions one may hold across a broad spectrum of issues.

The Restricted Topical Approach and Student Writing

A significant strength of the restricted topical approach is that it is particularly well suited to being taught as a course with writing emphasis. Focus on a single issue for the entire semester allows students to become acquainted with an abstract issue in great depth, and this, along with some study of the tools of elementary logic and in-class analysis of readings and examples, enables students to gradually build their critical acumen, and thus better express themselves in critical essays. We assign five or six short (two- to four-page) papers, with the demands made upon the students in the assignments graduated in difficulty according to how far along they are in the semester. For example, in the first paper students are required only to describe how the dilemma of determinism arises, and how in general libertarians and compatibilists attempt to avoid each horn of the dilemma; the second paper requires students to describe how determinists might argue from the perspective of Schopenhauer and Hume for the claim that human nature is causally structured. Evaluation of these early papers emphasizes clear exposition rather than critical analysis. Later assignments require students to consider problems more analytically and critically. For example, we ask students to consider the cogency and completeness of some scientific arguments for the determinism of human nature, such as the argument for determinism presented by Schopenhauer in his *Essay*. The final paper demands that the student defend or attack a particular solution to the free-will problem.

Conclusion

While the restricted topical approach probably is not suitable for all philosophy instructors and for all introductory-level students, we offer it in the spirit of exploration and as an alternative response to the sort of multifaceted concerns and classroom experiences that lie behind both Cahn's and Garver's articles. Having taught over the last dozen years more than fifty sections of introductory philosophy using the single-topic approach, we are confident that it is one that can benefit many instructors who for one reason or another have become disenchanted with more traditional approaches.[13]

NOTES

1. Cahn's article originally appeared in *The American Philosophical Association Newsletter on Teaching Philosophy* (fall 1986), 10-11; Garver's article appeared in *The American Philosophical Association Newsletter on Teaching Philosophy* (January 1988), 3-6. The articles are reproduced, in slightly revised form, in this volume as chapters 1 and 2.

2. Note that we are distinguishing between "topical areas" of philosophy, such as ethics, metaphysics, philosophy of religion, and so forth, and "topics" *simpliciter*, which we take to be more specific problems within those areas, such as those of free will, the existence of God, and so on.

3. The editor has pointed out to us, quite rightly, that given the onerous number of readings originally assigned, any reduction of such a workload would have to be an improvement! But the description of our initial course is no "straw man." Many instructors, for reasons of professional inertia or intractable expectations, continue throughout their careers to teach whole anthologies in introductory courses. We believe the restricted topical approach is an attractive and worthwhile alternative.

4. See *Newsweek* (13 April, 1981). Results of the trial are reported in "A Controversial Verdict," *Newsweek* (5 July, 1982), 30-31. An additional excellent resource is Peter W. Low, John Calvin Jefferies, Jr., and Richard

J. Bonnie, *The Trial of John W. Hinckley, Jr.: A Case Study in the Insanity Defense* (Mineola, NY: The Foundation Press, 1986).

5. William James, "The Dilemma of Determinism," in Arthur Minton, *Philosophy: Paradox and Discovery* (New York: McGraw-Hill, 1976), 305-13.

6. Schopenhauer's article is reproduced in Joel Feinberg, *Reason and Responsibility*, 7th ed. (Belmont, CA: Wadsworth, 1989), 351-62.

7. Feinberg, "Free Will and Psychoanalysis," ibid., 363-73.

8. "Liberty and Necessity," 374-83.

9. Ibid., "The Problem of Free Will," 387-91.

10. Ibid., "Freedom and Determinism," 392-97.

11. Ibid., "Has the Self 'Free Will'?" 398-408.

12. Harry G. Frankfurt, "Freedom of the Will and the Concept of a Person," *Journal of Philosophy* 68 (1971): 5-20.

13. One of the present authors attempts a more complete defense of the restricted topical approach in V. Alan White, "The Single-Issue Introduction to Philosophy," *Teaching Philosophy* 13, no. 1 (1990): 13-19, and "Single-Issue Introductory Philosophy: An Update," *Teaching Philosophy* 10, no. 22 (1996): 137-44. Another who has endorsed our "single-topic" approach is Mark T. Brown, "Focused Topic Introductory Philosophy Courses," *Teaching Philosophy* 10, no. 2 (1996): 145-53. Nathan Oaklander and Quentin Smith in *Time, Change, and Freedom* (London: Routledge, 1995) attempt an introduction to metaphysics that focuses only on issues in the philosophy of time. Martin Hollis's *Invitation to Philosophy* (Oxford: Blackwell, 1985), which we discovered some years after implementing the free-will version of our course, comes remarkably close to embodying the very same "single-topic" approach as presented in this paper.

PART II
Helping Our Students Improve

Chapter 4

How to Improve Your Teaching

Steven M. Cahn

I shall focus my remarks primarily on three common strategic mistakes to which we are prone.

First is the error of overestimating our audience's background knowledge, reasoning skills, powers of concentration, and interest in the subject. Beginning teachers are especially susceptible to this pitfall, because they typically come fresh from graduate school, where fellow students are well educated, skilled at argument, and deeply committed to philosophy. They know who St. Anselm was, how he formulated the ontological argument, and why Kant thought it unacceptable. Most important, they care deeply about such matters. Woe be it to instructors who walk into class assuming freshmen students share such knowledge and concerns.

I recall early in my teaching career discussing with an introductory class John Hospers's article, "Free Will and Psychoanalysis," in which he refers to the "Oedipus complex." I assumed my students would understand this reference and did not explain it. I soon realized my mistake, for not only was the Oedipus complex unfamiliar to them, but they also had never heard of Oedipus.

In such circumstances we tend to blame our students. But no matter how bright or well prepared they may be, they invariably do not know as much as we hope. Nor are they as interested in all aspects of the subject as we wish. These conditions are a given in any pedagogical situation. The challenge of teaching is to inform the uninformed and motivate the unmotivated. For a teacher to complain about such matters is akin to a surgeon complaining that the patients are all sick.

We should try to make our subjects as interesting and clear as they can be to as many of our students as possible. A good teacher directs instruction not only at the best student, or at the top 10 percent of the class, or even at the majority; instead, a good teacher aims to interest and instruct everyone in the class. All students pay tuition, not just the A students. Granted, we shall not succeed with every student. But when more than one or two students complain they are lost, many others, whether they realize so, are also in need of help.

Those who overestimate the audience may eventually become discouraged and fall prey to a second strategic error: underestimating the audience. As various experiments in educational psychology have demonstrated, the less expected from students, the less they accomplish. Ease soon brings boredom; challenge breeds interest and excitement.

Instead of leading students beyond what is familiar to them, the underestimator chooses topics and readings that allow students to remain mired in their own immediate interests. Admittedly, students may at first not be interested in the appropriate subject matter, but the aim of teaching is to make apparent the connections between seemingly esoteric material and the students' own sphere of experience. The proper subject then becomes the students' personal concern. A teacher is a guide, and a guide is expected to lead you into unfamiliar territory, not just stroll along as you revisit familiar haunts.

The underestimator, unwilling to treat students as responsible agents, typically fails to maintain deadlines; all excuses are accepted. One of the most popular teachers I have ever known, a man whose classes are packed semester after semester, insists that all papers be handed in by the announced time. Except in the direst circumstances, he accepts no late papers. Students admire his stance, for he is treating them as mature persons who are expected to take responsibility for their actions. Business people have deadlines to meet; so do doctors and lawyers. So should students.

The underestimator also engages in the all too common practice of inflating grades. At many schools today students are distinctive not when they are on the dean's list, but when they are off it. Were we to judge the intellectual state of the union by the number of A's awarded college students, our nation miraculously would seem to have been turned into a society of scholars.

Students deserve an honest appraisal of the quality of their work. To give an A to a student who has done mediocre work is pure deception. And those who unjustly receive high grades are hardly apt to learn the meaning of excellence.

But if overestimating and underestimating students are to be avoided, how to find the middle ground? No simple reply is available, just as Aristotle found no easy answer to the question of where the virtuous mean lies between the two extremes. But at the end of Book II of the *Nichomachean Ethics,* he remarks that "we must . . . examine what we ourselves drift into easily. . . . We must drag ourselves in the contrary direction; for if we pull far away from error . . . we shall reach the intermediate condition." So if you are inclined to overestimate the class, try underestimating. If you are inclined to underestimate, try overestimating. In both cases you are likely to achieve the sought-after mean.

A third strategic mistake is the failure to do justice to our intellectual opponents. Whenever a professor states opinions not shared by other reputable scholars, students ought to be so informed. They are entitled to know whether their teacher is expressing a consensus or only a majority or minority viewpoint. It is appropriate for an instructor to defend personal beliefs, but serious alternatives should not be neglected. A teacher should consider this question: if another qualified instructor were in my place, might that individual offer judgments that conflict with those I have presented? If the answer is yes, teachers should alert students, thereby increasing their understanding of the relevant issues.

For example, I believe that free will and determinism are incompatible, and when I teach this issue I argue for my own position. But I also emphasize that my view is, in fact, a minority opinion. And I do my best to explain as persuasively as possible the arguments that have been offered by those with whom I disagree.

To test your own fairness in presenting and examining ideas, imagine that your intellectual opponents were in the classroom. Would they agree that at least some of their arguments had been treated adequately? If not, you need to make greater efforts to be fair to the opposition.

Professors who are partisans usually display this failure in their manner of responding to questions. Instead of encouraging each student to think independently and raise challenges, they engage in intimidation and expect acquiescence. Their aim is not education but indoctrination. Such attempts to foster ideological zeal may be in order at a political rally, but they are entirely inappropriate in a classroom. Philosophy teachers are supposed to be guiding a critical inquiry, and an essential feature of this process is for all participants, including the faculty member, to be open-minded.

I have one final suggestion for pedagogical improvement. While we often seek our colleagues' advice about our scholarly endeavors, rarely do we ask their judgments about our teaching. I think it not only appropriate but also advisable for faculty members to share syllabi and examinations. Just as our colleagues can sometimes spot omissions or mistakes in our written arguments, so they can identify an unbalanced syllabus or an ambiguous examination question.

Most important, however, is for teachers to visit one another's classes. Professors typically allow as class visitors auditors, friends or relatives of students, and even faculty members from other departments. Why, then, should the doors be locked against those most qualified to understand what is going on? What would we think of surgeons who permitted their operating procedures to be observed by anyone except other surgeons?

A colleague in the back of the room watching the proceedings with an experienced and understanding eye can provide invaluable advice that will better our performance. Athletes improve by being observed; so do musicians; why shouldn't teachers?

The observer should not participate in the class unless invited but afterward should discuss with the instructor all aspects of the proceedings: how a question was well put, how discussion may have gone off the track, whether the instructor was audible, whether writing on the blackboard was visible, how a difficult concept might have been presented more clearly, or how an idea explained in one context could have been applied in another. The aim, of course, is not to destroy an individual's distinctive teaching style but to enhance it.

Let me conclude with one simple suggestion. Invite into your class someone you regard as an excellent teacher and a sympathetic soul. And explain to this person that you are seeking frank suggestions about how to improve your teaching. The experience will almost surely be revelatory.

NOTE

This paper was delivered at the 1987 Eastern Division Annual Meetings as part of a Special Panel on the topic "How to Improve Your Teaching," a panel arranged by the APA Committee on the Teaching of Philosophy.

Chapter 5

Reading and Interpretation: A Heuristic for Improving Students' Comprehension of Philosophy Texts

Jonathan E. Adler

I. An Assignment—Noticing Conflicts with One's Own Beliefs

One approach for improving students' comprehension of philosophy texts is, I expect, already embedded in the practices we all follow. But I think it valuable to have this practice explicitly and systematically presented to students. Essentially it is this: have students take special notice of claims or conclusions about ordinary concepts that appear incompatible with their own commonsense beliefs. An example would be the Socratic Paradox and its kin, one version of which we find in a standard introductory reading such as the *Meno* at 78b: "Nobody desires what is evil."[1]

To illustrate and develop the above suggestion, I will set out in detail and discuss a sample written assignment that I give my students.[1] This will serve as a handy way to introduce some general remarks about the teaching of philosophy. Whatever pretensions these remarks have, however, it is not to inflate the importance of the exercise. The exercise aspires to be but a small aid to teaching introductory philosophy. (More on this later.)

My interest is to improve the reading of philosophy, and my main claim is that this practical aim is furthered by explicitly appealing to one's own beliefs to test for the plausibility of one's interpretation of a text. The assignment is as follows:

A. Puzzle
In the text, find any claim or conclusion (or point of view) about an ordinary concept, for example, knowing, inquiry, virtue, desire, belief, good, wrong, freedom, that is strikingly different from what we (normally) believe, or that is puzzling or perplexing given what we believe.

B. What makes it puzzling?
State as precisely and informatively as possible what belief we have that is in conflict with the claim/conclusion. With respect to the example of "Nobody desires what is evil" in *Meno* 78b, a student might offer: "There are people who enjoy torturing others."[2]

C. What might make it less puzzling?
Offer some *alternative* interpretations, explanations, or background to the claim/conclusion that helps to impart intelligibility or plausibility to the claim or conclusion. This stage need not be too closely tied to the text.

D. What does the author actually (or most probably) believe that gives plausibility to the claim or conclusion?
Search the text, citing specific references from the text for your account. You should try to determine which of your alternatives, if any, comes closest to the author's own view. Obviously, if the claim or conclusion is contained in a forthright argument, your job is not difficult. But matters may not be that simple. From the material before you, there might not be sufficient evidence to fully determine an interpretation. Offer the best reconstruction you can.

E. Evaluation: Is it correct or well grounded?
Critically discuss the claim/conclusion in light of both the best account you have mustered (that is, answers to **C** and **D** above), and your own commonsense beliefs.

II. General Comments on the
Use of the Proposed Heuristic

If a passage fits the heuristic, that is pretty good evidence that it will be of philosophical significance. Philosophers are interested both in the nature of ordinary, even if abstract, concepts, and in fundamental assumptions about those concepts. But the exercise is intended only to highlight relevant passages. The justification for the exercise needs to go little beyond helping students *improve* their reading of texts. It need not focus on whether the highlighted passages are themselves philosophically illuminating.

However, I do not think the issue is entirely practical. Any suggested heuristic must not disrespect the integrity of the subject or text or, more generally, liberal education. (A useful heuristic—one that I would not offer—is to buy a used text from a bright student who had done a lot of underlining.)

III. Some Comments on Specifics
Regarding the Assignment

i. The exercise requires the use of whole classic works or large parts of them. A large chunk of a work is needed if a student is to try to get a good grip on how a concept is being used. The exercise will work less well, I expect, for problem-oriented courses, where texts are excerpted according to their specific views on a philosophical problem—for example, skepticism or free will. Once a work is located within a particular philosophical problem, students lose assurance of the relevance of their own beliefs, or of their competence to judge. The problems are not ones that they have systematically reflected upon, nor, more obviously, are they ones that arise in everyday discussions. In addition, as the work becomes more contemporary, it will be harder for students to find overtly puzzling or perplexing claims or conclusions, as it is likely that there will be less discrepancy in background beliefs or views.

ii. Students sometimes have difficulty with the exercise at the first step. In their initial use of the exercise, many cannot come up with good answers to **A**, which requires them to find a claim in the text that is at odds with what they normally believe. Since, without finding such claims, they cannot proceed with the exercise, I offer some examples, such as the following from the *Meno*:

73c: So everyone is good in the same way, since they become good by possessing the same qualities.

80e: [A] man cannot try to discover either what he knows or what he does not know.

81e: But what do you mean when you say that we don't learn anything, but that what we call learning is recollection?

87c: [A] man is not taught anything except knowledge.

87e: [I]f good, then advantageous. All good things are advantageous.

89a: [G]ood men cannot be good by nature.

But the exercise needs extension to the frequent cases in which it is difficult to recognize that a claim is in conflict with what one believes. Consider, for example, the opening of *Meditation I*, in which Descartes says "I should withhold my assent no less carefully from things which are not plainly certain and indubitable than I would to what is patently false." Although a natural interpretation of this would take it as the voicing of a healthy skepticism and not the opening for a radical one, really to make sense of Descartes' criterion, one must grasp his fundamental project. For it is only then that one is positioned to recognize and make sense of the very strong notion of certainty that he is proposing here.[3]

iii. Having students state precisely which of their beliefs the claim is not compatible with presses students to find and articulate the point of disagreement among themselves and the author of the text. The exercise invites clarification both of the contrary/contradictory distinction and of the scope of negation (that is, the differences between internal and external negation). Students will come to recognize that a belief opposed to 78b ("Nobody desires what is evil") such as "There are people who enjoy torturing others" is more specific, hence, more informative, than the weak, all-purpose, denial that nobody desires evil, which is the contradictory.

But students will also be taught that not all sharp disagreements take the form of direct negation—internal *or* external—of the content of the selected claim. Consider, for example, the claim from the *Protagoras* 330c, [4-8]: "Justice is just." Our opposing belief is not perspicuously or informatively represented as either the bland contradictory, "It's not the case that justice is not just" or even "Justice is not just." It is rather that we hold that justness is not the *kind* of thing that one predicates of, or attributes to, justice. The disagreement here is at a more abstract level than normal internal or external negation, and involves questions of both self-predication and category mistakes.

One of the puzzles about the claim from the *Protagoras* that "justice is just" is that it is found in a dialogue, none of whose participants find this *kind* of assertion puzzling. So here we have not just a puzzling claim or conclusion, but a puzzling presentation. This should indicate to students how wide a gap there is in shared background assumptions between themselves and the author. It also indicates the wide variety of differences or disagreements possible, besides simple "pro/con" opposition.

iv. The attempt to focus disagreements as narrowly as possible enforces the value of precision. But it also helps explain why the exercise works best with ordinary, even if abstract, concepts. We perk up when we find, within a rich and interesting presentation, bold and surprising claims regarding ordinary concepts.[4] Since there is a broad area of agreement in the application of ordinary concept terms, any disagreement about the application of these will stand out in sharp relief. In contrast, with concepts like God, the soul, Being, or the Good, extensive divergence or disagreement is expected, not surprising.

v. Step **D**, which requests students to reconstruct the background of a puzzling claim, is the most important. In the case of the Socratic Paradox (that no one does wrong knowingly), a supporting argument (that no one wants to harm oneself, and to do wrong is to harm oneself) is offered and should be presented. Of course, the conclusion remains puzzling, but the value of making the premise explicit becomes clear: students can now locate the source of divergence between themselves and the text at the premise "To do wrong is to harm oneself." So they are led to ask *why* Socrates believes that. Even the better students will have to search hard in the text for answers.

Expectations for step **D** cannot be lofty. Reconstructing the background of a philosopher's claim is, as we know, often enormously difficult. A good example is Descartes' claim (cited previously) "I should withhold my assent no less carefully from things which are not plainly certain and indubitable than I would to what is patently false." As already noted, without faculty guidance students will not recognize this claim as in conflict with their own beliefs since, taken out of context, there is a more harmonious interpretation available (namely, that Descartes is offering merely a healthy skeptical criterion). The single claim or conclusion that a student highlights as problematic given his or her beliefs is likely to be embedded within complex assumptions that are very distant from us. Without intense study, a proper understanding of the passage cannot be reached. The exercise aims to have students begin by recognizing resources and competencies for comprehension they already possess. But it does not claim that these resources and competencies are adequate to the task. Indeed, it is a lesson of this exercise that they are not.

vi. The last evaluation stage—step **E** of the assignment— reinforces the distinction between interpreting a claim so that it is understandable, intelligible, or plausible, and holding it to be true or justified. The earlier stages alone may wrongly encourage the view that so long as you can make sense of a claim, however unwarranted, it is acceptable. Again, here we are returning students to a distinction that they normally do respect—understanding someone is one thing, agreeing with him or her, another.

But aside from this value, I am least satisfied with this part of the exercise. Step **E** breaks the analogy to the ordinary understanding of another person, which ends with our making sense or seeking clarification of what has been said. We could reasonably expect steps **A** through **D** to become part of a habit or practice of "aggressive reading," in Bratman and Perry's apt phrase.[5] But step **E** requires aggressive and extended writing.

Furthermore, where understanding is improved, even if still very partial, not much is gained, I believe, by the additional demand to determine whether the claims are correct (as long as it is clearly recognized that the question of correctness is appropriate).

Someone may object that the above exercise shortcuts a valuable learning process: since we aim to aid students in locating philosophically relevant passages in their texts, the lessons that we supply should come more slowly and indirectly as they struggle through a text. Use of the exercise described here advances students by having them skip valuable, intermediate steps.

I offer no refutation of this serious objection, but I do not believe it is decisive. Rather, it exposes a cost in the approach I advocate. (It is one that I am willing to pay, since it promises to help my students, who have great difficulties with the material. The exercise lessens, but only a very little, the burdens upon them.)

IV. Interpretation

Central to the exercise is the notion of interpretation, especially as presented by Davidson.[6] In our classes, we regularly appeal to what we believe to justify difficult interpretations, with little—and sometimes, even conflicting—textual evidence. For example, in the opening section of the *Euthyphro* (4b), Socrates is taken aback by Euthyphro's prosecution of his father:

> Is then the man your father killed one of your relatives? Or is that obvious, for you would not prosecute your father for the murder of a stranger.[7]

In reply, Euthyphro accuses Socrates of violating something like a principle 'to treat like cases alike.' But despite the straightforward plausibility of Euthyphro's interpretation of Socrates' remark, we do not rest with it. For Socrates might be otherwise understood. He may be challenging the assumption that the duty to prosecute falls equally on all those in a position to do so. Our belief that a child's duty to the law does not always override filial loyalty may incline us to prefer this interpretation to one that understands Socrates as violating so basic a principle of formal justice. On the preferred interpretation then, Socrates' position comes more to resemble our own.

The first two, and often the first three, steps of the exercise are meant to connect the activity of (conversational) interpretation to students' reading. When a remark is anomalous (for example,

"Smith's test was a headache"), we immediately try to interpret it so that it appears intelligible or understandable. We quickly generate alternative interpretations (of a speaker's meaning) and select what is best. In introducing students to the assignment described, it is worthwhile to remind them that interpretation is at the heart of the very everyday activity of conversation. It illuminates complexities in students' own reasoning, which, within limits, they normally handle with ease. (But, unlike the exercise I am proposing, everyday literal anomalies that stimulate interpretation and the testing of alternatives hardly ever lead us to perk up. Since the remark is a contribution to a conversation, audiences must fix on a good interpretation quickly, so that the anomaly passes with hardly a notice.)

The assignment locates an area of overlap between the activity of interpretation in everyday conversation where anomalies are resolved instantaneously and what happens when controversial statements are made—statements that invite us to argue a claim. It points students to claims or conclusions that they should similarly perk up to, though these claims are hardly likely to surface in ordinary, "everyday" discussions or debates. (In fact, they do not even seem like the *kind* of claims that we debate at all—"No one desires evil." Huh?)

Having students be explicit about their interpretation of a particular text is valuable because it emphasizes that the understanding of a text—what is right there before one—is often subject to dispute. Nevertheless, there are better or worse interpretations and one should teach students to become self-conscious of the activity of interpretation and what they themselves bring to it.

In my experience (teaching at a public liberal arts college), unless students enter with a rich intellectual background and are able (and willing) to devote a lot of time to their studies, they are poor at discerning what is especially (philosophically) relevant in the texts they read. The heuristic suggested here is intended to arrest students' normal pattern of reading, which is fairly smooth and rapid. The exercise encourages students to become aware of and engage their own everyday beliefs in the comprehension and interpretation of texts. If successful, the exercise generates a barrier to students' bracketing these everyday beliefs and encourages them to recognize that in philosophy (as in everyday life) matters of truth and plausibility are not to be suspended, leaving good arguments to be merely a matter of validity rather than soundness. Many students enter philosophy expecting such abstract and distant ideas that a simple demand for truthfulness is suspended. They read the Socratic Paradox with hardly more notice than any of the surrounding statements. Or, if they do notice it, the wide disparity between it and their own beliefs is treated dismissively as either just the kind of thing one should expect in philosophy or a matter of special meanings attached to these terms.

As teachers, we should try to get our students to allow philosophical ideas to intersect with their own beliefs, to take notice of that intersection, and to draw out practical consequences from it. When presented with a foreign and difficult idea, students should learn to be disposed to try to draw from it concrete applications or implications. For example, confronted with Locke's claim that begins "universal assent . . . must needs be the necessary concomitant of all innate truth,"[8] the student should draw out from it a denial of the widespread contemporary belief that there can be nonconscious thoughts or rules. Where there is a wide disparity in beliefs between themselves and the author concerning concepts that are seemingly shared, this is indicative of an important gap in understanding. Students are familiar, from ordinary conversation and reading, with the need to lessen this gap through interpretation. From that familiar setting, we can show students that they are committed to a standard for reading comprehension. I remind them of this commitment and nudge them to transfer it to their study of philosophy.

The approach I am suggesting fits with traditional (Socratic) views about teaching and doing philosophy. Inquiry is motivated naturally or internally through perplexities, especially ones that hit home. We try to lessen our puzzlement to facilitate fruitful engagement with the ideas, relishing what remains.[9]

NOTES

1. I am grateful to the Editors of the *APA Newsletter on Teaching Philosophy*, especially Tziporah Kasachkoff, for helpful comments.

2. Plato, *Meno* in *Five Dialogues*, trans. G. M. A. Grube (Indianapolis: Hackett, 1981).

3. Aristotle, of course, also found the claim hard to swallow, though not as much as we do. See *Nicomachean Ethics*, trans. T. Irwin (Indianapolis: Hackett, 1985), 1145b-23-28. For a different reading, see Alasdair MacIntyre, "The Relationship of Philosophy to Its Past," in *Philosophy in History*, Richard Rorty, J. B. Schneewind, and Quentin Skinner, eds. (New York: Cambridge University Press, 1984), 31-48. See also 35-38.

4. For an appealing account, see Bernard Williams, *Descartes: The Project of Pure Inquiry* (New York: Penguin Books, 1978), chap. 2.

5. I am doubtful of the converse. Much that is philosophically interesting may not come in small bits, may fit well with, and develop commonsense beliefs, or may explore territory untouched by our ordinary beliefs.

6. John Perry and Michael Bratman, "Appendix: Reading Philosophy," in *Introduction to Philosophy: Classical and Contemporary Readings* (Oxford: Oxford University Press, 1989), 813-15.

7. See Donald Davidson, *Inquiries into Truth and Interpretation* (Oxford: Oxford University Press, 1984), especially essays 9 through 13. One might worry that to give prominence to one's own beliefs in interpretation will lead to distortions of the text, even when one does so judiciously. More study is needed to evaluate this concern. But I do take comfort in the more Davidsonian-than-thou approach advocated by Rorty, Schneewind, and Skinner (in "Introduction," *Philosophy in History*, 1-14) for the historiography of philosophy. They tell us that anyone who is writing history of western philosophy and who values contemporary philosophy, "must," in writing about philosopher X's views, filter out the sentences that are not worth translating while being conscientiously anachronistic in translating the remainder. This suggests that, in contrast to teaching, in historiography accuracy is of overriding importance, the audience is made up of professionals and the limitations on time and resources are not severe.

8. *Five Dialogues*.

9. John Locke, *An Essay Concerning Human Understanding*, ed. P. H. Nidditch (Oxford: Oxford University Press, 1975), bk. I, chap. 1.

10. On the importance of Socratic perplexity, see Gareth B. Matthews, "Perplexity in Plato, Aristotle, and Tarski," *Philosophical Studies* 85, nos. 2-3 (1997): 213-28.

Chapter 6

Improving Student Papers in 'Introduction to Philosophy' Courses

Juli Eflin

An important step in a student's education is learning how to rewrite a paper. In philosophy, learning how to rewrite a paper involves, at least partly, learning to identify and separate what is necessary for an argument from what is superfluous, ordering the presentation of points so that one point is seen to follow from another, and making sure that there are no jumps in reasoning that make the argument difficult to follow. Yet these are skills that most students lack.

To gain these skills, students need to be required to rewrite their papers based on helpful, critical comments. Unfortunately, writing comments on large numbers of student papers, reviewing the papers a second time once they have been revised in the light of one's comments, and then grading them is a task that can easily become overwhelming. I know that I am not alone in teaching Introduction to Philosophy to large numbers of freshmen without an assistant to help with grading. (In some terms I have 120 introductory philosophy students divided into three classes of forty each.) So the exercise that I have devised using peer review of papers may prove useful to others. It is an exercise designed to help students improve their papers without demanding that the instructor spend an inordinate amount of time commenting on and correcting them.

In my class, students are asked to write a five-page paper based on one of four assigned articles.[1] This paper is to be an exegesis of the author's claims and argument as well as a critical evaluation of these. I describe the assignment as a terse and lucid critical exegesis, called a TALCE for short. (Such a description, delivered with flair, seems to keep students focused on the kind of writing needed for a philosophy paper.)

The papers are to be "complete": they are to be typed (or word processed), have a title, and where called for, include footnotes and bibliography. I announce the following as my criteria for grading:

(1) *Comprehension of the Author's Claim and Its Justification*: does the student's paper display an accurate and complete understanding?

(2) *Use of Relevant Class Material*: is the author's view explicated and analyzed with the appropriate information from class discussions?

(3) *Evaluation*: does the paper give clear, cogent reasons for accepting or rejecting the author's view?

(4) *Mechanics*: does the paper have a thesis clearly stated, a clear structure, correct grammar, and a clear concluding paragraph?

One week before the final version of their papers is due to be turned in to me, students are to bring their papers to class for peer review. I build up the exercise as an event not to be missed, and stress that better papers and better grades are the likely outcomes of subjecting their papers to peer review.

The Exercise

Students are required to come to the peer review class session with duplicate copies of their papers. They are to turn in one copy to me and keep one copy for themselves to use during the (fifty-minute) class period. The instructions I give them are the following:

Round 1 (20 minutes)
1. Organize yourselves into groups of two, that is, pair up.
2. Read each other's papers.
3. Reader: Tell the writer what he or she has said. Do *not* say "I

like this part" and the like. Be descriptive, not evaluative.

4. Discuss any misunderstandings until it is clear that each has understood the other's argument. At this point, no evaluation of the paper is called for; the point is, rather, to be clear about what the author's position is and his or her argument for that position.

Round 2 (30 minutes)

1. Each pair join another pair (so now you are in groups of four).

2. Designate the original pairs as Group A and Group B.

3. Group A: explain one of your papers to Group B.

4. Collectively try to think of further arguments that could be added to strengthen the evaluative portion of the paper. Make two copies of the suggestions, one for the author of the paper and one for the professor.

5. Repeat steps 3 and 4 for the second paper of Group A and for both papers of Group B.

Once the students have assembled themselves into groups and are discussing each other's papers, I move from group to group to make sure that the members of each group keep focused on describing what is in each other's paper and on devising ways to strengthen further the papers. Even though I have not read the papers, it is easy to tell by "eavesdropping" whether the discussion has gone off track (or, as sometimes happens, degenerates into declarations of mutual admiration). If students get stuck in their efforts to improve an argument, I suggest examples that might help them develop the argument; if they have trouble putting their finger on what is wrong with an argument they think is faulty, I suggest they try to think of counterexamples. I also encourage them to think about whether the conclusions of the argument have implications for other issues we have studied. And I stress that they must keep the announced grading criteria in mind. (This usually results in a flurry of further discussion.)

Benefits of the Exercise

When forced to state explicitly what is in a fellow student's paper, there are many discoveries that students make, such as jumps in reasoning, inconsistencies (that might have gone unnoticed in merely quickly reading the paper), a lack of clear presentation, and a lack of logical order in the presentation of relevant points. Furthermore, simply hearing what another student *thinks* is in one's paper is quite revealing for most students. It brings home to them just how clear or unclear the presentation of their argument is or how good or thin the argument itself is. (Although students often come to class believing that they have a good paper, after this exercise with their peers they are usually eager to rewrite their papers.)

So, the first benefit of the exercise is that students gain practice in rethinking their work despite my not devoting extensive amounts of time to writing comments on their papers. The final papers I receive are of a much better quality than those I receive without using this exercise. My grading time is reduced and student grades are higher.

Second, there is the collaborative aspect of the work. Although students may, if they choose, turn in their papers without revising them in light of the comments of their peers, in my experience the majority of students do choose to rewrite their papers after the exercise. The collaboration and collective thinking that students engage in for the purpose of helping each other produce a good paper make the assignment more than just another term paper.

Finally, although I devised this exercise as a way to avoid the Herculean task of grading and regrading 120 freshman papers while having students achieve some critical awareness of the clarity and cogency of their philosophical writing, it has become clear that there are other—unanticipated but important—benefits for students who participate. Knowing that their papers will undergo review and comments by their peers before the final version is handed in to me, students regard the papers presented for peer review as "works in progress" and the comments they receive as comments on a still active project. Because of this, and the fact that feedback is immediate since students go home with comments on papers they presented that very day, there is no loss of momentum in their work. Students leave class still enthusiastically engaged in the project of writing their papers and have renewed interest in rewriting and improving those papers. In contrast, when I am the one who reads and writes comments on each student's paper, students must wait until their papers are returned to them—at which point, given the intervening time and the commitments to other projects in other courses, which, invariably, occupy students' attention, both energy and focus are somewhat lost.

This exercise will work with any kind of writing assignment, with one exception: longer papers will require more than one fifty-minute period. But even for short papers, it is not likely that the exercise can be completed in one class period if one does not prepare students in advance by telling them the nature of the exercise and how it works. Because of this possibility, I prepare students for the peer review session by explaining to them, in advance of that session, both the nature and the mechanics of the exercise.

Also, to save time in class, I do not try to organize how students pair up. I do, however, require that students do not pair up with someone who is a personal friend or who has read the paper beforehand. This helps promote a critical reading and assessment of the paper. (Too often, friends or students who know each other well sympathetically fill in each other's assumptions or jumps in reasoning. The result is that the argument is taken by the reader of the paper to be better, or better presented, than it actually is. Obviously, this sort of "kindness" undermines the purpose of the exercise.)

Some problems may arise. First, for a student whose writing and argumentative skills are much better than average, the in-class exercise described here may seem futile. A student who feels there is not much to be gained by the exercise is free to submit his or her paper as the final paper without revising it in the light of peer comments. However, I have found that only infrequently do students choose not to rewrite their papers.

Also, there may be some problems with compliance. A student may simply refuse to participate, either by not showing up for class on the day of discussion or by arriving without a paper to discuss. I put a student who comes to class without a paper with another pair of students so that he or she can participate in the discussion, even though his or her own paper will not have the benefit of others' comments. However, I have found that with a strong appeal to their self-interest and an approach to the exercise as a fun non-lecture day students willingly participate.

In the end, I am left with two sets of papers. One set, accompanied by peer suggestions, I now rarely read. The second set—the revised papers— I do read, comment on, and grade. They are usually well thought out papers with some creative arguments.

When I began using this exercise, I painstakingly compared each paper that was initially submitted with its "rewrite" and peer suggestions. I did this in order to see the way in which the presentation of information was reordered, logical connections were made more explicit, and argumentation was more fully developed and illustrated.[2] Now, however, I usually take the time to compare the revised papers with the paper initially submitted only if there is some special need to do so in a particular case (as might arise, for example, when an internal inconsistency results from an unwise revision, or the position taken in the paper seems at odds with what seemed to be the position of the author in class discussion). Nonetheless, comparing revised papers with the initially submitted ones always confirms the worth of the exercise.

One final comment: a question may arise as to how it is that students are capable of improving their papers through peer review when they may be no more skilled than their fellow students in detecting what is wrong with their arguments. To be sure, when asked such general questions as "How can this paper be improved?" beginning students are likely to be stumped. But they can usually point to a troublesome spot in a fellow student's paper even if they cannot articulate the trouble in some abstract way. The hope, which anecdotal evidence suggests is fulfilled, is that after practicing on the papers of others, students eventually become more adept at providing the same sort of critique for themselves.

NOTES

1. Some of the articles I assign are chap. 2 (which concerns ethical relativism and ethical objectivism) of Louis Pojman's *Ethics: Discovering Right and Wrong* (Belmont, CA: Wadsworth, 1990); John Searle, "Minds, Brains, and Programs," vol. 3 in *The Behavioral and Brain Sciences* (Cam-

bridge: Cambridge University Press, 1980), 417-24; Peter Singer, "Famine, Affluence, and Morality," *Philosophy and Public Affairs* 1, no. 3 (1972): 229-43; and J. J. Thomson, "A Defense of Abortion," *Philosophy and Public Affairs* 1, no. 1 (1971): 47-66.

2. There is a substantial body of literature on the use of peer review. The exercise discussed here and the positive results it achieves are consistent with this research. See Neil Ellman, "Peer Evaluation and Peer Grading," *English Journal* 64, no. 3 (1975): 79-80; and James Siders, "Instructor, Self and Peer Review: A Formative Evaluation Triad," *College Student Journal* 17, no. 2 (1983): 141-44. For a statistical model that evaluates the quality of peer reviews, see Hoyt Wilson, "Parameter Estimation for Peer Grading under Incomplete Design," *Educational and Psychological Measurement* 48, no. 1 (1988): 69-81.

Chapter 7

Using Essay Exams to Teach and Not Merely to Assess

Carrie Figdor

A former colleague of mine had a cartoon on his office door that showed one philosophy professor asking another about his final exam. "You haven't changed the questions in years," the first observes. "How do you get away with it?" "No problem," the other replies. "I just change the answers."

Anemic as it is, the joke turns on an assumption about what exams are and what they are for that the two professors, as many of us, take for granted. The assumption is that an exam is a method of evaluating student learning: its function is to elicit answers, even if there is no one right answer. I suggest that this focus on exams as tools for evaluation should be modified in the case of essay exams. An essay exam can be seen as a valuable way to promote learning and not just assess it. My remarks in this paper apply to essay exams designed for an introductory-level philosophy class with basic writing and reading skills of up to fifty students at an average four-year college or university. Except where I specifically discuss other types of classes, any reference in this chapter to "philosophy class," therefore, should be understood as a class that roughly fits this characterization.

For a variety of reasons, many students in college today are not as ideally prepared for college-level work as one might desire.[1]

Sometimes this is due to students not having learned basic critical thinking skills in high school, a lack that may leave otherwise motivated and prepared students at a loss when confronted with the idea—common to philosophy—that the main work of a discipline consists in defining a position and supporting it with facts and/or arguments. But in the worst case, students are unable even to write a grammatical sentence, let alone two that do not constitute a *non sequitur* or three that pass as a summary. Understandably enough, this situation has led professors in a variety of disciplines, including philosophy, to incorporate more writing-to-learn techniques into their classes, and thus, for example, to assign journal writing and to require multiple drafts of assigned papers.[2]

Philosophy teachers do not differ from those in other disciplines in facing this need to teach skills as well as content. This need is, if anything, more urgent for philosophy instructors since philosophy has no intrinsic factual content comparable to that found in other disciplines. (Such facts as are dealt with in philosophy are facts that are drawn from other disciplines.) Students who are adept at mastering factual content—say, a range of biological or historical facts—may be completely lost in a philosophy class if they do not quite grasp the concept of one thing being a reason for something else.[3] This may be why many introductory students are often eager to learn such philosophical 'facts' as there are—for example, that Descartes is a rationalist—and are uncomfortable when the teacher focuses on the status of a claim as either a premise for or a conclusion from some other claim.[4]

But philosophy teachers face two additional challenges. First, since many original philosophical works are difficult (not to say inscrutable), if a student finds reading difficult to begin with, problems of comprehension will only be magnified in a philosophy class that assigns these original works. Philosophy instructors constantly struggle to find effective ways for students to learn how to read original texts.[5]

Second, although a few students enroll in philosophy classes with a vague interest in the subject, most show up for reasons that have nothing to do with philosophy itself and everything to do with scheduling and graduation requirements. There is therefore (at least initially) little motivation other than the maintenance of a grade average for a student to perform well in a philosophy class. (Even this motivation can be considerably diluted by school policies that allow students to drop classes without academic penalty up to the day of the final exam.) Fortunately, while concern with grades may be all the motivation a philosophy teacher has to work with, this concern is often sufficient, at least at the introductory level, to induce students to work at mastering the material. It is not unusual for grade-motivated students to do what is required to get a good grade even if they are only mildly interested, while others who may find the material very engaging may not be able muster the time or energy to do the work necessary to succeed in the course. This is not to deny the importance of stimulating interest in philosophy, but only to emphasize that students need not be enthralled with the subject to do well in it.

It is clear, then, that often philosophy teachers must simultaneously teach philosophy and its associated skills to students who have, at most, a passing instrumental interest in the subject. My suggestions about rethinking essay examinations are made with this situation in mind.

Much has been written on how to teach critical thinking skills both critical-thinking and non-critical-thinking classes, with many of the strategies advocated being adopted from the writing-across-the-curriculum (WAC) movement.[6] Although some of the WAC literature has an annoying postmodernist slant (for example, professors are often subjected to belittlement-by-stereotype while students are extolled as knowledge-makers), it is valuable in its emphasis on process over product and in its concrete proposals for incorporating this viewpoint into pedagogical practice.

Among these proposals is the suggestion that explicit and incremental steps for producing an adequate, college-level, evaluable product (such as a term paper or some such graded assignment) be built right into the syllabus. Thus, term papers or other written assignments are "staged" or "sequenced" through of a series of due dates over a period of weeks so that students are required to submit items that, incrementally and progressively, lead to the production of the final paper. For example, a sequence of such steps might include, first, a two- or three-sentence statement of the position the student will take on the topic; second, a 250-word abstract of the central arguments that the student will develop; third, a first draft of the paper that is then returned to the student with suggestions for improvement; fourth, a final draft of the paper; and fifth, an optional rewrite of the final draft after it has been evaluated and graded. Ideally, each stage serves to reinforce both the content of some part of the course and a particular cognitive skill (such as the skill involved in articulating a particular position or in demonstrating how that position is or is not supported by particular reasons). In this way, the learning of skills and content come to complement one another.

The incremental process of writing described above captures the essential idea behind the view that essay exams may be used as tools for learning rather than as merely tools of evaluation. That is, essay exams can be part of a learning process and not just a product of learning.

Using Essay Exams as Part of the Learning Process

Just as one can teach the successful writing of term papers in stages, so one can have students learn to write a good essay examination in stages, though how much staging should be built into the exam process will depend on the skills possessed by the students in the class. If basic writing skills and minimal familiarity with making arguments can be assumed, a fairly simple sequence consists in having students (a) write practice essays; (b) model good essays; (c) model grading criteria; and (d) prepare notecards. I shall discuss each of these with examples drawn from how I employ them in the classroom.

Differences in skill levels among students in a single class will show up at each stage and can be addressed at each stage via more or less detailed verbal or written comments on how each student's work can be improved for the next stage. If the first step reveals that many students lack basic writing or reading skills, then the staging of assignments is, if anything, more rather than less important. I will return to this issue below.

A. Practice Essays

About three or four class periods before the exam date I provide a list of questions from which I will choose those questions that will appear on the exam. I ask students to prepare some rough notes that they might use to answer one of these questions. They all prepare notes for the same question for the practice essays. (They can prepare notecards for the other questions later. See D below on notecards.) In the following class session I set aside 20 minutes and have the students write an essay answering that question, using the notes that they have written at home. This gives the students a clear understanding of how much they can write during that time and of the pressure they will face during the exam itself. I inform the students that I plan to distribute two of the best essays written during this period to all members of the class.

I collect but do not grade this essay. It counts as an "informal" writing assignment—that is, it gets a checkmark and counts as part of each student's cumulative in-class "participation" grade. However, I do look through the essays briefly, without making comments, to find two essays that come closest to what I want. (See C below for what I look for in these essays.) I try to choose essays that differ from one another in how they answer the question, either in content or in organization. I photocopy these essays, names excluded, for the class. (The rationale behind "informal" or "low-stakes" writing—another bit of WAC terminology—is that while writing assignments that do not get grades often do not get done, assignments can still count—and get done—without being graded.)

B. Modeling Good Essays

An obvious problem with essay exams is that different teachers in different disciplines have different expectations of what constitutes a good essay. What counts as a good essay in one class may not in another. It is therefore important to make clear to students what your own criteria are. A "norming" session in class solves this problem neatly.

Before the class session when the exam is scheduled, I hand out photocopies of the selected practice essays. We read through each of the essays to discover what makes them good and how they might have been improved (keeping in mind that they were written in twenty minutes). As a variation, one can have the students make these discoveries in small discussion groups, after which everyone comes together for a whole-class discussion. I leave it to the students to compare the selected essays we go over in class with their own.

C. Modeling Grading Criteria

When we review the practice essays, I also distribute a 'grading sheet' listing the criteria that I will use when I grade the actual essay exam. I list my criteria under the main headings of 'Organization,' 'Content' and 'Style.' I demonstrate what each of these categories refers to with respect to the selected practice essays we have just discussed. I also explain why I think these criteria are important in assessing their work and why other considerations are not as crucial to me. For example, I make clear that while their essays must be readable, I do not expect perfect grammar since writing under time pressure usually induces mistakes. The practice essays and norming sessions are intended to give students an opportunity to make and learn from their most important errors—such as poorly organized answers or answers that do not address the question—without paying a penalty. They are not intended to teach grammar.

Not incidentally, establishing grading criteria also speeds the grading process itself. I write few if any comments on the exams themselves since, in my experience, students almost never read them. I have found that why a particular grade was earned (not 'given') is not normally an issue for students unless they are unhappy with their grade. Whatever comments I do wish to make, I put on the student's grading sheet (the same grading sheet introduced in the 'norming' session described above) that is returned to each student along with his or her graded test. Mostly, my comments are brief notes that can be used as reference points in case a student wants to retake some part of the exam (see below for retakes of exams). I have found that by making the criteria for the assessment of student essays clear ahead of time, student complaints about grades that are not requests for an exam retake are minimized.

D. Preparing Notecards

I recommend that students prepare a single 3 x 5 card of notes that they can bring with them to the exam. Having to fit their notes onto a 3 x 5 card can help students consider ahead of time what is important and how to organize that material. Some students write—or word-process—in unbelievably tiny font sizes and so are able to fit a good portion of their essay onto the card. Preparing notecards is wildly popular with students as it appears to give them license to prepare a 'cheat sheet.' But from a teacher's point of view this is an enormously effective way to encourage student preparation for the exam. When it comes to preparing 'crib sheets,' one man's cheating is another man's review. Very few students do not prepare these cards and hence very few do not do some preparation for their essay exams.

The minimal staging that I have just described for an essay examination can be varied and expanded in numerous ways. For example, to model good essays, the instructor can distribute photocopied examination essays from another class—essays which received grades varying from 'A' to 'D'—and have students, divided into small groups, try to figure out what grades the essays received and why. Practice essays can then be written after these essays are discussed by the class as a whole. Also, after discussing grading criteria, the instructor can ask students to rewrite their practice essays at home in accordance with the criteria discussed. Doing this would require beginning the staging process at least one class earlier. Alternatively, students can be given a few minutes in class to assess their practice essays according to the criteria discussed and be asked to write down what they would need to do to make their essay better conform to the criteria. Time can also be set aside for a peer review session in which students assess one another's essays according to the criteria.

As I noted above, the process that I describe here of preparing students for essay examinations assumes that one's students possess a level of reading comprehension and writing proficiency that allows their practice essays to be minimally coherent. If there are no—or too few—practice essays that demonstrate a minimal level of reading comprehension and writing skill, then the staging process would have to be further broken down and begun sooner. In fact, the lower the level of students' skill in writing and comprehension, the more necessary staging becomes if the essay examination is to be a useful type of evaluation at all. One suggestion for dealing with students of generally low-level skills is to provide examination questions along with each reading assignment from the very beginning, and then have the students rewrite the examination questions in their own words. (This is one way to discover poorly worded questions.) Students can also be asked to identify those portions of the readings that are most relevant to answering each question and why.[7] If the questions are well chosen, this can help students to focus on what is important in their readings. Classes in which students have only minimal levels of reading and writing skills are, of course, philosophy classes only in the sense that the subject being used to teach writing and reading happens to be philosophy. There is no genuine choice in these cases between teaching basic skills or covering the material, since where there are no skills, there is no learning, and where there is no learning, there is no coverage.

Staging need not stop once the exam that it has led up to is given. If optional examination retakes are allowed, students can earn extra points by explaining the mistakes that they made in selected essays.[8] I allow essay retakes in which students are required to explain what was wrong with their initial answer as well as provide the corrected one. It is not important for the rewritten assignment to deal with all of the errors on the previous exam or paper. Retakes can squeeze more learning out of an examination (or out of any written assignment) by giving students a second chance to do well.

In general, with staging, I get better essays and students get better grades. No doubt, this is in part because even minimal staging prevents students from waiting until the night before the exam to review the material. Staging exams also makes it clear to students what the instructor wants, and by what standards the work will be assessed. Finally, when I fail to receive good essays from my students, I am in a better position to diagnose the difficulties that students have, and can try to add stages into the preparation for the next exam (or the next version of the course) to work on those skills that are inadequate. Therefore, the basic sequence of essay examination preparation that I detailed above accomplishes two things: it eliminates or at least alleviates certain important sources of poor performance on essay exams and it helps reveal some specific cognitive weaknesses that would otherwise go unnoticed. The following example will illustrate this point.

On one essay examination I asked students to explain both how Descartes and Hume each accounts for our idea of God, and how Descartes' epistemology would be affected were he to admit that Hume was right (and vice versa). Most students did not draw the general implications for Descartes' epistemology were Descartes to have acknowledged that the idea of God is our own construction, as Hume maintained, and not innate. They did not see that a human-constructed idea of God need not have a referent, and that for Descartes this would have the unfortunate consequence of leaving his skepticism unresolved since a human-constructed idea of God would not entail a benevolent guarantor of the existence of anything that corresponded to his clear and distinct ideas.

I had initially thought that the process of sequential preparation of essay writing would challenge students to write more exploratory essays than they otherwise would have. But my hopes were unrealistic. I have come to realize that, at least at the introductory level, most essay exam-takers are sufficers, not maximizers. But I think the answers I received also reveal the difficulty that many students have in focusing on the important facts from which the correct implications might be drawn. Although I had stressed in class that—and why—Descartes needs to prove that God exists, no connection was made between this fact and the possibility that Hume's explanation of our idea of God is correct. I now realize that I should build into the assignments leading up to the exam more opportunities for making these kinds of connections and for drawing out their implications. My point here is that staging exams can help separate problems stemming from weaknesses in critical thinking skills from problems that stem from unfamiliarity either with the material or with the instructor's style. The latter types of problems can be fairly easily identified and addressed via the sort of staging suggested above; the former weaknesses are best addressed in exercises throughout the semester.

Finally, I should mention that staging is just one way of increasing the effectiveness of exams as learning tools. Another way is to simplify the examination itself by, for example, not asking a question trailed by hints or subquestions that can overwhelm students or lead them to answer each question in order rather than to write an essay on one clearly stated question.[9]

I also tend to have students answer the same questions, avoiding assessment problems that arise from inevitable differences in the difficulty of questions. Finally, I grade the exams "blind": students only put numbers on their blue books, 3 x 5 cards and examination sheets. This goes a very long way towards minimizing the "halo" effect: when I call out the numbers and match names with grades, I am often surprised at the results.

NOTES

1. A clear-eyed, yet hopeful, assessment of the difficulties many students have is provided in Jane Freimiller, "The One-Page Philosopher: Short Writing Assignments for Introductory Classes," *Teaching Philosophy*, vol. 20, no. 3 (September 1997): 269-76.

2. "Writing-to-learn" is part of the pedagogical vocabulary developed within the 'Writing Across the Curriculum' movement, which emphasizes the use of writing as a tool for teaching, not just evaluation. An early example of efforts to incorporate WAC techniques in the teaching of philosophy is Jeffrey Berger's "Writing to Learn in Philosophy," *Teaching Philosophy,* vol. 7, no. 3 (July 1984): 217-22. The approach to essay exams that I suggest in this paper stems from that pedagogical movement, and in particular owes a big debt to John C. Bean's *Engaging Ideas: The Professor's Guide to Integrating Writing, Critical Thinking and Active Learning in the Classroom* (San Francisco: Jossey-Bass Inc., 1996). Bean's book is an indispensable source of practical advice on using writing to improve student learning in any discipline.

3. Some of the difficulties that students can have in learning what it means to take a position and provide evidence for it are documented in B. Walvoord and J. Breihan, "Arguing and Debating: Breihan's History Course," in B. Walvoord and M. P. McCarthy, eds., *Thinking and Writing*

in College: A Naturalistic Study of Students in Four Disciplines (Urbana: NCTC, 1990): 97-143. Sensitivity to such issues of cognitive development is often missing in philosophical contexts. For example, Perry and Bratman, in their widely-used introductory text, include advice on how to read philosophical texts "aggressively," which in their terms means to "adopt the stance of the intelligent and perceptive opponent, thus coming to understand the case the philosopher is trying to make." (See J. Perry and M. Bratman, *Introduction to Philosophy: Classical and Contemporary Readings*, 3rd ed. {New York: Oxford University Press, 1999}: 2-6.) This advice could only be of use to a student who already understands what it is to make a case for something, not to mention what it is to adopt a critical attitude toward it.

4. An excellent article that examines the lack of basic epistemological education and—even more importantly—the resistance to critical thinking that often accompany the lack of critical thinking skills is Shelagh Crooks, "Developing the Critical Attitude," *Teaching Philosophy*, vol. 18, no. 4 (December 1995): 313-25. This article is a must-read for anyone in any discipline concerned with critical-thinking issues.

5. A heuristic for improving student comprehension of philosophy texts—based on having students focus on statements in their readings that are puzzling or incompatible with their beliefs—is suggested by Jonathan Adler in "Reading and Interpretation: A Heuristic for Improving Students' Comprehension of Philosophy Texts," in T. Kasachkoff, ed., *In The Socratic Tradition: Essays on Teaching Philosophy* (Lanham, MD: Rowman & Littlefield Publishers, Inc., 1998): 37-46. Bean (*op. cit.*) also suggests many reading strategies, such as developing reading guides that focus attention on critical aspects of the text. Adler, Bean, and Perry and Bratman (op. cit.) all agree that a critical factor in increasing comprehension is simply getting students to read slower. The introductory class that I have in mind in this essay has sufficient reading skill to be able to learn to read original works with the aid of such heuristics; I do not assume that they can already do this.

6. For a collection of important articles on WAC, see A. Young & T. Fulwiler, eds., *Writing Across the Disciplines* (Upper Montclair: Boynton/ Cook, 1986).

7. For a suggestion that daily essay quizzes can help increase learning, see P. A. Connor-Greene and J. W. Murdoch, "Does Writing Matter? Assessing the Impact of Daily Essay Quizzes in Enhancing Student Learning," *Language and Learning Across the Disciplines*, vol. 4, no. 1 (May 2000): 16-21. In the study reported here, psychology students who had

daily graded essays performed better than those who did not when given an essay quiz on a professional research article on an unfamiliar topic. The problem with such exercises, of course, is how to manage the grading load.

8. For suggestions on how multiple-choice exams can be used to bolster learning, see C. Bolt-Lee and S. D. Foster, "Examination Retakes in Accounting: Increasing Learning by Writing After the Exam," *Language and Learning Across the Disciplines,* vol. 4, no. 2 (August 2000): 40-46. The method described here of allowing students to "retake" missed questions by explaining why their original answer was incorrect could be adapted to essay exams or even to short-answer tests.

9. John C. Bean has many useful suggestions for improving essay questions to make them more effective. See *Engaging Ideas: The Professor's Guide to Integrating Writing, Critical Thinking. and Active Learning in the Classroom, op. cit.*: 191-92.

BIBLIOGRAPHY

Adler, J. E. "Reading and Interpretation: A Heuristic for Improving Students' Comprehension of Philosophy Texts." in T. Kasachkoff, ed., *In The Socratic Tradition: Essays on Teaching Philosophy*(Lanham, MD: Rowman & Littlefield Publishers, Inc. 1998): 37-46.

Bean, John C.. *Engaging Ideas: The Professor's Guide to Integrating Writing, Critical Thinking, and Active Learning in the Classroom* (San Francisco: Jossey-Bass Inc. 1996).

Berger, Jeffrey. "Writing to Learn in Philosophy," *Teaching Philosophy,* vol. 7 no. 3 (July 1984): 217-22.

Bolt-Lee, C. and Foster, S. D. "Examination Retakes in Accounting: Increasing Learning by Writing After the Exam," *Language and Learning Across the Disciplines,* vol. 4, no. 2 (August (2000): 40-46.

Connor-Greene, P. A. and Murdoch, J. W., "Does Writing Matter? Assessing the Impact of Daily Essay Quizzes in Enhancing Student Learning," *Language and Learning Across the Disciplines,* vol. 4, no. 1 (May, 2000): 16-21.

Crooks, Shelagh. "Developing the Critical Attitude," *Teaching Philosophy,* vol. 18, no. 4 (December 1995): 313-25.

Freimiller, Jane. "The One-Page Philosopher: Short Writing Assignments for Introductory Classes," *Teaching Philosophy,* vol. 20, no. 3 (September 1997): 269-76.

Perry, J. and Bratman, M. *Introduction to Philosophy: Classical and Contemporary Readings,* 3rd ed. (New York: Oxford University Press, 1999): 2-6.

Walvoord, B. and Breihan, J., "Arguing and Debating: Breihan's History Course," in B. Walvoord and McCarthy, M. P., eds., *Thinking and Writing in College: A Naturalistic Study of Students in Four Disciplines* (Urbana: NCTC, 1990): 97-143.

Young, A. & Fulwiler, T., eds., *Writing Across the Disciplines* (Upper Montclair: Boynton/Cook, 1986).

PART III
Teaching Applied Ethics

Chapter 8

From the "Applied" to the Practical: Teaching Ethics for Use

Joan C. Callahan

I. From the "Applied" to the Practical

So-called applied ethics has a bad reputation among some philosophers. This is puzzling, since many of the philosophers commonly studied in moral theory courses were concerned to address moral questions that were raised by the ideologies and practices of their times. Kant, for example, was concerned to secure reliability for moral judgments in a Newtonian world. And Bentham and Mill were committed to changing a number of the social attitudes and practices in nineteenth-century British society. Even Plato had "applied" worries about the social effects of the teaching of the sophists. And Plato, like all political philosophers since, intended that his political theory have application to the construction of public policy. Given the history of moral philosophy, it is odd, at best, that doing so-called applied ethics is often questioned as a properly philosophical enterprise.

Perhaps the problem is simply a stubborn residuum of moral philosophy's brush with logical positivism. More likely, the cause is some combination of that encounter and the misapprehension that follows from the name "applied ethics," which suggests that

doing this kind of ethics merely involves taking general normative theories and applying them to various questions of current
societal concern. This model takes "applied ethics" to ask what,
for example, Kant's theory or Mill's theory might have to say
about the morality of elective abortion, or what Aristotle's theory
might have to say about the morality of using certain drugs. It
may be that some instructors just beginning to teach so-called
applied ethics occupy their students with these kinds of questions; but (happily) this is not universally the case. Because of this
(and despite the fact that linguistic habits die hard), I shall mean
by "practical ethics" the kind of ethical inquiry that takes as its
direct concern the resolution of concrete morally problematic
cases and issues of moral urgency in the lived world.

Although practical ethics borrows insights from theories of
moral axiology, theories of moral obligation, and from metaethics,
the task is not simply to work out applications of existing ethical
theories. It is, rather, to attempt to find acceptable solutions to
moral problems of present and practical urgency. This involves
much more than merely doing some sort of philosophical technology where high-level theory is simply brought over to practice.
When done well, questions addressed within practical ethics con-
tinually raise important theoretical and methodological questions
for general theories of moral good, right, and for metaethics.[1] For
example, attempting to answer questions pertaining to securing
adequately informed and adequately voluntary consent to medical or surgical interventions in health-care provision raises a number of significant questions about what it means for *any* choice to
be rational and genuinely voluntary. Similarly, questions in professional ethics regarding the distribution of certain goods and
services raise deep questions regarding basic human goods and
the possibility maximizing the potential of characteristically human lives. In raising and addressing these questions, theorists
working in practical ethics are inseparable from theorists working
in more familiar areas of ethics. What is true, however, is that
good practical ethics teaching is in some important ways quite
different from good moral theory teaching. Specifically, there are
differences in content and focus, in goals, and in method.

II. Content and Focus

Although, historically, moral philosophers generally have been motivated to do their work out of concern about the practical moral questions of their times, the focus of moral theory courses is just what the kind name suggests—moral *theory*. One might teach an excellent course in traditional moral theory, yet never once discuss any practical moral dilemmas. For example, in a moral theory course, one might concentrate on the nature of different theories of moral obligation, such as Kant's and Mill's, focusing on the relative merits of a priori and empirical theories, asking if either type of theory is more likely to yield moral knowledge. In the same course, one might spend considerable time examining Mill's purported "proof" of the principle of utility and/or the purported equivalence of Kant's several formulations of the categorical imperative, and/or the logical differences between Ross' intuitionism and the intuitionism found in Rawls' method of reflective equilibrium or Nagel's pluralism. Alternatively, one might focus a moral theory course on questions having to do with the very nature of moral discourse or the analysis of moral terms or whether free action is possible. In short, concrete normative issues might never be addressed in a moral theory course, and this, of itself, would have nothing whatever to do with the appropriateness of the course's content or the value of the course. But things are different when it comes to practical ethics courses—courses in business ethics, health care ethics, legal ethics, and the like—within which the morally problematic issues of some "form of life" (more or less broadly construed) direct focus and content. In principle, a good practical ethics course need never concern itself with the finer points of theories drawn from the history of moral philosophy. Indeed, never even mentioning Aristotle, Kant, Mill, Rawls, or any other important moral theorist of itself says nothing about the quality of a practical ethics course.

III. Goal

The differences in content and focus in moral theory and practical ethics courses provide some clues as to how goals in teaching these courses might differ. A legitimate goal in moral theory courses might consist in acquainting students with one branch of the history of philosophy or one branch of systematic philosophy as a matter of purely intellectual interest, much as an academic course in religious studies might focus on exposing students to certain religious traditions as a way of deepening their appreciation of a culture's heritage. That is, a course in moral theory need not concern itself with helping students to resolve for themselves any real-life moral dilemmas, any more than an academic religious studies course need concern itself with helping students resolve for themselves any theological dilemmas. Practical ethics courses, on the other hand, can hardly remain neutral on the goal of helping students attempt to resolve some morally dilemmatic issues, since practical ethics takes the resolution of such issues as its proximate concern. There are several projects to be pursued in practical ethics courses if students are to be able to use such courses to help them attempt to resolve real-life moral dilemmas.

1. Recognizing Moral Issues

A first step in practical ethics courses needs to be getting students to *recognize* moral issues. Issues that have a moral content are those that (minimally) involve the rights and/or welfare of persons (and/or other sentient beings) and/or the character of the acting agent. Helping students to recognize such issues where they often go unnoticed is crucial. In a bioethics course, for example, it is important to get students to see that not all decisions commonly made by health-care providers are merely medical ones, and that providers sometimes inadvertently overstep the bounds of their authority and expertise by making important value judgments for patients. Such decisions might involve a physician's electing aggressive treatment for a severely damaged infant—a judgment that may be presented to the child's parents as a purely medical one, but which is really a moral judgment that may not be the physician's to make. Similarly, helping students to see that some rather standard behaviors in health-care provision are unjustifiably manipulative or even coercive is to make them aware of conventional, unreflective action—a point they might not discover without having it pointed out to them. An important first project in teaching practical ethics, then, is a kind of consciousness-raising that helps to sensitize students to the moral complexity of the world.

2. Stimulating the Moral Imagination

Closely connected to the task of helping students to recognize moral issues is the task of stimulating the moral imagination. As elementary as it may seem, students often need to be made aware that their attitudes toward (or indifference to) what is morally acceptable and what is not issue in actions or failures to act that can have serious effects on the rights and well-being of others. Thus, for example, people who do not realize that certain public policies or institutional policies are oppressive to women or members of certain minorities, or to persons generally, may support those policies or miss opportunities to oppose those policies. Such enlivening often requires stimulating students' capacity to imagine what it feels like to be a person directly affected by a certain practice or policy. For students to understand, say, the vulnerability of patients in hospital settings, they must be able imaginatively to assume the place of the hospitalized patient, who may be ill, bored, confused by complex machinery and terminology, feeling displaced, and affected by any number of the other daunting features of institutionalized life (even for just a little while).[2] Similarly, getting students to understand why conducting biomedical experiments on prisoners is morally problematic may require getting them to imagine what life in prison is like and how seductive various benefits of participating in experiments can be—breaks from routine, a little money, and some extra attention in the infirmary—and how this raises serious worries about prisoners giving genuinely informed consent to such experiments.

The goal of stimulating the moral imagination is closely related to the first—recognizing moral issues—since it is in the exercise of such imagination that we often come to see moral issues where we saw none before.

3. Sharpening Analytical/Critical Skills

At least two more goals of practical ethics courses are connected to the relativism that is so often suggested by students in beginning ethics courses—a relativism reflected in remarks such as: "Well, it is right for him but not right for her." I assume I am not alone in having used the example of the Holocaust to make some point about justice or gross immorality, only to have students say things like "It was right for Hitler," or "Who's to say what's right?" Many students are extremely reluctant to call *any* action (or practice) morally wrong. To be sure, calling another person's action morally wrong does amount to a strong and important claim. And establishing exact criteria for moral rightness and wrongness has eluded philosophers for centuries, and continues to elude us. Aware of the hazards of moral evaluation, students often do not want to "pass judgment"—they want to be careful about condemning the actions of other persons, the practices of other societies, and practices in earlier stages of our own society. Students want to be tolerant of differences, and this is a good thing. But when "tolerance" becomes so extensive that we are left morally resourceless, the virtue of tolerance swells into its excess and everything becomes permissible.

One of the goals of practical ethics courses is to help students see that even though moral questions are difficult, we can go a long way before we need to say, "Well, we just disagree on our fundamental moral commitments." By helping students hone their analytical and imaginative skills, we can help them to see that we share a large common moral ground that can be defended on the basis of reasonable moral principles, and that ground can provide us with reasons for ruling out certain kinds of actions and practices as morally unacceptable. This is not to suggest, of course, that all morally aware, imaginative, and reasonable persons will always agree on how morally dilemmatic cases and issues are to be decided. But it is to suggest that we can help our students to see that careful reflection on what might initially seem to be an utterly unresolvable case or issue will often at least reveal that some potential resolutions are not consistent with moral principles to which they are committed, or that what was initially thought to be a case or issue requiring one sort of resolution might be given a different sort of resolution, say, as in some cases involving severely defective newborns, where the proper resolution lies not in determining *what* should be done, but in determining *who* should decide what should be done. Thus, sharpening students' conceptual and imaginative skills can help them to rule out certain potential resolutions that might initially seem acceptable to them, and can help them to consider potential resolutions that were not initially apparent to them.

4. Sorting Out Disagreements

Hard moral questions *are* hard because they tend to leave residues of disagreement among even the most sensitive and astute moral agents. No matter how refined students' analytical skills become, such residues will tend to remain. It is here that tolerance in ethics has its proper place. The instructor in a practical ethics course assumes a twofold task: her job is not just to help students put *themselves* in the position of others, but to help them put themselves in the position of *others*. That is, to get them to realize that there are legitimately differing ways of ordering values and that some differences in value judgment may be inevitable and may also be acceptable. An important part of an instructor's task, then, is to encourage students to express their moral misgivings about proposed resolutions to morally dilemmatic cases and issues, to sort out disagreements that are morally reasonable from those that are not, and to work toward acceptable moral closure despite some residual disagreement. Indeed, often decisions will need to be made despite serious and morally responsible disagreements. The practical ethics course is the perfect laboratory for learning how to reduce disagreements that are not well justified and to make moral progress despite reasonable disagreements.

5. Influencing Decisions and Behavior

The goals I have so far suggested as proper to practical ethics courses are generally accepted as appropriate. But the goal of influencing decisions and behavior is controversial. Daniel Callahan, who has offered his own version of the goals I have sketched, has argued that the goal of changing behavior is a dubious one for ethics courses.[3] *Changing* behavior is certainly a dubious goal, since it assumes that all students in such courses behave in morally unacceptable ways. But the goal of *influencing* behavior is different; and if practical ethics courses are to be useful to students, then they are to be useful in the real and hard business of moral decision making. (I certainly hope that my courses in business ethics, biomedical ethics, and professional ethics—as well as my graduate courses in topics that raise questions about rights and public policies—will help students to take moral care in their personal, professional, and political lives.) The reluctance of philosophers to admit influencing decision making and behavior as a legitimate goal of practical ethics courses strikes me as odd, at best. It is reminiscent of the unwillingness of moral philosophers earlier in this century to address any normative questions whatever. If practical ethics is worth doing and worth doing well, it is precisely because doing practical ethics holds out the promise of influencing individual behavior (as well as public policy) in a morally positive way. Helping students to decide and behave in ways that are reflective, well reasoned, intellectually responsible, and sensitive is not only a legitimate goal of practical ethics teaching, it is also the goal that underpins all the others and that gives practical ethics teaching (and scholarship) its reason for being.

IV. Implementation

If we accept the goals I have sketched as proper to practical ethics teaching, what kinds of problems might be expected in pursuing them, and what might be some strategies for avoiding these problems?

1. *Practicing Coming to Closure*: I have already touched on one potential problem in practical ethics teaching—the problem of hasty relativism. Given the pluralism of our society, the desire to be tolerant, and the very real problems that intra-personal and intra-societal disagreements about morality raise, students may retreat into a relativism or subjectivism where everything is permitted, or they may resort to the "pragmatic" view that morality is one thing, getting through life is another. It is important, then, in any course (or course component) in practical ethics to discuss and experiment with moral closure and concrete suggestions for action. By "closure" I mean the *resolution* of a moral dilemma or debate, a resolution that is supported by the best reasons available and recognized by the disputants as a morally responsible solution that takes seriously the positions of those who may still disagree. In this regard, a potentially useful exercise is to break students into small groups and instruct them to assume that their

group makes up a committee that *must* make a decision on some morally dilemmatic case or policy. The groups can be directed to work together until they come to a decision that everyone can "live with," even though not everyone might agree that the solution is ideal. Of course, it may sometimes turn out that a group simply is not able to come to such an agreement. But this happens in real life as well, and if it happens in a class, this does not reflect badly on the merits of the exercise. In such cases, the reasons for failure to come to closure can be explored by the whole class. Is the remaining disagreement one that can be well defended? If not, why? If so, can any of the other groups offer a solution that avoids the problem(s) giving rise to the disagreement? If not, given that a decision *must* be made, what can the class suggest to ensure that the least morally problematic decision is made? Exercises like this make the ethics class a practice ground for the real-life work of making hard but reasoned choices. At the same time, they can help students see that reflective morality is workable, and that there can be considerably more agreement in ethics than they might have suspected.

2. *Creating a "Safe Place"*: Attempts to come to moral closure and the goal of influencing behavior raise the potential problems of closing prematurely and of indoctrination. Connected to these problems is what can be the threatening nature of practical ethics courses and the danger of suppressing those students who may have unpopular views.

The very nature of practical ethics courses is such that they tend to touch on people's most deeply held moral convictions. Because of this and because of the need to have students practice forming and defending moral judgments on specific cases and issues, practical ethics courses can be threatening to students in a way that moral theory courses may not be. Practical ethics courses press students to become clear about their own biases and to examine the reliability of their own ways of making moral decisions, and this, unavoidably, makes students feel vulnerable. It is crucial, then, that instructors guard against letting their own views settle issues, and against allowing students with unpopular views to think that they should yield to more popular ones. This is important to keep in mind when selecting texts. Students should be exposed to a range of positions on issues and to the best possible defenses of conflicting views. Being able to respond to the strongest objections to one's own view is necessary if one is to have confidence in one's own view; no less important is encouraging the participation of students who hold views that conflict with what the majority thinks. Fostering genuine dialogue requires the creation of a safe place—a place where students can expect that their views will be heard and taken seriously. This responsibility, of course, is not extraordinary; all philosophy courses should encourage dialogue. It is, however, particularly important to set a tone that creates a safe place in classes where people's basic moral convictions may be up for public examination.

3. *Structuring Discussions*: One way of creating a safe place is to build into the structure of discussions a protection for those in the minority. Since practical ethics courses are concerned to foster resolution of concrete moral problems, it is appropriate to include in them a good number of discussions on particular cases. One helpful way of doing this is to assign written case analyses before the cases will be discussed in class. (I will suggest a formula for writing these analyses in the next section.) Before beginning the discussion, a poll can be taken asking where students came out on the case, and students in the minority can be asked to justify their position first. The next portion of the discussion can be limited to replies to the arguments given, and students in the minority can then be asked to respond to those replies. A procedure like this ensures that the minority view will be kept before the class through most of a case discussion, and it assures students that minority views will be taken seriously.

I believe that the goals and suggestions that I have sketched can best be served by using both readings that address the issues systematically *and* cases that raise the issues concretely. One helpful structure involves first introducing a hard case that raises the issue, then looking at some various ways of addressing the issue, and then having the students do a case analysis that concretizes the problem—either the case that was initially used to introduce the issue or some other case. It is extremely helpful to have students write out their analyses before discussing cases in class. Students often need more than simply an opportunity to think about a case in advance of discussing it. And they often need considerable guidance on how to go about doing that thinking.

V. Teaching Ethics for Use

Most helpful to most students is providing a clear formula that they can use for case analyses. One such formula directs students in the following way.[4]

1. *Set out the various possible resolutions of the case.* Be sure to tax your imagination. The case may admit of more alternatives than are initially obvious.

2. *Set out the facts relevant to supporting each resolution you have identified.* Generate as complete a set of lists as possible of the *facts* (known, possible, probable) that might be used to support *each* of the options you have identified on how the case might be resolved. Relevant facts might include the following: someone will or is likely to be harmed (physically, emotionally, financially, in reputation, and so on) if a certain resolution is chosen; limited resources expended in one way could be expended in another way, meeting some other pressing need; some decision will interfere with the liberty of an individual; a proposed resolution involves coercion, deception, manipulation, breach of trust, breaking a promise, exploitation, unequal treatment, and so on.

3. *Set out the moral principles that underpin the selection of the facts on your lists.* That is, each fact that you identify as supportive of a possible resolution will be relevant because of some underlying moral principle. Articulate these principles clearly. Relevant principles might include the following: Prevent harm; Do good; Be fair; Be loyal; Keep your promises; Do not inflict harm on other persons/sentient beings; Maintain integrity; Be candid; Live up to the requirements of your office or role; It is permissible to protect one's own interests; Respect the liberty/autonomy of persons, and so on. Combining these principles with the relevant facts you have selected provides moral arguments for the possible resolutions you have identified. So, for example, an argument from your lists for one resolution for a case might look like this:

Premise 1: Principle: Keep promises
Premise 2: Fact: Doing X, which will be done if Option A is selected, involves keeping a promise
Conclusion: Choose Option A

4. Reflect on the options you have identified and on your lists. Ask yourself (again) if you have included all potentially acceptable options and if your lists of facts and the principles that lead you to select those facts as supportive of the options you have identified include all the plausible arguments for each of the alternatives you have identified. Are the lists of facts and principles supporting the view you are inclined to take longer than your other lists? If so, *be sure* that you have been as thorough as possible in laying out the facts and principles supportive of the resolutions that differ from the one you are inclined to favor.

5. Make and articulate your decision. After careful consideration of the options you have identified and the arguments supporting each, select the option you think is the one that should be chosen.

6. Justify your decision. Set out your *positive* reasons for the decision you have made. This will take you back to your lists. Say which considerations on your lists of facts and principles you found the most compelling.

7. Anticipate and respond to the most serious potential objection to your decision. Go back to the lists supporting the option(s) other than the one you have chosen. Use these lists to help you clarify what you take to be the strongest potential objection to your position or to your positive argument for your decision. Offer your reply to that objection.

8. Clarify the costs or downside of your decision. Go back to your lists a final time and use them to help you articulate what you take to be the most morally significant cost(s) of your decision. (This may be related to what you take to be the strongest potential objection to your decision.)

A procedure incorporating such steps goes a long way toward fulfilling the goals I have suggested are proper to practical ethics courses and will nicely prepare students to engage in a lively, sophisticated class discussion. Most important, providing students with a method for helping them systematically sort through morally dilemmatic cases gives them a procedure they can use long after the course is over and they are confronted with the hard moral questions that inevitably challenge us all.[5]

NOTES

1. See, for example, Arthur L. Caplan, "Ethical Engineers Need Not Apply: The State of Applied Ethics Today," *Science, Technology, and Human Values* 6, no. 33 (1980): 24-32.

2. See, for example, Samuel Gorovitz, *Doctors' Dilemmas: Moral Conflict and Medical Care* (New York: Oxford University Press, 1985).

3. Daniel Callahan, "Goals in the Teaching of Ethics," in *Ethics Teaching in Higher Education*, ed. Daniel Callahan and Sissela Bok (New York: Plenum, 1980), 61-80.

4. See Joan C. Callahan, ed., *Ethical Issues in Professional Life* (Oxford: Oxford University Press, 1988), appendix 2, for a fuller discussion.

5. This paper was revised in September 1996. Thanks to Tziporah Kasachkoff for encouraging me to write the first version and for her helpful suggestions for revising it.

Chapter 9

A Social Dilemma Game for an Ethics Class

Marshall Missner

Introduction

One of the most troubling problems in ethics is what can be termed "the social dilemma." This dilemma may be stated as follows: there are some goods that we as individuals want that can only be achieved by the action (or inaction) of a large number of individuals. It would therefore seem that each individual who desires these goods has a good reason for joining in the collective action (or restraint) that is necessary for obtaining them. However, if there are enough *other* people who are doing (or refraining from doing) what has to be done so that these goods are produced, then these goods will be forthcoming no matter how one behaves. So given others' conduct, an individual may be the beneficiary of certain goods without himself or herself having to act in the ways that are necessary to produce them. But although this is true with respect to any particular individual, not *every* individual can rationally engage in this line of reasoning, for were every individual to reason and act in this way, the benefits producible only if a large number of people act (or refrain from acting) in a particular way would not be forthcoming. Sometimes this dilemma is called the "problem of the free rider." The "free-rider" problem has been discussed by many philosophers from Thomas Hobbes[1] to David Gauthier.[2] It is also the subject of discussion among sociologists[3] and decision theorists.[4]

In the ethics class that I teach, I raise this social dilemma when we discuss the Gyges story in Book II of Plato's *Republic*[5] (the story of someone who can make himself invisible, thereby allowing him to commit adultery, theft and murder, while remaining immune from discovery). Although the Gyges story does not concern cheating in its relation to collective or public goods such as lower prices for everyone, it does focus on the question of whether it is important to act justly even when no one else knows how one is acting. The Gyges story is relevant to the free-rider issue because the free rider can benefit from collective action only because his or her noncontribution is not known.

Typically, students view the Gyges story as one of theoretical interest only, as they rightly see that no one actually has, as Gyges does, both unlimited opportunity to do evil and complete certainty that he or she can get away with it. I point out to them, however, that often we are in the Gyges-like position of having the opportunity to conduct ourselves, without discovery by others, in ways that are less than admirable (such as when we falsely fill out our income tax forms to avoid paying our rightful share of taxes, litter when no one is looking, and do not cast our vote in public elections). In all of these cases, the free rider seems to come out ahead, for the free rider gets some benefit without paying the cost, and if enough other people are free riders, it seems that one might as well cheat, because the public good is going to disappear anyway.

Although class discussion of the free-rider issue is often quite lively, I wanted to make it even more vivid and less hypothetical by having students face this problem themselves. Fortunately, I came across a "social dilemma game" in Howard Raiffa's *The Art and Science of Negotiation* that he says is based on work by Thomas Schelling.[6] The social dilemma game goes like this: a number of people are each given the choice of voting 'nobly' or 'selfishly.' They are told that if all the individuals choose to be 'noble,' all get a monetary reward. But if all individuals but one choose to be 'noble,' the 'noble' ones get a smaller reward, and the 'selfish' free rider gets a greater reward. The rewards keep scaling down with increasing percentages of 'selfish' voters until at some point the 'noble' voters begin to lose money. No matter how many people vote to be 'noble,' the ones who vote 'selfish' always do better, but if all vote to be 'selfish,' all suffer. With this information, the individuals in the group are asked to vote either 'noble' or 'selfish.' (Raiffa reports that when he used this game in his class, he was disturbed by how many of his students said that, in this situation, they would vote 'selfish.')

I could have presented this game "as is," but it is more gripping when students experience the free-rider problem as a real one. To do this, I have the rewards and penalties involve the their grades. At the beginning of the course, I told my students that I would give eleven un-announced quizzes concerning the assigned class readings and that the average of the best ten scores would be 20 percent of the final grade. I now presented them with the following social dilemma: rather than have the grade that each student receives be a straight average of his or her earned grades on the quizzes, every student would be given a ballot in which he or she must vote either 'noble' or 'selfish.' The following are the rules governing how votes will translate into grades:

(a) If every student votes 'noble,' then the entire class will be better off, as the grade of each student will be raised.

(b) But if every student but one votes 'noble,' the student who voted 'selfish' will be even better off, as that student's grade will be raised in a greater amount than would be the case in situation (a).

(c) If no student votes 'noble,' all students will be worse, for each will lose some percentage of his or her grade.

(d) If all students but oneself votes 'selfish,' one had better be 'selfish' too; otherwise, one will be worse off than every other student, for one will receive a lower grade than the rest.

Putting the Game into Practice

First, everyone votes on a paper ballot to be 'noble' or 'selfish.' Second, everyone signs his or her ballot so that I, the instructor, cannot see the names of the voters at the same time that the vote—'noble' or 'selfish'—can itself be seen. Immediately after the voting, I tally the ballots without looking at the names of the voters. However, at the end of the semester, I do look at the names on the ballots and I distribute points to students according to the following schedule, which has been made known to students in advance:

% who are selfish	% who are noble	score for each noble person	score for each selfish person
100%	0%	—	-1.0
99%	1%	-2.0	-0.5
80%	20%	-1.5	0
70%	30%	-1.0	+0.5
60%	40%	-0.5	+1.0
50%	50%	0	+1.5
40%	60%	+0.5	+2.0
30%	70%	+1.0	+2.5
20%	80%	+1.5	+3.0
1%	99%	+2.0	+3.5
0%	100%	+2.5	—

Explanation of the Scoring System

The plus and minus numbers represent the number of points added or subtracted to the final average of each student's best unannounced quizzes. At the maximum, 3.5 points will be added to a student's grade, which means that three of that student's quizzes will be increased by one letter grade and one quiz will be increased by half of a grade. At the minimum end (-2.0), two of a student's quizzes will be lowered by one letter grade. If a student's grades are already all A's and the student voted in a way that would produce an increase in his or her grade, the added points will be counted as extra credit and added to that student's final average.

Points to notice:

    (a) If everyone is selfish, everyone suffers.
    (b) If everyone is noble, everyone prospers.
    (c) At each percentage level, the individual who votes 'selfish'does better than the individual who votes 'noble,' so the 'noble' students suffer in this situation.
    (d) If one looks carefully at the payoff schedule, one will see that no matter how one votes, the more other people that vote 'noble,' the better off one is.
    (e) From (d) it follows that if a student wants to benefit his or her classmates, that student should vote 'noble.'
    (f) If one looks carefully at the payoff schedule, one will also see that no matter how one votes, the more other people that vote 'selfish,' the worse off one is.
    (g) From (f) it follows that if one votes 'selfish,' no matter what one's intentions are, one will be harming one's classmates.

Every time that I have used this game, there has been intense interest in it. Students pay careful attention and usually take it very seriously. (I was once asked, "Are you really going to do this?" My reply was that Yes, I was really going to.)

I encourage discussion in the class *before* the vote. At this point students usually offer some interesting arguments as to why everyone should vote 'noble.' Since we have already examined the ethical views of Kant, Aristotle, and the utilitarians, some students draw on these views to try to convince their classmates to vote 'noble.' Sometimes I am asked to leave the room, so that the discussion can be more candid. I always agree to, but I am usually told later that, while I was out, the students tried to figure out a way to make sure that everyone *would* vote 'noble.' However, given that the voting is secret, it is difficult to see how there could be a way to enforce nobility.

The most common result of the vote is that about 80 percent vote 'noble' and 20 percent vote 'selfish.' That means that everyone gains at least a point or two. (I once had a class in which everyone voted 'noble,' but in another class 70 percent voted 'selfish.' In the latter case, the 'noble' voters each lost one point. There was some unhappiness about that, and it was directed toward me.)

Discussion after the Game

It is worthwhile noting that many students claim they vote 'noble' only because they have agreed to vote 'noble' (even though they know the agreement to be unenforceable). Some say that had they voted immediately after being presented with the game, they would have voted 'selfish,' but once they had agreed to vote 'noble,' they felt obligated to stick to their agreement. This is in line with what I usually find: if members of a class make an explicit agreement with each other to vote 'noble,' then the percentage of 'noble' voters is higher than if no explicit agreement is made.

When some students cheat and vote 'selfish' after it is agreed that everyone in the class will vote 'noble' (the 'selfish' voters thereby gaining points for themselves at the expense of their classmates), some 'noble'-voting students express resentment. Even though the 'noble'-voting students gain extra credit on account of the way the class voted (since most of the class has voted 'noble'), some of these students still feel taken advantage of because the few students who voted 'selfish' gain even more. A more serious concern arises when students actually lose points because of the cheating of their classmates. This happened in one class that I taught. In that class, there were enough 'selfish' voters to actually cost other students points. (However, since the number of points lost did not amount to much, students in that class were not greatly upset about the results of the vote.) It may be worth discussing with the class the difference between resenting another when one loses out because that other has cheated and the resentment one might feel toward freeloaders, even when one is not disadvantaged (much) by their conduct.

Finally, there is a point to be made here about trust. The

'noble' voters exhibit a good deal of trust in their classmates, but the 'selfish' voters also display trust. After all, the 'selfish' voters only vote 'selfish' because they believe me when I say that no one will ever find out. I could easily betray this trust, but clearly I am taken at my word, as no one who votes 'selfish' thinks that I will reveal what he or she has done. (And of course, I don't.) It may be of some value discussing with students the apparent fact that the people who cheat in everyday situations trust that those few people who know about what they are doing, or are helping them do it, will not betray them.

Assessment of the Game

The main reason that I use this game is that I think it serves as a pedagogical device for illustrating the free-rider problem in a realistic and gripping way. The problem of the commons,[7] polluting the environment, overpopulation, and cheating on one's taxes all have the same free-rider/social dilemma structure. But although these problems may be of interest to students, they remain abstract. However, as the students play the game that I have described, they see very clearly what is involved in these situations—just how easy it is in real life sometimes to be a free rider, and how difficult it is in practice to convince others not to cheat.

Second, the game serves as a context for examining the ethical theories we study, as well as for discussions concerning ethical egoism, the nature and costs of altruism, and the social costs of everyone acting selfishly.

Third, the game certainly enlivens the course. Students pay very close attention to what is going on, and their attention is heightened by the suspense of trying to guess what will happen. After using the game a few times, the suspense factor has diminished for me, but still there are often some surprises. It always intrigues me to see how the dynamics of a particular class are affected by the development of students' discussion concerning how best to respond to this game.

Finally, the game has some effect on the self-consciousness of the students. They are put in a situation where they have an ethical choice to make and have to consider various reasons for the way they will act. This sometimes leads them to reflect on their own character and, often, on the characters of their classmates.

An Ethical Objection

In the several times that I have used the game, I have always asked my students afterward if anyone felt that it was emotionally unsettling. Some students do report feeling hurt a bit. But since almost all students actually gain a point or two, and the penalties, if they are incurred at all, are very small, it is very unlikely that the results of the game will significantly affect anyone's final grade.

Nevertheless, I am bothered by the possibility of the following scenario: A righteously indignant student confronts me and complains, "I took an ethics course in order to learn about what is the right thing to do. And then you had us play this Social Dilemma game, and I voted 'noble.' Since everyone else voted 'selfish,' I lost two points on my average, and that means that I am going to get a B instead of an A. Is that fair? Should I be penalized, particularly in an ethics class for being noble?"

A good reply, I believe, would deal with the understanding that is supposed to be the result of an ethics class. Ethics deals with the perennial problems of why it is so difficult for human beings to just do the right thing and why it is so hard to get people to cooperate. A complete answer to these questions would have to deal with psychological and sociological matters such as the nature of motivators and inducements in human action and the nature and extent of environmental influences on what we choose to do. But there is also a logical aspect to these problems that involves the meaning of "rationality" and the structure of the cooperative situation. It does seem to be the case that the indignant student has gained some understanding of why cooperation is problematical and why it is that everyone else is not simply just good.

But the real issue the indignant student is probably raising is this: why be noble if it will not be rewarded? The student might well conclude that nobility without reward is worthless. All I can say to this student is that he or she now sees that avoiding the free-rider choice is not always rewarded and that this might be an important point to learn. But note also that if enough people are selfish and try to get the free-rider benefit, then everyone could very well end up suffering; and that is also an important lesson.

NOTES

1. Thomas Hobbes, *The Leviathan; or The Matter, Forme and Power of a Commonwealth, Eccliasticall and Civil* (Oxford: Basil Blackwell, 1946).

2. David Gauthier, *Morals by Agreement* (New York: Oxford University Press, 1986).

3. The classic statement of the free-rider problem is to be found in Mancur Olson, *The Logic of Collective Action* (Cambridge, MA: Harvard University Press, 1965), 55-56.

4. A very fine anthology that contains a useful bibliography is in Richard Campbell and Lanning Snowden, *Paradoxes of Rationality and Cooperation* (Vancouver: The University of British Columbia Press, 1985). For a very clear and readable introduction to this field, see Morton Davis, *Game Theory: A Non-Technical Introduction* (New York: Basic Books, 1983).

5. Plato, *The Republic*, trans. G. M. A. Grube (Indianapolis: Hackett, 1974), 31-33.

6. Howard Raiffa, *The Art and Science of Negotiation* (Cambridge, MA: Harvard University Press, 1982), 347.

7. Garrett Hardin, "The Tragedy of the Commons," *Science* 162 (1968): 1243-48.

PART IV
Teaching Philosophy with Computers

Chapter 10

Teaching with a Screen

Lawrence M. Hinman

Introduction

Four years ago I began teaching with a screen, that is, teaching classes with a computer and projector and screen in the front of the room. Initially, conditions were primitive. The computer for the classroom was kept in a locked storage room down the hall. Before each class, it was necessary to get it out of the room, roll it down to the classroom, hook it up, and then pray that the internet connection worked. There were no speakers, and our academic computing services looked puzzled when asked about sound capabilities. (Napster changed all that.) Now, at least in the newer classrooms, all is changed. The computers are built into the front podium desk, room-darkening shades are on all the windows, the sound system is excellent, the projectors are brighter. All that is necessary is a little key to open the cabinet in the desk.

In the following remarks, I would like to reflect on some of the ways in which the presence of a screen in the classroom has had an effect on my teaching. In the course of these reflections, I shall talk about some of the technology, especially the software, and indicate some of its strengths and weaknesses.

In my experience, the impact of the screen in the classroom varies with the type of course being taught. I have found teaching with a screen most helpful and least intrusive in logic courses but more problematic in ethics courses where the screen is a positive factor in some respects but an impediment in other respects. Let us look at these issues in more detail.

Teaching Logic

For the past twenty-five years, I have taught introductory logic every year. Teaching a basic course in logic involves helping students to develop certain skills. But in order to develop these skills, students need to acquire a certain amount of knowledge of logical conventions and symbols and what they stand for and an understanding of how to manipulate these symbols. Teaching logic thus involves (a) conveying the requisite information (such as the conventions for Venn diagrams) to the students, (b) helping students to understand the relevant information through explanations and examples, and (c) helping students to develop proficiency in the application of the concepts they have studied. Classroom time is devoted primarily to the first two tasks but since the amount of information conveyed in an introductory course in logic is in fact relatively small, much of class time is devoted to understanding the key concepts that are presented. Proficiency in using these concepts is principally accomplished through homework exercises which are later reviewed in class, a review usually directed toward uncovering student misunderstandings of the concept.

I have found teaching with a screen to be a tremendous help in the logic classroom. My use of the screen in this (and in other courses) has gradually evolved to have the several components. First, I have integrated my logic (as well as some other) courses with a course website that I have developed.

(I started running my own web server in 1994, primarily because the support of our university's academic computing center was so bad it came closer to resistance than support. Being forced to develop a course website on my own, however, has turned out to be fortuitous since it has made web publishing and the development of further course websites far easier than it would otherwise have been.)

On-line Syllabus, Schedule, and 'Handouts'

I post the full syllabus for the class on the website, including the schedule of all classes and class assignments. This turns out to be particularly useful as last-minute changes to the schedule or to assignments can easily be posted on the web thus making the information easily available even to students who miss class. My on-line syllabus has quickly evolved into a substitute for class handouts generally. Many of the materials that I previously would have duplicated on paper and distributed in class—for example, sample quizzes and exams, review questions, and case studies—I now put on the web for easy student access and use. It is also easy to include links to other on-line logic resources that are beneficial to students. For example, I can now easily send students to Ron Blatt's elegant Java application for teaching moods and figures using Venn diagrams (an application to which Blatt is happy to have links).[1]

Answer Keys

I can post answer keys for homework assignments on the web. Although students are advised not to consult the answer keys while they are doing their homework, they are encouraged to refer to the answer key when checking their work to see where they might have made mistakes. Not only is this advantageous to students who miss class, it makes reviewing homework answers in the classroom easier as well. For instead of my students having to grapple with my semilegible writings on the board, they can now view neatly typed or computer-drawn answers to homework assignments. When it is time to go over homework assignments in class, all I have to do is click on the appropriate link on the web-based class schedule and the answer key for that set of exercises pops up on the screen.

My putting answer keys on my website proved to be a problem in a way that I had not initially anticipated: because my websites are open sites that are accessible to everyone, students in courses other than my own had access to the answer keys that I posted on my site even when their instructors (who were using the same logic book as I opposed their students' having access to the answer keys. 'Dedicated' course software packages (which I do not use) solve this problem by restricting access to the whole site to authenticated users only. My own solution is to have access to answer keys password-protected so that only my students can access these files.

This issue raised for me a number of new questions about academic integrity. Is it cheating for students in a course to surf the web and find other course sites that can help them, perhaps in ways that their instructor would not like but which the instructor did not explicitly forbid? Jim Moor has argued that new computer technologies can create "policy vacuums," areas in which we have yet to develop explicit rules to guide conduct.[2] The example I cited above is an example of such an area. Often instructors do not have an explicit policy forbidding students from accessing other course sites or restricting the ways in which they can use those sites, and usually this is because the instructors have not even thought of the possibility.

When issues such as this arise, all three groups involved have responsibilities. First, webmasters must be responsible in choosing what is to be put on the web and what kind of access will be permitted. Second, instructors need to be aware of new technologies and the ways in which they may be used by their students and to publish clear policies about these matters for their students. Third, students who have some reason to doubt whether it is appropriate to use a particular electronic source must act responsibly by asking their instructors whether use of that web-based resource is permitted. In some classes (such as mine), students are encouraged to use answer keys responsibly to help them to better understand the material; they are not to be used as a substitute for doing the work. In other classes, especially where homework is graded, instructors may prefer students not to have access to answer keys at all. Responsible students should always ask instructors to clarify what their particular policy is.

PowerPoint Presentations

A third on-line component which I include in the class schedule are PowerPoint presentations of the material.[3] PowerPoint is designed to be an electronic overhead program, flashing up one page of text or drawings after another. Over the years I have developed a set of PowerPoint presentations that cover all the topics to be covered in class. These are tightly integrated into the on-line schedule. For each class meeting, there may be one or more PowerPoint presentations, depending on the number of specific topics covered that day. For example, on a day where we will be dealing with fallacies, I will have prepared a Power Point presentation that deals with fallacies of relevance, another with fallacies of weak induction, and so on. As a result, all the lecture material for the course is on the web in a format that allows students to find specific topics easily and quickly. It is possible to save Power-Point presentations on the web in such a way that users of the website can play these presentations full-screen, moving through each slide a click at a time or using a navigator to go to a particular slide. Instructors should be aware of the fact that it is also possible to put PowerPoint presentations on the web so that students can simply right-click on the link and download the presentations to their own computer. This option enables students who have only dial-up access to the web at home, the convenience of downloading the website while connected to the university network and viewing the downloaded file off-line at a later time.

PowerPoint presentations of basic logical concepts work well in the classroom: they are useful for popping up definitions of fallacies, examples of particular fallacies, and the like. Typically, when we are analyzing arguments in ordinary language, it is easy just to 'pop up' the passage on a screen so that everyone can see it in the front of the room in legible form. Key words or phrases can be highlighted, and it is often useful to have two versions of the same slide—one without any markups or comments, and the other showing the various points in the passage that one wants to emphasize. (See below for a discussion of the way in which SmartBoard technology can further improve the use of Power-Point's in such situations.) And PowerPoint presentations can be helpful in more formal areas as well: Venn diagrams can be presented, one premise at a time, in a neat and colorful fashion. (At this stage of the technology, a certain amount of animation can be added to the individual slides, but this is still fairly limited.) Furthermore, PowerPoint presentations are extremely easy to create. Nonetheless although the ease of using PowerPoint in the presentation of logical concepts makes PowerPoint highly efficient in terms of time spent in developing a presentation, PowerPoint has the disadvantage of being inflexible in two ways.

First, as noted above, it has very limited animation capabilities. Basically, PowerPoint is designed to be an electronic overhead program, flashing up one page of text or drawings after another. Although, often, this is precisely what we want to do, sometimes in teaching logic we want to do more than this, and then PowerPoint falls short. For example, if we want to capture the flow of a particular argument or demonstrate the logical impact that one premise has on another (which, when I taught with a blackboard or whiteboard, I tried to do by means of drawing arrows) then it is precisely this dynamic sense that is difficult to capture in a static program such as PowerPoint.

Second, PowerPoint is not interactive: it is not possible to click a button and interact with the program, except in the limited sense that one chooses when to move from one slide to the next. For classroom presentations, this is usually not a major issue as the students are interacting not with the program but with the instructor and each other, but for on-line use by students when they are not in the classroom, interactivity is often highly desirable.

Other Presentation Packages

In light of the above deficiencies of PowerPoint, let me indicate some alternative possibilities for electronic presentations. There are at least two good ways to create animations for the web.

First, the most powerful way—in the sense of allowing tremendous flexibility in drawing and animation, far more than one can get in PowerPoint—is through the use of a dedicated animation program, that is, a program whose sole purpose is to produce animations. The best animation program now available is one from Macromedia called 'Flash'[4] (though recently Adobe has released a competing product, 'LiveMotion,'[5] that can create movies in the popular Flash format). Flash is highly powerful, has a full programming language that allows one to control virtually all aspects of the ways in which animations are created and played and allows one to create very sophisticated on-line animations that stream over the web quite efficiently. Whereas PowerPoint uses the metaphor of a slide or page as its basic unit, Flash uses a timeline and divides a movie into individual scenes.

Flash creates its drawings in what are called 'vector graphics.' Vector graphics create pictures through mathematical equations that describe how lines should be drawn (and, generally, how the picture should be constructed). As a result, the clarity of a drawing or picture created with vector graphics is independent of size. Thus, vector graphics provides the tremendous advantage of allowing you to zoom in on a particular part of a very detailed drawing, such as a complicated argument diagram or timeline, without losing clarity. You could, for example, easily zoom in on a region of a picture or drawing with a magnification of fifty and the zoomed-in region would remain as clear and crisp as it was originally. (The crystal clarity of zoomed-in areas of vector graphics stands in stark contrast to 'bitmaps' which are electronic drawings and pictures made up of a series of dots with each dot (or 'pixel') having a specific numeric value that indicates a particular color. Bitmaps do not resize very well and quickly become grainy if enlarged.)

Flash is also a great program for creating web-based interactions that involve responses from the user. One can, for example, create a quiz in Flash that records student responses to a database or file that is then sent to the instructor while at the same time giving immediate feedback to the student. This makes it easy to combine quizzing students with teaching them.

The other way in which you can create dynamic information is by using a program called 'Dynamic HTML.'[6] The advantage of DHTML is that it does not require any special software, whereas Flash requires the Flash player to be installed on the viewer's computer. The disadvantage of DHTML is that it does not behave the same way with all browsers. Because of this, an operation that works perfectly in Internet Explorer 5.5 may not work at all in Netscape Navigator 6. DHTML does, however, easily handle such things as on-line quizzes and interactions. For example, one can set up an interaction in which students can drag and drop premise or conclusion indicator words onto a particular icon as a way for students to practice identifying premise and conclusion indicators. In my experience, the best program for creating DHTML and on-line interactions such as the one described above is Macromedia's Dreamweaver MX. (The earlier version of this program was called 'Dreamweaver Ultradev.') It even has a free extension (a supplemental program or plug-in) called "CourseBuilder" that makes the process of creating on-line quizzes and exams much easier.[7]

The Interactive Whiteboard

Typically, when we teach with a screen, there is both a screen and a whiteboard in the front of the room. The whiteboard is clearly the direct instrument of the professor, whereas the screen is not (though of course, what is displayed on the screen will have been programmed or designed by the instructor beforehand). Recently, the whiteboard and the screen have been combined into one. The most successful version of this combination is called 'SmartBoard' which allows the teacher to project PowerPoint slides onto the board and then draw on the board to bring out particular points.[8] SmartBoard allows the instructor to save the slide with the writing on it to a file by simply tapping the screen. The result is that instructors can interact dynamically with the screen and then easily save and archive the results of these interactions so that they can be made available to students.

Many Boards vs. One Screen

When you teach with a whiteboard, it is often possible (if you have enough whiteboards in the classroom) to fill up several boards before having to erase anything. During a logic class, I have often filled one or two boards with reference material helpful to that day's material while using one or two more boards to work out problems. One of the limitations of teaching with a screen is that you can only have one screen visible to students at any given time. This poses a difficulty when you are working on material that cannot fit on a single screen.

The Darkened Classroom

One of the more interesting aspects of teaching with a screen is that it alters the space of the classroom. The room is usually darkened, especially when the projector is old-fashioned. In addition, there is often noise generated by both the computer and the projector (although this will diminish as equipment improves). Most interestingly, the lived space of the classroom is altered: prior to the use of a screen, the classroom space was typically divided into two areas: the instructor's turf and the students' turf. With the addition of a screen, students and teacher are often put to one side while the screen is on the other. (I shall comment on the strangeness of both students and professor staring at the inanimate screen in my discussion of teaching ethics, below.)

Student Access to Computers

It is important to consider the issue of equal access to computers. Clearly, if not all students have access to computers or do not know how to use the computers that they may have access to, then a course that depends on computer use will disadvantage some students relative to others in the class. One has to be careful not to create unfair requirements that put some student on unequal footing with others. Until two years ago, I dealt with this problem by ensuring that students who did not have access to computers or have the requisite skills to use a computer received a 'hard copy' of the same materials as I made available in electronic form to my computer-savvy students. But in the last two years two factors have prompted me to change this policy. First, at our university we now have sufficient computer-lab access that students can get on a workstation at any time of the day and work at a computer for as long as they want. Second, increasingly, I have come to believe that students who do not use a computer are precisely those students who need to be encouraged to become computer-literate and so should not be exempt from the computer-related aspects of the course. Typically, at the beginning of the term, I conduct one class period in a computer lab where all the students have workstations. This is a perfect time to set up a buddy system in which the more computer-savvy students can help those who are less comfortable with the technology. (Indeed, for this generation of students, the buddy system has often been the principal way in which computer skills have been developed.)

This does not, however, always solve the problem, especially for students who work and are only on campus while they are taking classes. On our campus, which has many resident students, this is much less severe a problem than it is at other institutions, particularly urban schools with a very high percentage of commuter students. In such circumstances, it is important to remain sensitive to the needs of students who still do not have ready access to computers and the Internet. For both ethical and pedagogical reasons, we should avoid reinforcing the "digital divide" in our classrooms and disadvantaging students who are already at a competitive disadvantage with their more affluent counterparts.

Teaching Ethics

I am somewhat more ambivalent about teaching with a screen in my ethics classes than I am about teaching logic with a screen. This is all the more surprising to me because I spend a significant portion of my day working on my ethics websites, Ethics Updates[9] and Ethics Videos.[10] Since I have been a strong and active proponent of putting ethics-related materials on the web, I was clearly well disposed toward teaching ethics with a screen, and expected my teaching the subject with a screen to be a smashing success. But my experience was otherwise.

To be sure, the experience certainly was not terrible. Student evaluations were fine, and in many ways the course offered students a rich experience: on-line videos, including interviews with authors of some of the articles in our anthology; videos of many of the class lectures; on-line PowerPoint presentations on, for example, current newspaper articles relevant to the topics being considered in class; case studies; discussion forums; and student journals in which they write about their reactions to the readings and the course ideas. But I found myself discontent with the classroom experience. I set out my reasons below.

Teaching Ethics and Teaching Logic with a Screen: Important Differences

My discontent with teaching ethics with a screen centers on the use of PowerPoint presentations in the classroom. The presentations locked me into a strict—perhaps constricting—agenda. While this did not pose any special problem for the teaching of logic, it did so for teaching ethics. This led me to asking why having a fixed teaching agenda is less important in ethics than in logic. Is it simply that the material in ethics is far more interesting and thus digressions into related material are more attractive? Although the answer to this question is 'yes,' this answer does not capture the full or even primary issue. It is rather that the process of teaching ethics involves an important element that is quite minimal in the teaching of logic. Recall the three elements in teaching logic discussed above: (a) conveying information, (b) fostering understanding, and (c) developing proficiency in applications. All of these elements are certainly present in teaching ethics, but in addition, one needs to conduce students to self-reflection.

In teaching ethics, it is, of course, necessary and important for students to understand the concepts and arguments being considered in the course. But in the study of ethics, understanding involves self-understanding. That is, the grasp and evaluation of moral concepts and theories necessitates our understanding the content of our own beliefs and practices. Fostering self-understanding can be done very effectively in the classroom. But the need to do so points to the root problem with presentation software, whether PowerPoint or some other version: it locks the class into a fixed path that can often prevent instructors from exploring issues that relate to the interplay between the self-understanding of one's students and their understanding of the moral concepts.

If this sounds like Socrates, that is because it is. In his early dialogues, Socrates clearly saw the intimate link between understanding and self-understanding. For him, philosophy is fundamentally a dialogue or conversation, and the basic movement of philosophical discourse is not the lecture from one to the other but the back-and-forth movement between discussants of an issue. It is precisely this "to and fro" movement that is disrupted by presentation software.

Consider an example: When considering issues of animal rights and welfare, students often find themselves forced to look at some of their most basic suppositions about personhood and respect. For many Christian students, there is a deep ontological divide between human beings, who have immortal souls and who have been distinguished by the fact that the Son of God became a human being, and all other living beings, who possess neither of these characteristics. We often discuss traditions that contrast with this understanding of the Christian view, such as, for example, Hinduism, according to which both animals and humans have immortal souls, in which the same soul may be incarnated at one time as an animal and at another time as a human being, and in which some Gods (such as Ganesh) take animal form. This is precisely a moment when students are likely to reach deep into their own experience and respond with a "yes, but. . . ." objection that can lead to the heart of their beliefs. When they are in the passive mindset encouraged by presentations, they are much less likely not merely to voice but even to have such a response.

Of course, the issue of self-understanding is not limited to ethics. There are many areas of study, such as literature, where self-reflection is crucial, and teaching in these areas is subject to the same considerations outlined here for teaching ethics.

Expectations Created by the Screen

There is a natural reply to some of the problems that I have raised above: "Simply turn off the projector and enter into a dialogue with the students." This is exactly the right thing to do, and one of the secrets of teaching well with a screen is knowing when to shut it off. However, when a class begins with a PowerPoint presentation, students often settle into a passive mindset. The presentation seems to conduce to their viewing themselves as passive absorbers of information: they may ask questions for clarification (and even this seems intrusive to some students) but generally they take their job as one of sitting, listening, and taking notes. I have found that it is often difficult to shift students from this passive modality to a more active one without providing some strong stimulus.

The Ideal Screen

Some of the problems I have noted here will, no doubt, eventually be addressed by better technology. I noted above one such move—the introduction of the combining of a traditional whiteboard with an interactive screen that allows the instructor to write, draw, and annotate on the whiteboard in a way that can be integrated with the presentation software, and which can then be archived for students. Undoubtedly there will be many similar developments in the future.

(I should mention that my remarks are not meant as the endorsement of any particular product—-such as SmartBoard, discussed above—but rather as an endorsement of a specific kind of product. We need products such as SmartBoard that allow the instructor to deal with the dynamics of the classroom as it actually unfolds, and not merely present what was planned, in advance, to happen.) What we need is the development of electronic technologies that can be responsive to the responses of students, a technology that will not only aid students in mastering certain material but also help them to reflect on their own responses to this material and so enlarge their capacity for self-reflection and understanding.

An additional, albeit small, way in which technology might be improved so as to allow greater responsiveness to students' questions would involve creating an on-line bank of mini-responses to specific questions that could be called up easily. Currently, presentations tend to be bulky and capable of being used only in their entirety. It would be helpful to be able easily to pull up a set of only three or four slides that address a specific question. (This is not a difficult programming task—though to the best of my knowledge no such program now exists—and it would be more and more useful as we come more and more to depend on presentation software in the classroom.)

Conclusion: Teaching Well with a Screen

Teaching with a screen is here to stay. Increasingly we will find ourselves using computer-equipped classrooms that actually work well and easily, and as these classrooms become more common it is reasonable to expect that their use will expand. This expanded use will, in some cases, no doubt prove helpful in improving the quality of classroom education. Yet there is a danger that teaching with the aid of computers will encourage students to be passive and to see their role in life primarily as absorbers of knowledge rather than as active thinkers. Particularly in courses where self-knowledge is an important component, it is important to preserve the classroom space for dialogue and interaction, for the back-and-forth movement of conversation that has been at the heart of philosophy since Plato's dialogues.

The Medium and the Message

In teaching with a screen it is important to consider the question of the extent to which the use of computers transforms not only how we teach but also what we teach. Years ago Marshall McLuhan told us that "the medium is the message." Teaching with a screen brings home how true this is in the classroom. No doubt, in our teaching with a screen we gravitate toward what we can put on a screen, especially what we can put on a screen in a compelling manner that commands students' attention. Students (and teachers, for that matter) are talented in many different ways, and we must be careful not to overlook or devalue talents that do not manifest themselves in computer-mediated communication.

NOTES

1. The Ron Blatt Java application is available free on-line at: http://ronblatt.tripod.com/venndiagram.html

2. James H. Moor, "What is Computer Ethics?" This article first appeared in Terrell Ward Bynum, ed., *Computers & Ethics*, (New York: Blackwell, 1985) 266-75. It is online at: http://www/southernct.edu /organizations/rccs/resources/teaching/teaching_mono/moor/moor/ definition.html

3. PowerPoint is available as part of Microsoft Office MX. Academic prices should be available through campus bookstores or on the web at: http://www.microsoft.com/office/

4. Flash is available at academic discount from Macromedia: http://www.macromedia.com/resources/education/store

5. Information on Adobe's LiveMotion is available at: http://www. adobe.com/products/livemotion/main.html

For information about educational pricing, see: http://www/adobe. com/store/general/otherplaces/uscanada/educlist/jhtml

6. Dynamic DHML is a genera l standard (like HTML) that is supported by various programs.

7. Dreamweaver is available at an academic discount from Macromedia, *op. cit.* CourseBuilder is available free of charge as an add-on to Dreamweaver.

8. Information about SmartBoard is available at: http://www.smart tech.com/products/smartboard/index.asp

9. http://ethics.sandiego.edu

10. http://ethics.sandiego.edu/video/ This and the website noted in the immediately preceding endnote now receive about two million visits a year.

PART V
Teaching Aesthetics

Chapter 11

The Case Method Approach to the Teaching of Aesthetics

Ronald Moore

Two key aims of any aesthetics course are to engage the curiosity of students about aesthetic problems and to induce in them a desire to seek solutions to these problems. One of the most effective means of achieving these aims is the "case method." This is a pedagogical technique intermittently used in some philosophy classes, but more commonly employed in other disciplines, such as business, medicine, and law. In the case method, a student studies a problem consisting of a set of real or hypothetical facts and assesses various possible solutions to this problem. Sometimes several proposed solutions are presented along with the facts of the case; sometimes only one or none is, and it is left to the student to invent as well as to assess alternative solutions. Whatever the student's response, the teacher can draw out its implications by asking whether other, similar cases should be decided in quite the same way, by "ringing changes" (that is, altering facts or assumptions) in the case to test the limits of the position the student has taken, or by inviting the student to formulate a covering rule that he or she would be prepared to apply more generally. Solutions the student proposes will suggest or create further problems, which will, in turn, invite further assessment and conjecture, and so on. In this way, points of principle, rudimentary arguments and the beginning outlines of possible theories emerge in classroom discussion, rather than full armored from the text.

By beginning with cases—and only after students have discussed the cases and the principles or general ideas that arise out of them, turning to the aesthetic theories that take up these principles and ideas—the teacher can easily make clear both the motivation behind the relevant aesthetic theories and the reasons these theories can properly be said to respond to the evidence they are meant to explain. When, in due course, students examine some element of aesthetic theory, say, Bullough's theory of "psychic distance" (the view that suspension or truncation of the usual patterns of experience is required for the aesthetic appreciation of an object),[1] they will presumably already have formed opinions about, and perhaps even debated, some of the important themes that that theory takes up (such as the claims that "underdistancing" and "overdistancing" can radically impair or altogether thwart aesthetic experience). They will regard Bullough's theory as part of an ongoing philosophical discussion, a confrontation of ideas that is directly inspired by the problems presented in cases considered. And they will regard themselves as parties to this discussion in that they have already grappled with the conceptual problems that animate it. Being in on the discussion, they will very likely want to carry it forward. This the teacher can facilitate by supplying more case problems, which may usefully be interspersed with texts or combined with them in various ways. For example, the teacher might invite the students to consider ways in which "psychic distance" seems to be involved in the twentieth-century theater. (Do the well-known "spell-breaking moments" in *Peter Pan, Our Town, A Taste of Honey,* and other plays show us that there *is*, or rather that there *isn't* a requirement of distance in the audience's appreciation of the dramatic performance?)

I. Why the Case Method Works

Since its inception a century ago, the case method has grown to be the prevalent mode of instruction at nearly every American law school. The method is far from uncontroversial, but it has proven to be a lively and effective means of teaching heterogeneous student bodies fundamental principles of law. Before the introduction of the case method, students learned law by reading treatises, compendious theoretical tracts that purported authoritatively to set out the principles governing all the fields of law. It is now generally thought that these early students learned the what, but not the why, of law. They could recite the rules, but, not having involved themselves with the arguments in the cases out of which the rules arose, they did not know fully what these rules stood for and where they were going. (Of course, today's law students still turn to treatises—or hornbooks and outlines, their contemporary progeny—to round off their study of law; but they now do so in order to determine the scope of principles whose point and tendency they have already learned from grappling with them in cases.)

The chief perceived advantages to the law school case method are these: First, students are required to put themselves in the position of deciding hard conceptual problems, rather than reviewing others' solutions. Second, students are made aware of how certain legal principles relate to particular concrete, practical applications. For example, the question of whether a particular defendant is, in a particular case, actually civilly liable to an injured plaintiff might depend on whether a fire hydrant was weatherproof against normally adverse winter conditions or against historically extreme weather conditions.[2] Third, in such judicial opinions as may accompany the statement of facts in a case, the students see a line of reasoning reflecting a selection of premises favoring an outcome, and frequently an alternative line of reasoning, proposed in dissent. And fourth, they can see in a series of cases (and particularly cases reporting dissenting opinions) the ongoing debate within which all legal decisions enjoy at best a provisional status.

These advantages have clear correlates in the application of case method to the study of aesthetics: first, students are stimulated to confront the great aesthetic problems themselves; second, aesthetic cases appeal to students as intellectual puzzles whose solutions bear directly upon the practical contexts of art and aesthetic judgment; third, in trying to resolve these puzzles, students are frequently led to express lines of reasoning going well beyond present cases and to appreciate divergent lines of argument that may be brought to bear on present cases; and fourth, students who are presented with a series of aesthetic cases, or with a series of variations on the facts of a given case, can come to sense for themselves the continuing drama of conflict and growth that characterizes this field.

As in law, the case method in aesthetics is not meant to displace theory or theoretical texts. Rather, it reverses the usual order of instruction by seeing to it that students struggle with the questions before they struggle with their answers. In aesthetics as elsewhere, one of the great enemies to learning is complacency. Well-chosen exotic cases, or made-up cases, serve to jar students' prereflective convictions by wrenching them out of familiar contexts in which their commonsensical hunches are generally reliable. This dislocation is, arguably, more important in understanding art than in understanding anything else.

II. Illustrations of This Method

The case method in aesthetics draws upon three kinds of material: (1) genuine cases *at law* involving art and aesthetic issues, such as James McNeill Whistler's suit against John Ruskin, in which the famous painter sued the eminent art critic for defamation for claiming (in a published pamphlet) that Whistler had been guilty of "flinging a pot of paint in the public's face," or the customs dispute involving Constantin Brancusi's metal sculpture *Bird in Space*, in which government authorities sought to subject that metal sculpture to an import tariff as a piece of metal rather than letting it pass duty-free as a work of art, or Supreme Court deliberations dealing with the suppression of *Ulysses, Fanny Hill*, and other such materials;[3] (2) *normative*, but not legal, accounts involving aesthetic problems (the question of whether Betsy the Chimp's "paintings" are art, the issue of whether mountains were beautiful before Romantic poets and philosophers began to regard them as such, and so on);[4] (3) *fictitious* cases, involving made-up facts aimed at highlighting specific aesthetic issues or at testing prereflective judgments.[5]

It should not be presumed that "real" cases are pedagogically superior to made-up ones. The objective of the case method is to raise and address issues of general principle (such as the question of whether works not regarded by the majority of informed spectators as works of art might nevertheless *be* works of art, or the question of whether a performance of an eighteenth-century musical composition on modern instruments can be considered a performance of the same piece), rather than to settle points of controversy rooted in any specific set of facts (for example, whether one particularly well-regarded work of art, say Leonardo's *Mona Lisa*, is superior in its brushwork to another well-regarded work of art, say Rembrandt's *Night Watch*). Sometimes the description of real facts will work best in bringing home the practical bearing of theory on reality; in particular, a law case may dramatize most effectively the serious economic and social consequences of decisions that have to be made respecting art and aesthetic values.

But sometimes fiction works better than fact. Rather than lose its point in a welter of (philosophically) extraneous detail (as all too often happens in legal case material), a made-up case can be carefully framed to focus on a specific theoretical issue clearly and directly. Moreover, the fabricator can add to the allure of the case by making it sardonic, witty, outrageous, and so on. Most students will rise to a puzzle; they will rise faster to a funny puzzle.

The effectiveness of the fictitious case is, of course, well recognized in legal pedagogy. Some of the best-known and most informative cases studied in law schools are fictitious,[6] and fictitious cases are created whenever a law professor "rings the changes" on a set of facts in a real case. In aesthetic education as in law, the *kind* of case chosen for examination should be dictated by features of the problem or issue under examination. If the fact pattern of a real case is likely to propel discussion in the desired direction, well and good; but if no real case presents itself as likely to do so, it is useful to invent one that does. In what follows, I present a sample case from each of the previously mentioned categories. I append to each case a series of questions a teacher might use to get the discussion rolling.

A. The Bare Chest (law case)

In 1938, Alfred Crimi, a well-known muralist, was comissioned by the Rutgers Presbyterian Church to paint a fresco mural on the rear chancel wall of its church building in Manhattan. The mural turned out to be controversial, some parishioners maintaining that "a portrayal of Christ with so much of His chest bare placed more emphasis on His physical attributes than on His spiritual qualities." The number of those objecting increased, and in 1946 the mural was painted over without first giving notice to the artist. Hearing of this action, Crimi brought an action for equitable relief, seeking:

1. To compel the defendant to remove the obliterating paints on the fresco mural; and

2. In the alternative, to permit the plaintiff to take the fresco mural from the defendant's church at the cost and expense of the defendant.

3. In the event that the fresco mural cannot be thus removed (as detailed in #2), for judgment against the defendant for $150,000.

On his behalf, the artist maintained that "certain general customs and usages [exist] between artists and those who contract with them for the creation of a work to which the artist's name and reputation will be attached, . . . the gist of [which] is that the work, if accepted as being of high artistic standard, will not be altered, mutilated, obliterated or destroyed." The defendant church, however, argued that "the mural, under the terms of the contract, became part of the building owned by the church," and that the contract reserved no rights to the artist upon completion of its terms.[7]

Is there, or ought there to be, any special "right of integrity" (that is, a right that "a work, if accepted as being of high artistic standard, will not be altered, mutilated, obliterated, or destroyed")[8] inhering in artistic creations? Is an agreement between an artist and his patron to be treated as a service contract between, say, a mechanic and a car owner? Would it make any difference to the outcome of this case if the artist were dead? Does it make sense to suppose that a work of art might, *itself*, be actionably injured, even in absence of injury to its creator? That is, is it conceivable that the artwork's rights to preservation or protection against harm and change survive those of the artist? Does it make sense to suppose that a work of art might itself (through guardians) prevail as a plaintiff in a lawsuit to protect itself against mutilation, alteration, and the like? Also, should it have made any difference to the outcome if the defendant were an art museum, rather than a church?

This case is useful in drawing attention to a problem of considerable interest to contemporary aestheticians: do artworks have rights? Legal arguments have been advanced that nonhuman animate objects (for example, trees) have rights and should have standing to sue in their own right (through guardians),[9] but these arguments have not so far extended to artworks. Should they? Or are other, and perhaps better, arguments available here?

A similar, but perhaps somewhat differently focused case, could be built around the plight of Alexander Calder's mobile *Pittsburgh*. In 1958 Calder's mobile was donated by a private collector to Allegheny County, Pennsylvania, for installation in the Greater Pittsburgh International Airport. The mobile was originally painted black and white; but it was, upon installation, repainted green and gold, the official colors of Allegheny County. Calder protested, but the work was not restored in his lifetime.[10]

This Calder case (though it never reached a court of law) highlights certain features of the problem of aesthetic rights (for example, rights against alteration, as opposed to obliteration; rights surviving the death of the artist) that the *Crimi* case does not. And it is not difficult to conceive of additional (fictional) cases that would carry the discussion in other worthwhile directions.

B. Colored Glass (factual case)

Recent research has established that the iridescence which is characteristic of much ancient glass—for instance that originating in Syria between the 7th and 3rd centuries B.C. is not, as had previously been thought, the product of a now-lost coloration technique, but rather the product of a chemical leaching of the glass. The original glass was clear or slightly greenish in color; the leaching process, called "layering," occurs when the glass is buried for long periods; and the iridescent colors which have been highly prized by collectors are not the product of artistic efforts, but of natural processes. Museum curators dealing with classical antiquities now face a dilemma: Should they display their collections of ancient iridescent glass "as found," preserving its peculiar surface beauty, but obscuring the original glass, or should they remove the leached surface to reveal the clear original glass and sacrifice the dazzling iridescence?[11]

How important is fidelity to original form in the presentation of artworks? Is it more important in some genres than in others? Do we, for instance, think it more worthwhile to try to preserve the text of *Pride and Prejudice* exactly as Jane Austen wrote it than it is to play Handel's *Water Music* with original instrumentation, technique, and tempi? In some art forms (for example, landscape architecture), it is very hard to say what should count as the original state; in trying to preserve or restore such art forms, what should guide our selection of the form toward which we should bend our efforts? Some critics allege that Michelangelo's Sistine Chapel frescos became much more powerful and beautiful with the accretion of varnish and dirt over the ages and that this acquired beauty has now been sacrificed in the course of their restoration. Suppose that, somehow, Michelangelo himself had been able to tell us that he agreed with this judgment. Should that have negatively affected the decision to proceed with the planned restoration?

This case can be used to develop inquiry into a number of important problems in aesthetics. One is the problem of what the authentic work of art *is*, that which was conceived and originally executed by the artist (perhaps regretting the inferior performers, instruments, pigments, or such, on hand), or that which the work becomes at some later time. Another is the problem of weighing the value of beauty currently perceived against historical fidelity. A third is the problem of the role the artist's opinion is to be given in these matters: is he or she (or our estimate of what he or she would have said) the final arbiter?

Obviously, other problems are not hard to reach from this beginning as well.

C. Plum Loco (fictitious case)

Prominently displayed in the fine arts museum of major midwest city is *Plum Loco*, a painting by Z. Z. Smith. In all the years that it has been hanging there, well over one million museum visitors have seen it. Remarkably, however, not one viewer in all this time has found the work to be beautiful, moving, fascinating, or pleasing in any way. Indeed, not one person has stood before it and felt the slightest twinge of a tingle of aesthetic appreciation. An exit poll conducted by the museum demonstrates a striking uniformity of response to *Plum Loco*. Almost everyone says of it "It leaves me cold," or "It's boring," or words to that effect. A. A. Jones, art critic for a major art magazine, recently devoted an entire article to *Plum Loco*. He argued that all audience response notwithstanding, *Plum Loco* is a great artwork, and indeed a very beautiful one. He writes: "It doesn't matter one whit that no one likes it. Probably no one ever will. In fact, I don't like it myself, and can't imagine that I ever will. Nevertheless, I understand enough about what makes for greatness and beauty in art to realize that this painting is great and beautiful, in and of itself. Its greatness lies in what it is, purely apart from anyone's response to it."

Does Jones' point of view make sense? Could *Plum Loco* be art even if it always leaves everyone cold? Could *Plum Loco* be beautiful even if no one ever finds it so?

This case is obviously aimed at drawing attention to a time-honored quandary in aesthetic theory: the role of subjective response in the evaluation of artworks. On the one hand, it seems clear that "immediacy of enjoyment" ought not to be the criterion of aesthetic merit; on the other, it is also clear that *total* absence of subjective response counts heavily against artistic merit.

III. Using the Case at Different Instructional Levels

One of the pedagogic virtues of simple cases such as the ones I have already described is that they can easily be modified to make them appealing and accessible to different age groups. Take the *Plum Loco* case, for example. Very young students (sixth graders, say) might be invited to look at a series of pictures and to announce in each instance whether they like it or not. When one is found that no one likes, the teacher might ask whether it still could be a good picture, reminding them that there are some things (medicine, for example) that are good even though people do not like them. This question leads, of course, to a consideration of the different criteria in virtue of which we determine that art (as opposed to medicine, say) is or is not good. Older students (tenth graders, for instance) might be asked to imagine themselves to be writers on the school newspaper, assigned the job of writing a critical evaluation of *Plum Loco*, on temporary loan to the school. Should the fact that students and teachers uniformly do not like the work affect the writer's assessment of its merit as an artwork? Advanced students (undergraduate, or even graduate students) might be asked to consider the case in the light of the arguments that Nelson Goodman and Kendall Walton have advanced dealing with its central problem, namely, that although critical appraisal of an artwork undeniably involves aesthetic experience of some sort, this experience may involve knowledge (say, acquaintance with aesthetic categories, styles, movements) as much as, or in place of, feeling. If critical appraisal of an artwork *does* involve knowledge as well as feeling, we may be left wondering how much knowledge and how much feeling are demanded, and whether these sometimes opposing elements of experience might nullify each other.[12]

Or students might be invited to consider the *Plum Loco* case in the light of psychological, critical, or even political theories with which they are familiar. For example, they might consider whether certain factors not evident on *Plum Loco*'s surface—say (drawing on Freudian theory), autobiographical revelations about Z. Z. Smith's subconscious attitude toward his siblings, or (drawing on feminist theory) his status as a male artist in a generally aggressive, competitive, male-dominated world, or (drawing on Marxist theory) the painting's status as a commodity in a luxury art market, should color our appraisal of the painting.

Additionally, students might also be induced to think about some of the underlying epistemological issues: what do we mean when we speak of a "thing in itself"? Is it the way a thing "looks" to the untrained eye? Or to a trained eye? Or is it the "internal struc-ture," that is, the atomic or molecular structure of the thing that causes the "look"? And so on. There is no end to the stimulating and worthwhile questions a case like *Plum Loco* can generate at all instructional levels. And this is because the central question the case raises,—namely, to what degree are the aesthetic features of a work functions of viewers' response, and to what degree are they integral to the work itself?—is a question that is pertinent and meaningful at every level.

It should be evident that a limitless number of cases might be reported or devised to expose and illustrate points of theoretic interest in aesthetics. Some cases (for example, the *Plum Loco* case) are relatively elastic and open-ended. Other cases (for example, the "Bare Chest" case) focus attention on issues specific to individual genres, periods, controversies, and so on. It is sometimes useful for cases to involve more than one problem, or to invite comparison between modes of analysis or styles of criticism from different fields. Cases drawn from neighboring fields, such as ethical theory, or political theory, can be used to throw refracted light on aesthetic concerns and can sometimes be modified to reach those concerns directly. For example, students might be asked whether it should be regarded as permissible or morally proper for a person to require that certain personal possessions be buried with him or her at death, and whether the answer to the question changes if the possessions in question are artworks—say, priceless Impressionist drawings. Or students might be asked whether principles of evaluation drawn from the world of art can be used to provide standards of measure-ment for aesthetic factors in, say, legally mandated environmental protection programs or in scenic vista protection programs. Or students might be asked whether performance artworks that pose threats to the health or safety of performers and audiences should for that reason be prohibited.[13] Finally, in addition to their great *propaedeutic* value in classroom discussion, problem cases provide a useful means of stimulating creative and enthusiastically argued responses on exams.

NOTES

1. See Edward Bullough, "'Psychical Distance' as a Factor in Art and as an Aesthetic Principle," *British Journal of Psychology* 5 (1912): 87-98. This essay is widely reprinted in basic aesthetics anthologies.

2. *Blyth v. Birmingham Waterworks Co.,* 11 Exch. 781, 156 Eng. Rep. 1047 (1856).

3. *Whistler v. Ruskin* is well described in Laurie Adams, *Art on Trial* (New York: Walker, 1976); *Brancusi v. United States* is reported as 54 Treas. Dec. 428 (Cust. Ct. 1928); and the two famous censorship cases appear as *United States v. One Book Entitled Ulysses,* 5 F. Supp. 182 (1933), and *Memoirs of a Woman of Pleasure v. the Commonwealth of Massachusetts,* 383 U.S. 413 (1966).

4. Betsy's "oeuvre" is discussed briefly by George Dickie in *Art and the Aesthetic: An Institutional Analysis* (Ithaca: Cornell University Press, 1974), 45-46; the issue of when mountains came to be regarded as beautiful is examined at length in Marjorie Hope Nicolson, *Mountain Gloom and Glory: The Development of the Aesthetics of the Infinite* (Ithaca: Cornell University Press, 1959).

5. A large variety of such cases (as well as cases of the former two sorts) is presented in Margaret Battin, et al., *Puzzles about Art: An Aesthetics Casebook* (New York: St. Martin's Press, 1989).

For a discussion of the uses to which these cases can be put in the K-12 classroom, see Margaret Battin, "Cases for Kids: Using Puzzles to Teach Aesthetics to Children," in *Aesthetics for Young People,* ed. Ronald Moore (Reston, VA: National Art Education Association, 1995), 89-104.

6. For example, "The Case of the Speluncean Explorers," "The Case of the Contract Signed on Book Day," and "The Case of the Interrupted Whambler," all celebrated creations of Lon Fuller, a consummate legal theorist and teacher at the Harvard Law School. The first appears in *Harvard Law Review* 62 (1969); the other two appear in Fuller's *The Problems of Jurisprudence,* temp. ed., (Brooklyn: Foundation Press, 1949).

7. *Crimi v. Rutgers Presbyterian Church,* 194 Misc. 570, 89 N.Y.S. 2d 813 (Sup. Ct. 1949).

8. Franklin Feldman, Stephen E. Wei, and Susan Duke Biederman, *Art*

Law: Rights and Liabilities of Creators and Collectors (Boston: Little, Brown & Co., 1986), 496.

9. See Christopher Stone, *Should Trees Have Standing? Toward Legal Rights for Natural Objects* (Los Altos, CA: Williams Kaufmann, 1974).

10. The Pittsburgh scandal is discussed in Stephen Weil, "The 'Moral Right' Comes to California," *ARTnews* 78 (December 1979).

11. I owe this case to Margaret Pabst Battin, who bases her description on information supplied by the Walters Art Museum, Baltimore, Maryland, regarding its collection of Syrian Glass.

12. In a celebrated analysis of critical appraisal, Nelson Goodman ridicules the notion that the aesthetic potency of a work can be gauged by the intensity of the "tingle" that results when we suspend our knowledge and submerge ourselves in it. He calls this notion the "Tingle-Immersion theory," and puckishly attributes it to Immanuel Tingle and Joseph Immersion (*Languages of Art: An Approach to a Theory of Symbols* [Indianapolis: Hackett, 1976], 112).

Kendall Walton argues that critical questions about works of art cannot be separated from questions about their histories because "certain facts about the origins of works of art have an essential role in criticism [in] that aesthetic judgments rest on them in an absolutely fundamental way" ("Categories of Art," *Philosophical Review* 68 [1959], reprinted in Alex Neil and Aaron Ridley, eds., *The Philosophy of Art: Readings Ancient and Modern* [New York: McGraw-Hill, 1995], 334).

13. Examples of such works include Chris Burden's "Transfixed" (1974), in which the artist had himself "crucified" with nails in his hands on the back roof of a Volkswagon automobile; "Still Life" (ca. 1980), in which Ed Kienholz arranged a chair facing a gun set to go off randomly sometime during the next one hundred years and invited members of the audience to sit in the chair; and the notorious acts of self-mutilation presented from time to time in the 1960s as "artistic nudes—similar to wreckage" by the Wiener Aktionismus group (resulting in the death of the group's leader, Rudolf Schwarzkogler, in 1969).

PART VI
Teaching Philosophy of Religion

Chapter 12

Teaching Philosophy of Religion (either as a full course or pas part of an 'Introduction to Philosophy')

Louis P. Pojman

The Ultimate Metaphysical Issue

Questions connected with the existence of God may be the most important that we can ask and try to answer. If God, an omni-benevolent, supremely powerful being who interacts with the world, exists, then it is of paramount importance that we come to know that fact and as much as possible about God and his plan. Implications follow that affect our understanding of the world and ourselves. If God exists, the world is not accidental, a product of mere chance and necessity, but a home that has been designed for rational and sentient beings, a place of personal purposeful-ness. If there is a God, we ought to do everything possible to discover this fact, including using our reason in the discovery itself or to test the validity of the putative discovery.

On the other hand, it may be that a supreme, benevolent being does not exist. If there is no God, we want to know this too. Whether we believe in God or not will make a difference in the way we view the universe and in the way we live.

Many people live happy, moral lives without believing in God. La Place, when asked about his faith, is reported to have replied, "I have no need of that hypothesis." But the testimony of the vast majority of humankind is against him. Millions have needed and been inspired by this notion. So great is the inspiration issuing from the idea of God that we could say that if God does not exist, the idea is the greatest invention of the human mind. What are all the world's works of literature, art, music, drama, architecture, science, and philosophy compared to this simple concept? To quote Anthony Kenny:

> If there is no God, then God is incalculably the greatest single creation of the human imagination. No other creation of the imagination has been so fertile of ideas, so great an inspiration to philosophy, to literature, to painting, sculpture, architecture, and drama. Set beside the idea of God, the most original inventions of mathematicians and the most unforgettable characters in drama are minor products of the imagination: Hamlet and the square root of minus one pale into insignificance by comparison.[1]

The field of philosophy of religion documents the history of humanity's quest for a supreme being. Even if God does not exist, the arguments centering on this quest are interesting in their own right for their ingenuity and subtlety, apart from whether or not they are valid or sound. It may be argued that the Judeo-Christian tradition has informed our self-understanding to such a degree that every person who wishes to be well-informed must come to grips with the arguments and counterarguments surrounding its claims. Hence, even if one rejects the assertions of religion, it is important to understand what is being rejected and why.

Whether religious beliefs are true or justified is the overarching concern of the area of philosophy of religion.

Curriculum

Traditionally eight topics have constituted the domain of philosophy of religion. They are (1) The "Proofs" for the Existence of God: The Cosmological, Teleological, and Ontological Arguments; (2) Religious Experience (sometimes seen as a proof of God's existence); (3) The Problem of Evil, as constituting evidence against the thesis that God exists; (4) The Meaning of the Attributes of God (for example, omnipotence, omniscience, omnibenevolence, eternity, and aseity); (5) Miracles; (6) Immortality; (7) Faith and Reason (Is religious faith for the most part irrational? transrational? rational?); and (8) Ethics and Religion (In what way, if any, does religion make a difference to morality?).

The field has a natural order (beginning with arguments for and against a deity to the nature of God's attributes to the implications of his existence—miracles, immortality, questions about the need for faith, and ethics—as they are set forth above), but one cannot adequately cover all of these topics in a single semester. Topics (1 and 2) the "Proofs" and (3) the "Counter-Proof" have traditionally been given preeminence, for it is the existence of a God that really is the pivotal post on which the rest of the material hinges. Topics (4) and (5), while they must be touched on, deserve less emphasis in an introductory course, and (8) may be left to a course in ethical theory. Topic (6) concerns immortality—the question of What is it within us, if anything, that survives our death?—is the second major metaphysical issue in philosophy of religion that deserves close analysis. It is here that philosophy of religion touches philosophy of mind and, especially, the problem of personal identity. Finally, topic (7), the problem of faith and reason, merits considerable attention, for unless religion is to some extent accessible to rational investigation, philosophy of religion as a discipline may be an entirely wrongheaded approach, as, indeed, many students believe it is. I generally find that topics (1) to (3), (6) and (7) are all I have time for in a semester-long course.

Methodology

Because of the sensitive nature of the material, philosophy of religion demands a somewhat more sensitive approach than most other subjects, for the material tends to arouse great passion and teachers and students alike tend to take strong stands on these issues. If one is not careful, this can get in the way of rational discussion, though it can also open up an opportunity for the teacher to show how philosophy can cut through emotional fog.

Out of this highly charged state, the teacher faces two challenges: (1) to respect the individual student's personal religious heritage and worldview while also challenging it, and (2) to combine passionate feeling with dispassionate reasoning.

There are no easy answers to these problems, but some guidelines may be suggested. With regard to (1), the tension between respect and challenge, the Socratic method is a great boon. By using a question and response heuristic, the teacher can distance himself or herself from the need to take a stand. Presenting arguments on behalf of different sides of the issue and using an anthology with readings on different sides of the issue are helpful here. Encouraging students to participate in the process of developing and criticizing the arguments allows students to come to their own conclusions without undue influence from the instructor. It sometimes angers or annoys students that teachers will not declare their own particular position with respect to belief or nonbelief, but in the long run I have found it to be the best way to compel the student to develop his or her own ideas. Of course, "compelling" students to develop their own ideas puts the emphasis on student autonomy, but there is no doubt that the kinds of questions one raises reveals, at least to some degree, one's own biases. These biases cannot be helped, but self-awareness and a commitment to fairness serve as countermeasures.

I begin the course with a lecture on the social and personal functions of religion, discussing the role of religion as an explanation of the world and our existence, as a mechanism for social control, and as a system offering a meaning to life. Then I discuss some critiques of religion: the Presocratic Critias's[2] suggestion that religion is an invention for social control, Marx's thesis that religion is the opium of the people,[3] Freud's hypothesis that it is a product of wish-fulfillment concerning the father figure,[4] and Nietzsche's discussion of the death of God (in *Joyful Wisdom*).[5] Most students agree—to varying degrees—that none of these interesting hypotheses, while suggestive, has been shown to be true.

Next, I turn to the arguments for the existence of God, the cosmological, teleological, and ontological arguments, as well as the argument from religious experience. I have found that the assignment of a written essay (given early on in the course) on the question "Does God exist?" concentrates the mind on philosophical reasoning. Usually, the class has already worked through basic forms of deductive argument (for example, the basic syllogisms, *modus ponens, reductio ad absurdum*) by this point, and students are ready to try out their skills in arguing for their position. I encourage students to present their own views, but I do not insist on it. Whether they try to present both sides of an issue or only their own position, the aim is to get them to support whichever views they present with good arguments.

I require the first essay to be turned in around the fourth week of the semester. I read it for its argumentative prowess, challenging its undefended statements and encouraging the students to develop their thoughts further. Generally, my Philosophy of Religion class has an enrollment of fewer than twenty-five students, so that I am able to schedule an interview (twenty minutes to a half an hour) with each student in which we discuss the essay (as well as the student's progress to that point). I often use one class period in addition to extra office-hour time to allow myself sufficient time for each student. (It is not feasible to use this interview method with large introductory classes. For large classes I write detailed comments and invite those who need help to see me during my office hours.) This interview process generally takes me about three days. I allow students to revise their papers until the end of the semester, regrading the essay each time. (I used to allow unlimited revisions, but that became unwieldy as some students brought long drafts to me weekly. I now allow only two revisions.) Virtually all essays show improvement by the end of the course. (On class evaluations, students have reported that this exercise of reworking their papers was one of the best aspects of the class.)

I generally assign only one other essay during the course: either on faith and reason (whether religious belief is rational or irrational or somewhere in between) or on ethics and religion, or on immortality. I do not allow revisions on these essays, but I do give "free looks" (that is, ungraded responses) at outlines and rough drafts turned in ahead of the deadline.

Sometimes, in order to provide students with a focus for their thinking about their religious beliefs, I have assigned Bertrand Russell's "Why I Am Not a Christian"[6] (or a pseudonymous essay that I have written for this purpose, not necessarily representing my own point of view), and have asked the religious students to respond to it in essay form. For atheists and agnostics, I have assigned Richard Taylor's Cosmological Argument[7] or C. S. Lewis's "On Obstinacy in Belief."[8] (A questionnaire given at the beginning of the course clues me in to the students' general orientation.)

The second challenge mentioned, namely, teaching students to think clearly and critically on issues for which they have passionate feelings, has been a more difficult, but not impossible, task. I have had students come to me the day before their essay on the existence of God was due either to confess that they were unable to write an essay because they felt too passionately about the subject (or to request a second copy of that "damn atheist's essay"—Bertrand Russell's—since they had destroyed their first copy in a religious act of holy anger). It is not uncommon for religious students to feel quite uncomfortable treating "sacred oracles" from a neutral, detached perspective.

The teacher must attempt to show that one can be respectful (even reverential) and, at the same time, remain a rational inquirer after truth. Religious students in the Judeo-Christian tradition can be reminded that they are supposed to love God with their whole *mind* as well as their whole *heart* (Deut. 6:5; Matt. 22:37), and that this includes honest questioning and the giving of reasons for one's positions.

Exposing students to opposite points of view, and gradually getting them to appreciate the ingenuity and weight of opposing arguments helps somewhat. But there is no easy road here. One method that I have found fruitful is to get students to appreciate the difference between being neutral and being impartial. I ask students to imagine a football game between Southern Methodist University (SMU) and Notre Dame. (This illustration has not worked as well since SMU was penalized by the NCAA.) The model of a neutral person is the atheist in the stands who is indifferent to the outcome. The model of a partial person is the coach who always sees the referee's decision against his team as entirely unfair and the decisions for his team as entirely justified. The fans are also partial (to various degrees). But the model of the impartial person is the referee in the game, who, though knowing that his wife has bet their life savings on the underdog (SMU, of course), still manages to call what any reasonable spectator would judge to be a fair game. He does not let his wants or self-interest influence his judgments. The atheist spectators are neutral and impartial; the coaches are interested and partial, but the referee is both passionately interested and impartial. Becoming a fair-minded or impartial person is one of the virtues that philosophy should help inculcate in college students, a character trait consistent with caring deeply about the outcome of the arguments. In this way I try to get students to see that trying to discover which beliefs are best justified in these important matters does not commit one to neutrality. One can care desperately about the outcome of an argument and still be fair about its appraisal.

Material

The goal of my course in Philosophy of Religion is to get the student to think for himself or herself, to develop a philosophy of religion (or nonreligion—a completely secular worldview) for oneself. To do this the teacher needs to expose students to the best arguments on various sides of the issues in question. Sometimes this can be done by using a single-authored text where the author has set forth the arguments fairly on both sides of the question, but more often than not bias shows through such a text as one side will not be as developed as well as it should. For this reason, I favor a dialogic form: readings on both sides of the issue, where each author tries to convince you that his or her position is the correct one. Here selections from the classics are irreplaceable, and I appeal to the following to set up the desired contrasting positions: both Aquinas's "Five Ways"[9] and Anselm's Ontological Argument offered as proof for God's existence,[10] together with Kant's critique of both;[11] Paley's teleological argument for God's existence (known as "the Watch Argument"),[12] together with the skeptical view of that argument offered by Hume in his *Dialogues*;[13] William James's[14] appeal to Religious Experience as evidence for God's existence and Wallace Matson's[15]denial of the significance of such experience; Hume and Hick[16] on opposite sides of the question of whether evil in the universe counts against God's existence; Bertrand Russell's argument against the view that there is immortality and John Hick's contrary argument;[17] Pascal's and William James's argument that belief in God is not an unreasonable belief even in the absence of positive evidence for His existence—the former known as "Pascal's Wager,"[18] the latter presented in James's "The Will to Believe"[19]—countered by W. K. Clifford's essay, "The Ethics of Belief," which calls into question the ethical legitimacy of using 'pragmatic' grounds as the basis for deciding what to believe;[20] and finally, the famous Oxford University debate between Antony Flew, R. M. Hare, and Basil Mitchell[21] on the question of the meaningfulness of religious utterances and the way in which immunity from empirical falsification might or might not affect that meaningfulness. These essays, together with John Mackie's[22] and Alvin Plantinga's[23] respective arguments concerning the religious implications of evil in the universe, Richard Swinburne on the Teleological Argument,[24] and essays on the relationship of religion to morality by Patrick Nowell-Smith and George Mavrodes,[25] bring a rich array of philosophical argument to both sides of the issues and give the student ample room for developing and criticizing arguments.

NOTES

1. Anthony Kenny, *Faith and Reason* (New York: Columbia University Press, 1983), 59.
2. Kathleen Freeman, ed., *Ancilla to the Pre-Socratic Philosophers* (Cambridge, MA: Harvard University Press, 1983), 157.
3. Karl Marx, "Towards a Critique of Hegel's *'Philosophy of Right'*" in *Karl Marx: Selected Writings,* ed. David McClellan (Oxford: Oxford University Press, 1977), 63.

4. Sigmund Freud, *The Future of an Illusion*, trans. James Strachey (New York: W. W. Norton, 1963).

5. Friedrich Nietzsche, *Joyful Wisdom*, trans. T. Common (New York: Frederick Unger, 1960), 167.

6. Bertrand Russell, *Why I Am Not A Christian* (New York: Simon & Schuster, 1957).

7. Richard Taylor, in *Metaphysics* (Englewood Cliffs, NJ: Prentice Hall, 1983). Reprinted in *Philosophy of Religion: An Anthology*, ed. Louis Pojman (Belmont, CA: Wadsworth, 1994).

8. C. S. Lewis, "On Obstinacy in Belief," in *The World's Last Night and Other Essay* (New York: Harcourt, Brace, Jovanovich, 1960). Reprinted in *Philosophy of Religion: An Anthology*.

9. St. Thomas Aquinas, *Summa Theologica*, Part I, trans. Dominican Fathers of English Province (New York: Benzinger Bros., 1947).

10. St. Anselm, *Proslogium* in *Anselm's Basic Writings*, trans. S. W. Deane (La Salle, IL: Open Court Publishing Company, 1962).

11. Immanuel Kant, *Critique of Pure Reason*, trans. J. M. D. Meiklejohn (New York: Colonial Press, 1900).

12. William Paley, in *Natural Theology or Evidences of the Existence and Attributes of the Deity* (London: R. Faulder, 1802). Reprinted in *Philosophy of Religion: An Anthology*.

13. David Hume, *Dialogues Concerning Natural Religion* (Edinburgh, Scotland: Adam Black and William Tait, 1876). Reprinted in *Philosophy of Religion: An Anthology*.

14. William James, *The Varieties of Religious Experience* (New York: Longmans, Green & Co., 1902).

15. Wallace Matson, *The Existence of God* (Ithaca, NY: Cornell University Press, 1965), chap. 2. Reprinted in *Philosophy of Religion: An Anthology*.

16. David Hume, *Dialogues on Natural Religion* (London: Longman Green, 1878); and John Hick, *Evil and the God of Love* (New York: Harper & Row, 1966). These are reprinted in *Philosophy of Religion: An Anthology*.

17. Bertrand Russell, "The Finality of Death," in *Why I Am Not a Christian* (New York: Simon & Schuster, 1957). John Hick, *Philosophy of Religion* (Englewood Cliffs, NJ: Prentice Hall, 1983). These are reprinted in *Philosophy of Religion: An Anthology*.

18. Blaise Pascal, *Thoughts*, trans. W. F. Trotter (New York: Collier & Son, 1910).

19. William James, *The Will to Believe* (New York: Longmans, Green & Co., 1897).

20. W. K. Clifford, *Lectures and Essays* (London: Macmillan, 1879).

120   *Louis P. Pojman*

21. Antony Flew, R. M. Hare, and Basil Mitchell, "Theology and Falsifi-cation," in *New Essays in Philosophical Theology*, ed. Antony Flew and Alasdair MacIntyre (London: SCM Press, 1955), 96-108.

22. J. L. Mackie, "Evil and Omnipotence," *Mind* LXIV(1955): 254.

23. Alvin Plantinga, *God, Freedom and Evil* (New York: Harper & Row, 1974).

24. Richard Swinburne, *The Existence of God* (Oxford: Oxford University Press, 1979).

25. Patrick Nowell-Smith, "Morality: Religious and Secular," in *The Rationalist Annual* (London: Pemberton Publishing Co., 1961); and George Mavrodes, "Religion and the Queerness of Morality," in *Rationality, Religious Belief and Moral Commitment: Essays in the Philosophy of Religion*, ed. Robert Audi and William Wainwright (Ithaca, NY: Cornell University Press, 1986).

A SELECTED AND ANNOTATED BIBLIOGRAPHY

Adams, Marilyn McCord, and Robert Merrihew Adams, eds. *The Problem of Evil* (Oxford: Oxford University Press, 1990). Contains important essays on the problem of evil by J. L. Mackie, Alvin Plantinga, William Rowe, John Hick and others.

Audi, Robert, and William J. Wainwright, eds. *Rationality, Religious Belief and Moral Commitment* (Ithaca, NY: Cornell University Press, 1986). Contains important essays by Plantinga and Mavrodes. Mavrodes' "Religion and the Queerness of Morality" is reprinted in Pojman (1994).

Broad, C. D. *Religion, Philosophy and Psychical Research* (New York: Harcourt, Brace, 1953). The essay on Religious Experience is one of the finest in the literature. Reprinted in Pojman (1994) and Rowe and Wainwright (1989).

Brody, Baruch. *Readings in the Philosophy of Religion* (Englewood Cliffs, NJ: Prentice Hall, 1974). A comprehensive anthology, especially good selections of the classics.

Clifford, W. K. *Lectures and Essays* (London: Macmillan, 1879). His classic essay "The Ethics of Belief" is reprinted in Pojman (1994) and Rowe and Wainwright (1989).

Davies, Brian. *An Introduction to the Philosophy of Religion* (Oxford: Oxford University Press, 1982). This is readable and reliable and written from a distinctive theistic framework.

Flew, Antony, and Alasdair MacIntyre. *New Essays in Philosophical Theology* (London: SCM Press, 1955). Contains the classic exchange between Flew, R. M. Hare, and Basil Mitchell, in "Theology and Falsification," reprinted in Pojman (1994) and Rowe and Wainwright (1989).

Gale, Richard. *On the Nature and Existence of God* (Cambridge: Cambridge University Press, 1991). A probing, cogent critique of contemporary theistic arguments.

Geivett, R. Douglas, and Brendan Sweetman, eds. *Contemporary Perspectives on Religious Epistemology* (Oxford: Oxford University Press, 1992). This is an important selection of essays on religious epistemology, including such topics as atheism, Wittgensteinian fideism, reformed epistemology, natural theology, prudential justification, and religious experience.

Gutting, Gary. *Religious Belief and Religious Skepticism* (Notre Dame, IN: University of Notre Dame Press, 1982).

Hick, John. *Arguments for the Existence of God* (London: Macmillan, 1971). A clearly written, insightful examination. The chapter "Rational Theistic Belief without Proof" is reprinted in Pojman (1994).

Hick, John. *Philosophy of Religion* (Englewood Cliffs, NJ: Prentice Hall, 1983). A lively and succinct work.

Howard-Snyder, Daniel, ed. *The Evidential Argument from Evil* (Bloomington, IN: Indiana University Press, 1996). Contains recent work on the problem of evil.

Hume, David. *Dialogues Concerning Natural Religion* (1779). There are several good editions, including the one edited by Richard Popkin (Indianapolis: Hackett, 1980). A selection is reprinted in Brody (1992), Pojman (1994), and Rowe and Wainwright (1989).

James, William. *The Varieties of Religious Experience* (New York: Longmans, Green & Co., 1902).

Kenny, Anthony. *Faith and Reason* (New York: Columbia University Press, 1983). A rationalist examination of religious belief.

Lewis, C. S. "On Obstinacy in Belief." In *The World's Last Night and Other Essays* (New York: Harcourt, Brace, Jovanovich, 1960). Reprinted in Pojman (1994).

Loades, Ann, and Loyal D. Rue, eds. *Contemporary Classics in Philosophy of Religion* (La Salle, IL: Open Court, 1991). This anthology contains 27 papers chosen by 22 leading philosophers of religion.

Mackie, J. L. "Evil and Omnipotence." *Mind* LXIV (1955): 254. Reprinted in Pojman (1994) and Rowe and Wainwright (1989).

Mackie, J. L. *The Miracle of Theism* (Oxford: Oxford University Press,

1982). A lively discussion of the proofs by one of the ablest atheist philosophers of our time, but uneven.

Martin, Michael. *Atheism: A Philosophical Justification* (Philadelphia: Temple University Press, 1990). A comprehensive and well-argued critique of theism and defense of atheism.

Matson, Wallace. *The Existence of God* (Ithaca, NY: Cornell University Press, 1965). A cogent attack on the traditional arguments for the existence of God. The chapter on Religious Experience is reprinted in Pojman (1994).

Moreland, J. P. *Scaling the Secular City* (Grand Rapids, MI: Baker Books, 1987). An accessible and well-argued defense of theism.

Plantinga, Alvin. *God, Freedom and Evil* (New York: Harper and Row, 1974). A clear, detailed treatment of the problem of evil and the ontological argument from a theistic point of view.

Plantinga, Alvin, and Nicholas Wolterstorff, eds. *Faith and Rationality* (Notre Dame, IN: University of Notre Dame Press, 1983). Part of Plantinga's essay "Religious Belief without Evidence" is abridged in Geivett and Sweetman (1992) and Pojman (1994).

Plato. *Euthyphro* (several good translations by Jowett, Cooper, Grube, and Tredennick, among others). Contains the famous challenge to the Divine Command Theory of Ethics: "Is the Good because God loves it, or does God love the Good because it is good?" Reprinted in Brody (1992) and Pojman (1994).

Perry, John. *Personal Identity and Immortality* (Indianapolis: Hackett, 1979). An excellent dialogue on the subject.

Pojman, Louis. *Philosophy of Religion: An Anthology* (Belmont, CA: Wadsworth, 1994). A comprehensive anthology.

Pojman, Louis. "Faith, Doubt and Hope" from his *Religious Belief and the Will* (London: Routledge & Kegan Paul, 1986).

Purtill, Richard. *Thinking about Religion* (Englewood Cliffs, NJ: Prentice-Hall, 1978). A very basic account of the major problems from a theistic point of view, containing a fascinating defense of the Christian notion of life after death.

Ross, James. *Philosophical Theology* (Indianapolis: Hackett, 1969). This is to be recommended for its discussion of the medieval sources, as well as for its contemporary relevance.

Rowe, William. *Philosophy of Religion: An Introduction* (Belmont, CA: Wadsworth, 1978). A judicious, comprehensive, and lucid presentation of the major issues, useful for beginners and more advanced undergraduates.

Rowe, William, and William Wainwright. *Philosophy of Religion: Selected*

Readings (New York: Harcourt, Brace, Jovanovich, 1989). A comprehensive anthology.

Russell, Bertrand. *Why I Am Not a Christian* (New York: Simon & Schuster, 1957).

Stewart, J. David. *Philosophy of Religion* (Englewood Cliffs, NJ: Prentice Hall, 1977). Anthology with short selections and long introductions; nicely set out.

Swinburne, Richard. *The Existence of God* (Oxford: Clarendon Press, 1979). Perhaps the most sustained, if not the overall best, defense of the traditional arguments available. Suitable for upper-division courses.

Taylor, Richard. *Metaphysics* (Englewood Cliffs, NJ: Prentice Hall, 1983).

Wainwright, William. *Philosophy of Religion* (Belmont, CA: Wadsworth, 1988). A rich and detailed as well as comprehensive treatment of the central issues from a theistic perspective.

Chapter 13

Three Courses in Philosophy of Religion

Michael Martin

Over a teaching career of thirty years at Boston University, I have taught courses in the philosophy of religion at three different levels. In this chapter I will briefly describe the content of these courses, the teaching methods used, and some of the problems I have encountered. I hope that my experience will be useful to other philosophy teachers.

The Introductory Course

On at least three different occasions in the last ten years, I taught an introduction to the philosophy of religion course, titled "Philosophy and Religion." Although this course was not intended to be an introductory course in philosophy, several students in the class had had no previous acquaintance with philosophy so that the course served as their introduction to the field. The texts used were William Rowe, *Philosophy of Religion*,[1] and Louis Pojman, *Philosophy of Religion: An Anthology*.[2] Rowe's introductory book and Pojman's anthology complement each other nicely. On the one hand, the classical and contemporary articles in Pojman, although difficult and demanding, are illuminated by Rowe's clear expositions. On the other hand, Rowe's introductory exposition is given depth and historical perspective by the selections in Pojman. The topics covered in the course—the nature of God; the ontological, cosmological, teleological arguments; the argument from miracles; religious experience; the presumption of atheism; the argument from evil, faith, life after death; and religion and ethics—were derived from these books.

As a supplement to these readings, I distributed several handouts during the semester in which I formulated an argument that was being discussed informally in class. Here is a sample handout:

The Argument from Knowledge by Acquaintance

1. If God is all knowing, He has all factual knowledge and all knowledge by acquaintance.

2. If God has all knowledge by acquaintance, then He knows (by acquaintance) torturing someone gratuitously.

3. But if God knows (by acquaintance) torturing someone gratuitously, then He would have had to have tortured someone gratuitously.

4. If God is all good, He would never torture someone gratuitously.

5. If God would never torture someone gratuitously, then He does not know (by acquaintance) torturing someone gratuitously.

6. Therefore, God cannot be both all knowing and all good.

7. But by definition God is both all knowing and all good.

8. Hence, God does not exist.

Ways of Escaping the Conclusion

(a) Deny premise 1. God has only all factual knowledge. But then one must say that an all-knowing being lacks knowledge, and this is paradoxical.

(b) Deny premise 3. God could know by acquaintance torturing someone gratuitously without actually having engaged in torture. But how? By definition one can know x by acquaintance (where x is some activity) only by engaging in it. Even God cannot do what is logically impossible.

(c) Deny premise 4. God might be justified in torturing someone because it is necessary to some larger good. But by definition gratuitous torture is not justified.

(d) Deny premise 4. God might be all good in some different sense of "good" than the human sense of "good." In this different sense, gratuitous torture is morally permissible. But in this case why worship God? We worship God because we suppose he is good in *our* sense.

(e) Deny premise 7. God in the Judeo-Christian tradition is by definition all good and all powerful. However, there are other religious traditions in which this is not true. Perhaps; but the argument purports only to refute the existence of God in the Judeo-Christian tradition.

The goal of "Philosophy and Religion" was to introduce students to philosophical issues connected with the Judeo-Christian religious tradition, as well as to get students to think philosophically and critically about these issues. There is no doubt that the first goal was achieved: most students finished the course with at least a passing knowledge of the topic listed above. Yet, the second goal was harder both to achieve and to measure. Though I am certain that some students did come to think philosophically and critically outside of the classroom about religious issues, I doubt that most did. However, it is perhaps unrealistic to suppose that an introductory course in the philosophy of religion can alone turn most students into critical philosophical thinkers concerning religion.

The teaching methods used in the introductory course were determined to a large extent by the size of the class—which ranged from between thirty and seventy students. Lectures and discussion occupied most of class time. I tended to call on students who raised their hands in response to my questions, but I also made an effort to call on students who did not raise their hands—the majority—in order to engage them. On occasion, I divided the class into small groups (of five or six) to discuss, for about a half-hour, such questions as whether there are objections to the view that there is life after death. Each group then reported the results of its deliberations back to the class as a whole.

Another technique that I sometimes used was to have students "act out" philosophical positions. For example, to illustrate the contrast between being free and not being free on the compatibilist view, I would have a student try to leave the classroom with other students blocking the way. I would point out that the student trying to leave lacked freedom in the compatibilist sense. Then I would have the student leave the room without the way being blocked, and point out that the student had freedom *in this sense* to walk out the door. Another technique I have used is to turn off the lights and then, to stimulate students' imaginations, ask them to close their eyes. ("Can you imagine world in which human beings never did anything immoral? If you can, how does this affect the freewill defense for the problem of evil? Can you imagine God creating this world?")

To encourage students to challenge what I said, I stated at the beginning of the course that I would offer extra credit to those who wrote out their objections to the views that I expressed in class. I responded to these objections in writing (and, more recently, by electronic mail).

Grading

The grading policy in the class was structured so that students had to both achieve certain grades on the midterms and take-home final and *also* do additional work, in order to receive a grade in the A or B range. For example, to receive a grade of A or A minus, students had to write a term paper and successfully answer two sets of questions taken from the *Questions for Discussion* at the end of Rowe's chapters. Typical questions for discussion were (1) "Which of the several objections to the Ontological Argument strikes you as most plausible? Which strikes you as the least plausible? For what reasons?" and (2) "Of the various arguments for and against personal survival, select what you think is the strongest for and the strongest against. Carefully discuss each of these arguments, and indicate which of the two, in your judgment, is the most plausible."

My requiring additional work in order to qualify for an A or B grade quickly separated the highly motivated students from those who were simply good exam takers. It also allowed students to adjust their grade expectations to their capacity for work.

Graduate-Level Seminar on Christianity

A number of years ago, I taught a graduate-level course on philosophical issues connected with Christianity. At the time, I was completing the manuscript of *The Case Against Christianity*,[3] and so I structured the course around topics covered in that book. The seminar considered questions such as Did Jesus exist? Was Jesus a miracle worker or a magician? Was Jesus resurrected from the dead? Could Jesus, a finite human being, be God Incarnate? Was Jesus an ideal moral teacher?

Texts for the course were Michael Arnheim's *Is Christianity True?*;[4] Rudolf Bultmann's *Jesus Christ and Mythology*;[5] Thomas Morris's *The Logic of God Incarnate*;[6] Paul Ramsey's *Basic Christian Ethics*;[7] Morton Smith's *Jesus the Magician*;[8] and George Albert Wells's *Did Jesus Exist*.[9] In addition, students were required to buy a packet of photocopied articles and book chapters that included William Frankena's "The Ethics of Love" from his *Ethics*;[10] Paul Kurtz's "The Jesus Myth" from his *The Transcendental Temptation*;[11] Richard Robinson's "The Ethics of the Synoptic Gospels" and "Criticism of the Synoptic Gospels," both from his *An Atheist's Values*;[12] a selection from Bertrand Russell's *Why I Am Not a Christian*;[13] George Albert Wells's "Myth and Authenticity in the New Testament" from his *The Historical Evidence for Jesus*,[14] as well as his "The Historicity of Jesus" from *The Encyclopedia of Unbelief*;[15] and, Ian Wilson's "Did Jesus Even Exist?" from his *Jesus: The Evidence*.[16]

The course was run as a seminar with student reports, several short papers, and lots of class discussion and student participation. The topics for student presentations were chosen by me. Typically, they consisted in a report on the readings and students' critical reaction to the readings. For example, I asked one student to expound Wells's argument against the historicity of Jesus and to raise some critical questions against Wells's argument. Another assignment was to evaluate several criticisms that Robinson raises against Christian ethics. I graded the reports on the basis of the clarity of their thought and the critical acumen displayed.

My goal for the course was twofold: that students become acquainted with some of the problems connected with Christian belief and that they learn to think critically about these issues. The first goal was certainly achieved, and judging from the student papers, the second goal was, to a limited extent, realized.

Were I to teach this seminar again, I would probably cover the same questions and topics, but I would certainly update the readings. An update is warranted because work has appeared recently that raises arguments and points that I did not consider in the seminar. This update would include my own book, *The Case Against Christianity*,[17] as well as papers from the journal *Faith and Philosophy* that include material on the Resurrection, such as Robert Greg Cavin's "Is There Sufficient Historical Evidence to Establish the Resurrection of Jesus?"[18] and Stephen T. Davis's "Is it Possible to Know that Jesus Was Raised from the Dead?"[19] The first two works argue that because the initial probability of the Resurrection is low, extremely strong evidence is needed to justify belief in it.

Middle-Level Seminar on Religious Epistemology

In the fall semester of 1996, I taught a middle-level seminar on religious epistemology that was open to graduate students and advanced undergraduates. The required texts were Louis Pojman's *What Can We Know?*;[20] R. Douglas Geivett and Brendan Sweetman's *Contemporary Perspectives on Religious Epistemology*;[21] William Alston's *Perceiving God*;[22] and Alvin Plantinga's *Warrant and Proper Function*.[23] The following books were on reserve: D(ewi) Z(ephaniah) Phillips's *Faith after Foundationalism*;[24] Michael Martin's *Atheism*;[25] and Alvin Plantinga's *Warrant: The Current Debate* and *Warrant and Proper Function*.[26]

In addition, a number of articles that are critical of Plantinga's and Alston's positions were placed on reserve, including a symposium on Plantinga's *Warrant and Proper Function* that appeared in *Philosophy and Phenomenological Research*,[27] and a symposium on *Perceiving God* that also appeared in that journal.[28]

The goals of the course were the same as those for the graduate-level seminar described previously. Like that seminar, this class too was conducted as a seminar. Four basic topics were covered: (a) reformed epistemology; (b) Wittgensteinian fideism; (c) religious experience; and (d) proper function and supernaturalism. (For the latter two topics, the readings were restricted to Alston's *Perceiving God* and its critics and Plantinga's *Warrant and*

Proper Function and its critics.) Several short papers were assigned during the semester and a long fifteen-page paper was due at the end of the course.

One problem that arose in this course—it is a potential problem in any course in which there are both graduate and undergraduate students—was the tendency of graduate students to dominate the discussion at the expense of the undergraduate students, the former tending, as a result, to feel intimidated. (In my particular course, this was perhaps exacerbated by the fact that there was only one undergraduate student in the course.) I know no easy way to handle this. (I tried to take special care to include the undergraduate student in the discussion and hold graduate-student domination in check, but I am not sure how successful I was. I also gave the undergraduate tutorials during my office hours to help with difficult material.)

Because the seminar met three times a week, I thought it necessary to organize the discussions carefully. Hence, I handed out a day-by-day schedule of the readings and the questions to be covered. There follows a sample schedule of four class meetings that I distributed on the very first day of the seminar.

Assignments for First Four Meetings

Assignment for first meeting:

Read Pojman's *What Can We Know?*, Chapter 6 [which concerns classical foundationalism]. Be sure you consider *Questions for Discussion* 1-5 and be prepared to answer these questions orally in class. [The *Questions for Discussion* help the students to focus on the main critical points of the chapter. For example, *Question for Discussion* #4 is "Go over the critique of foundationalism. What is the 'ascent' problem?" (This chapter was not discussed in class before the students were asked to answer the questions concerning it.)]

Assignment for second meeting:

Read Pojman's *What Can We Know?*, Chapter 7 [which concerns coherentism and modest foundationalism]. Be sure you consider *Questions for Discussion* 1-9 and be prepared to answer *Questions for Discussion* 6-9 orally in class. [*Questions for Discussion* help the students to focus on the main critical points. For example, *Question #3* is "Go over the three main criticisms of coherentism in this chapter. How might the coherentist respond to these objections?" (This chapter was not discussed in class before the students were asked to answer these questions.)]

Assignment for third meeting:
Read Plantinga's paper "Is Belief in God Properly Basic?" in R. Douglas Geivett and Brendan Sweetman's *Contemporary Perspectives on Religious Epistemology*. Be prepared to orally answer the following in class:

1. What is classical foundationalism according to Plantinga? What are his objections to it?

2. Could foundationalism be modified in such a way that it would meet Plantinga's objections and yet block theological beliefs from being properly basic?

3. What does Plantinga mean when he says that properly basic beliefs are not groundless? What is the difference between groundless beliefs and basic beliefs? Is this distinction tenable?

4. What does Plantinga mean by saying that the criteria of properly basic beliefs should be arrived at inductively? Has Plantinga followed his own advice? What are the problems with this inductive method?

Assignment for fourth meeting:
Write a critique of Plantinga's paper of no more than two pages. Be prepared to read your paper in class.

Teaching Philosophy of Religion While Being an Atheist

Although I am an atheist, my atheism was not an issue in teaching philosophy of religion. Indeed, most students in the introductory course did not even realize that I am a nonbeliever. In general, I did not tell students in my introductory class my position unless they asked. (Most students in the more advanced courses seemed to know my position, and some perceptive students in my introductory course inferred my views from the titles of my books and articles.) Although I offered critiques of the arguments for the existence of God, I also presented objections to the atheistic arguments (for example, objections to the argument from evil). However, I also tried to show how many of these objections can be answered. I try to present atheism fairly and pick textbooks that give atheism its due. For example, of the books that I assign, Rowe's is sympathetic to atheism, and Pojman's anthology has selections that are critical of theistic positions.

NOTES

1. William Rowe, *Philosophy of Religion*, 2nd ed. (Belmont, CA: Wadsworth, 1993).

2. Louis Pojman, ed., *Philosophy of Religion: An Anthology*, 2nd ed. (Belmont, CA: Wadsworth, 1994).

3. Michael Martin, *The Case Against Christianity* (Philadelphia, PA: Temple University Press, 1991).

4. Michael Arnheim, *Is Christianity True?* (Buffalo, NY: Prometheus Books, 1984).

5. Rudolf Bultmann, *Jesus Christ and Mythology* (New York: Charles Scribner's Sons, 1958).

6. Thomas Morris, *The Logic of God Incarnate* (Ithaca, NY: Cornell University Press, 1986).

7. Paul Ramsey, *Basic Christian Ethics* (New York, Charles Scribner's Sons, 1950).

8. Morton Smith, *Jesus the Magician* (San Francisco, Harper and Row, 1978).

9. George Albert Wells, *Did Jesus Exist?* (London, Pemberton, 1975).

10. William Frankena, *Ethics* (Englewood Cliffs, NJ: Prentice Hall, 1973).

11. Paul Kurtz, *The Transcendental Temptation* (Buffalo, NY: Prometheus Books, 1986).

12. Richard Robinson, *An Atheist's Values* (Oxford, Basil Blackwell, 1964).

13. Bertrand Russell, *Why I Am Not a Christian* (New York: Simon and Schuster, 1957).

14. George Albert Wells, *The Historical Evidence for Jesus* (Buffalo, NY: Prometheus Books, 1982).

15. *The Encyclopedia of Unbelief*, vol. 1, ed., Gordon Stein, (Buffalo, NY: Prometheus Books, 1985).

16. Ian Wilson, *Jesus: The Evidence* (San Francisco: Harper and Row, 1984).

17. Michael Martin, *The Case Against Christianity* (Philadelphia, PA: Temple University Press, 1991).

18. Robert Greg Cavin, "Is There Sufficient Historical Evidence to Establish the Resurrection of Jesus?" *Faith and Philosophy* 12, no. 3 (1995): 361-79.

19. Stephen T. Davis, "Is it Possible to Know that Jesus Was Raised from the Dead?" *Faith and Philosophy* 1, no. 2 (1984): 147-159.

20. Louis Pojman, *What Can We Know?* (Belmont, CA: Wadsworth, 1995).

21. R. Douglas Geivett and Brendan Sweetman, eds., *Contemporary Perspectives on Religious Epistemology* (NY: Oxford University Press, 1992).

22. William Alson, *Perceiving God* (Ithaca, NY: Cornell University Press, 1991).

23. Alvin Plantinga, *Warrant and Proper Function* (New York: Oxford University Press, 1993).

24. D. Z. Phillips, *Faith after Foundationalism* (Boulder, CO: Westview Press, 1990).

25. Michael Martin, *Atheism* (Philadelphia: Temple University Press, 1990).

26. Alvin Plantinga, *Warrant: The Current Debate* (New York: Oxford University Press, 1993).

27. *Philosophy and Phenomenological Research* LV, no. 2 (1995): 393-464. The symposium on Plantinga's *Warrant: The Current Debate* and *Warrant and Proper Function* consisted of the following papers: "Précis of *Warrant: The Current Debate* and *Warrant and Proper Function*," by Alvin Platinga; "Epistemic Warrant as Proper Function," by William Alston; "Comments on Platinga's Two-Volume Work on Warrant," by Carl Ginet; "Proper and Improper Use of Cognitive Faculties: A Counterexample to Platinga's Proper Functioning Theory," by Matthias Steup; "Response to *Warrant*," by Richard Swinburne; "Platinga on Epistemic Warrant," by James E. Taylor; and "Reliabilism, Analysis and Defeaters," by Alvin Plantinga

28. *Philosophy and Phenomenological Research* LIV, no. 4 (1994): 863-99. The symposium on Alston's *Perceiving God: The Epistemology of Religious Experience* consisted of the following papers: "Précis of *Perceiving God*," by William P. Alston; "Why Alston's Mystical Doxastic Practice is Subjective," by Richard M. Gale; "Perception and Mystical Experience," by George S. Pappas; "Religious Disagreements and Doxastic Practices," by Robert M. Adams; and "Reply to Commentators," by William P. Alston.

PART VII
Teaching Critical Thinking

Chapter 14

Using Pseudoscience in a Critical Thinking Class

Kathleen Dean Moore

From the amazing claims of grocery store tabloids to dorm room conversations about star signs for lovers, students are subjected to the hard sell of popular pseudoscientific theories. Philosophy professors have a responsibility to teach the logical skills that will help students evaluate these usually poor and sometimes pernicious arguments. However, this can be an opportunity rather than a burden, because pseudoscientific theories provide a useful vehicle for teaching critical thinking. Using popular pseudoscientific theories as examples in a critical thinking course is an effective way to teach students how to distinguish good from bad arguments.

I offer here a suggestion for a critical thinking class that uses egregious examples of pseudoscience to teach techniques of critical thinking, and to sharpen students' appreciation of the characteristics an inductive argument must have before it deserves assent. What follows is the rationale for such a course, a summary of the course plan, a sample class exercise, and advice on resources.

Rationale

Using pseudoscience in a logic class is a compromise between two common practices: the exclusive focus—in many formal logic courses—on ideal forms of argument (such as, for example, the categorical syllogism, the disjunctive syllogism, *modus ponens*), and the exclusive focus—in many critical thinking courses—on fallacies. The approach offered here encourages students to examine faulty pseudoscientific arguments in order to discover for themselves the characteristics of a good argument, and thus learn about ideal forms of argument by studying arguments that are decidedly less than ideal.

One good reason for using pseudoscientific arguments in a critical thinking class is that they are fascinating and often funny. They attract and hold students' attention. A further reason is that taking on the pernicious or poor arguments of pseudoscience falls to the philosophy professor, if only by default, since, with few exceptions, scientists have not bothered to disown or refute bogus theories. Being trained in critical analysis, having wondered about the relation between belief and truth, and being blessed with elegant arguments as old friends, professional philosophers are particularly suited to the task of exposing poor arguments for what they are.

Course Plan

For each pseudoscientific claim, we study a technique of critical thinking that can be used to evaluate it, as follows:

- *Clairvoyance.* Super Psychics from Hollywood See Tomorrow's Headlines Today.

    How to Reason to a Reliable Generalization: the pitfalls of enumerative induction.

- *Unidentified Flying Objects.* The Evidence of Invasions from Outer Space Is Startling.

    How to Use Observations as Evidence for or against a Hypothesis: the formulation and design of a good test of a hypothesis.

- *Remote Viewing.* Some People Have an Eerie Ability to "See" a Distant Scene by Tuning in to Psychic Bea- cons Beaming Back a Vision from Afar.

    How to Avoid a Common Mistake in Hypothesis-Testing, namely assuming that a con- confirmed prediction pro- vides decisive evidence for a hypothesis.

- *Spoon Bending.* A Psychic Can Use His Mind's Energy to Turn Spoons and Keys into Twisted Curls of Metal, but Never in the Presence of Skeptics.

  How to Avoid Another Common Mistake in Hypothesis-Testing: special traps laid by hypotheses that are not falsifiable.

- *Surgeons without Scalpels.* Healers in the Philippine Islands Remove Tumors, Excise Peptic Ulcers, and Cure Earaches without Surgery or Drugs.

  How to Reason from Effect to Cause: designing experiments to test causal relationships.

Given the nature of the material, the course format varies from topic to topic. Generally the first order of business, for each pseudoscientific claim, is to become acquainted with several of the arguments offered in its support. For some of the topics, I have asked students to find flawed arguments in the "literature"—grocery store tabloids, popular magazines, used paperbacks. More often, as explained below, I provide a class exercise that draws students into misusing evidence themselves, or a homework assignment in which the students observe others making mistakes. Then, we work together to expose the weaknesses of the resulting faulty arguments. On the basis of their new insight into the weakness of particular kinds of evidence, I ask students to think about what would constitute strong evidence for the claim in question.

Sample Class Exercise: Remote Viewing

The following class exercise serves to illustrate how study of a pseudoscientific claim—in this case, that "remote viewing" is possible—can be integrated with the teaching of techniques of critical thinking and inductive reasoning. In this exercise, the students first divide into small groups, do an experiment (explained later), and draw their own conclusions. Then, the groups discuss and write answers to a set of questions that draw out the logic lessons of the experiment. Finally, the professor leads a whole class discussion of student groups' responses to the questions.

Background Information for Instructors

A current fad among psychics is "remote viewing." This is the ability to "'see" a remote location without using any of the five senses. A psychic 'sender' goes to a location—a park, a building, a street corner—and at a prearranged time, 'sends' a visual image of that location to a psychic 'receiver' who is waiting with experimenters in a closed room. The receiver draws a rough sketch of the image in his or her mind; the sender or an assistant takes a photograph or draws a picture of the location. The two visual images are searched for similarities. The results of these "tests" are often striking, providing evidence—the psychics say—for extrasensory perception.[1]

The reasoning process is, as instructors will recognize, a classic case of the fallacy of affirming the consequent. If remote viewing really works, the argument goes, then there will be matches between the sender's and the receiver's drawings. When such matches occur, as they inevitably will, they are often taken as convincing evidence for the existence of the mysterious psychic powers. The absence of matches, or the ratio of matches to mismatches, is usually ignored. The following experiment is designed to illustrate the dangers of using a correct prediction as evidence for a hypothesis.

Instructions to Class

- Divide into groups of five or six.
- From the members of your group, choose a 'sender.' The rest of you will be 'receivers.'
- Coordinate your watches. Get out a pencil and a clean sheet of paper.
- The sender leaves the room and goes to some place beyond the view of the receivers.
- At a prearranged time, the sender focuses on a particular scene and draws a simple sketch of the subject.
- At the same prearranged time, each of the receivers in the group should draw the image that is in his or her mind. If nothing is *in* your mind, draw whatever *comes* to mind.
- When the sender returns, compare the receivers sketches to the sender's drawing.
- As a group, discuss and write answers to the questions.

Questions for Students; Sample Student Answers; Suggestions for Using Student Answers to Make Points about Inductive Reasoning

1. In what specific ways are the receivers' sketches like the sender's sketch?

Students will find all sorts of matches if they look closely enough. If not, help them out: perhaps a small part of one drawing is repeated on a larger scale in another; perhaps a rectangle is present in both drawings; perhaps letters appear in two drawings, and so on.

Once it is clear to the students that they are actively looking for matches *of any kind*, they will be able to find them, no matter how minor. Moreover, in my experience, students systematically disregard mismatches. The point, of course, is to lure students into a misleading search for confirming evidence and a suppression of disconfirming evidence.

2. What argument might you offer to convince someone that remote viewing really works?

Sample student response:

"If a person really can beam a visual image to another person, then there should be lots of similarities between the drawings of the sender and receivers. This is just what our experiment found: many of us had matches, and one receiver was right on the money. So there probably is something to remote viewing."

To the Instructor: Make sure the students understand that this argument has the form of a conditional syllogism and that the first premise is a conditional statement, with the hypothesis as the antecedent and the prediction as the consequent.

3. In what ways could receivers increase the chances of matches with the sender (without peeking at the sender's drawings)?

Sample answer:

Matches are more likely when the receivers make a drawing as vague or "sketchy" as possible, when they draw a common shape with few details, or when—relying on their knowledge of the vicinity—they draw an object likely to be chosen by the sender.

To the Instructor: It should be pointed out to students that those who answer question 2 in the above manner make a common mistake in hypothetical reasoning: they formulate a prediction in such a way that it is difficult to falsify, not because it is true but because of the characteristics of the statement itself. The result is a test that will probably not show a hypothesis to be false, but cannot be used as evidence that a hypothesis is true.

4. What various explanations might you offer for any matches you may have had, other than the explanation that is offered by the psychics.

Sample answer:

Maybe the matches occurred by chance alone. After all, there are a limited number of simple geometric shapes, so some are likely to match up. Maybe the psychic energy of the receivers influenced the sender's choice of subject, rather than the reverse. Maybe the group members knew the sender and the vicinity well enough to guess what subject the sender would choose. Maybe there was a secret prior agreement between sender and receivers.

To the Instructor: The important point here is for students to understand that there are an indefinite number of alternative explanations for any true prediction. If students understand this, they will understand the primary problem with affirming the consequent.

5. Given your answers to questions 3 and 4, what central weaknesses do you find in the argument formulated in question 2?

To the Instructor: Explain to students that if remote viewing were true, the group would have had matches. But even if remote viewing is false, the group would have had matches—so long as one of the alternative explanations that students gave in response to question 4 is the true one. If a prediction is consistent with a number of different hypotheses, then the fact that the prediction is true cannot be used to determine *which* of those hypotheses is the correct one. Help the students draw a general conclusion about using the argument form, affirming the consequent, to confirm a hypothesis.

6. If you selected the pairs of drawings that display the best sender/receiver matches and used these as evidence to try to convince your friends that remote viewing works, do you think they would be impressed by the evidence? If they were impressed by the evidence, what mistake would they be making?

To the Instructor: It is to be hoped that after discussion of the above example, students can now name and understand the logical error their friends may be eager to make.

7. Give at least one example of when you have been fooled by the same general kind of argument you formulated in question above.

To the Instructor: It is important for students to recognize that the same general sorts of errors can occur in different contexts. If students are unable to come up with an example for themselves, tell them that you are a graphologist and ask for a handwriting sample. Tell the writer that his or her handwriting reveals the following: *You have a great deal of unused capacity which you have not turned to your advantage. You have a tendency to be critical of yourself. You have a strong need for other people to like you and for them to admire you. At times you are extroverted, affable, sociable, while at other times you are introverted, wary, and reserved.* This description was written by psychologist Bertram Forer, who based it on descriptions found in astrology books.[2] Essentially flattering, it probably describes how we all think of ourselves. Does the aptness of the character reading convince your students of your graphological powers? If students have learned their lessons, they will not only be unconvinced, but also will be able to explain exactly why.

RESOURCES

A number of resources are available for critical thinking courses based on analyses of pseudoscientific reasoning. *Understanding Scientific Reasoning,*[3] by Ronald Giere, makes effective use of pseudoscientific theories as illustrations and provides an excellent explanation of hypothetico-deductive reasoning and its fallacies. *Science and Unreason,*[4] by Daisie and Michael Radner, is a particularly useful lecture resource because of its critical analyses of pseudo-scientific arguments. Other lecture resources are Martin Gardner's *Fads and Fallacies in the Name of Science*[5] and James Randi's *Flim-Flam!*[6] Many of the intellectual swindles recounted in these sources make errors that are monumental in scope, classic in form, and important enough to warrant serious refutation. Two recent books, *How to Think about Weird Things,*[7] by Theodore Schick and Lewis Vaughn, and *Thinking Critically about New Age Ideas,*[8] by William D. Gray, offer students wise advice on (as their names suggest) the evaluation of claims concerning weird and unusual things.

As a resource for awful arguments, grocery store tabloids such as *The National Enquirer*, *The Star*, and *The Globe* are good. Also, used bookstores usually have many shelves devoted to short-lived pseudoscientific or self-improvement fads. Look under such categories as "occult" and "paranormal," or—in some book-stores—"psychology" and "philosophy." Finally, *The Skeptical Inquirer*[9] is a journal devoted to the scientific investigation of paranormal claims; its bad examples are often hilarious.

NOTES

1. For more information, see David F. Marks, "Remote Viewing Revisited," *The Skeptical Inquirer* (summer 1982): 18-20.

2. For more information, see Ray Hyman, "'Cold Reading': How to Convince Strangers That You Know All about Them," *The Zetetic* (spring/summer 1977): 18-37.

3. Ronald Giere, *Understanding Scientific Reasoning*, 2nd ed. (New York: Holt, Rinehart, and Winston, 1984).

4. Daisie Radner and Michael Radner, *Science and Unreason* (Belmont, CA: Wadsworth, 1982).

5. Martin Gardner, *Fads and Fallacies in the Name of Science* (New York: Dover Publications, Inc., 1957).

6. James Randi, *Flim-Flam!* (Buffalo, NY: Prometheus Books, 1982).

7. Theodore Schick and Lewis Vaughn, *How to Think about Weird Things* (Mountain View, CA: Mayfield Publishing Company, 1995).

8. William D. Gray, *Thinking Critically about New Age Ideas* (Belmont, CA: Wadsworth, 1991).

9. For information about subscriptions to *The Skeptical Inquirer*, contact the Committee for the Scientific Investigation of Claims of the Paranormal, Kendrick Frazier, Director, P.O. Box 703, Amherst, New York 14226-9974.

Chapter 15

A Critical Thinking Portfolio

Theodore A. Gracyk

In my first years of teaching, I was regularly assigned to teach a course in critical thinking. After nine consecutive quarters teaching such a course, I decided to overhaul it to reflect my sympathy with John E. McPeck's view that general critical thinking skills are "by no means sufficient for thinking critically." Being able to think critically in one discipline has little or no bearing on being able to do so in another.[1] How well one thinks about a specific topic is primarily a function of one's grasp of that specific subject: "critical thinking is tied more closely to specific knowledge and understanding than to any specific set of allegedly transferable skills."[2] This is so because effective assessment of complex, "real-life" arguments typically requires knowledge of information that is not part of the argument itself—"extra-argument information" that is left unstated but is understood to be relevant by informed parties to the discussion.[3] The relevance of such information is unrecognizable if the argument is assessed as a context-free bundle of premises and conclusions. (To illustrate this point, I suggest that my students look at a newspaper of some distant city and try to make sense of its Letters to the Editor concerning local politics. Assessing the reasoning and premises of these letters is almost always impossible; general skills are not enough.)

How, then, to combine skills and subject matter in a worthwhile manner? During the first class session, I give students the following assignment: they are to begin assembling a file—a "portfolio"—of the identification and assessment of the reasoning in twelve distinct pieces of discourse, each drawn from the student's everyday reading, such as advertisements, Letters to the Editor, news articles, and so forth.[4] The items for the portfolio can be drawn from any printed material the student chooses other than books about logic or books on critical thinking.[5] (Items are typically obtained from a magazine or newspaper, but interesting cases have come from management textbooks, self-help books, novels, and even the Bible. Magazines have ranged from *Playboy* to *Good Housekeeping*; students have diverse reading habits.) But the twelve pieces of discourse are not to be chosen randomly. Rather, each piece that is chosen is to illustrate a specific sort of reasoning or mistake in reasoning that is named on an assignment sheet that I distribute to each student. The sheet lists twenty-four types of reasoning and pseudoreasoning that will be covered in the course, divided into four groups. Group I names four types of valid deductive inference: *modus ponens, modus tollens*, disjunctive syllogism, and hypothetical syllogism. (While these are not the only types of deductive inference that we take up during the term, I have found that students rarely choose passages that illustrate inferences other than these for inclusion in their portfolios. So I have eliminated the others as choices.) Group II names four types of nondeductive inference: statistical generalization, universal generalization, causal argument, and analogical argument. Groups III and IV each name eight fallacies or types of pseudoreasoning. (When I designed the portfolio assignment, I separated the fallacies into the groups "Sleight of Hand" and "Motive in Place of Support."[6] But now I separate fallacies into Groups III and IV on the basis of when they are covered in the course, forcing students to find examples from both the earlier and later weeks of the term.) Each student must construct his or her portfolio so that, of the twelve items chosen, there are examples of three of the four kinds of inferences listed in Group I, three of the four kinds of inferences listed in Group II, and three of the four sorts of mistakes in reasoning listed in each of Groups III and IV. (The element of choice is important since a particular student may not come across a clear example of some categories or, as McPeck warns, come across an example but might not recognize it due to a lack of relevant information.)

For pieces of discourse that illustrate inferences named in Groups I and II, students must, with respect to each discourse chosen, reconstruct the argument in a clear fashion and then write a paragraph assessing its soundness. Dealing with the discourses that are chosen to illustrate the mistakes in reasoning listed under groups III and IV is easier, since it requires only an explanation of how the fallacy or problem arises in the particular discourse.

Students are to turn in their portfolio the day before the final examination. They are told that fulfillment of the assignment is worth one third of their final course grade. (I think that it must be worth at least that much in order that students take it seriously.)

Homework and traditional exams are used to reinforce what will be expected in the portfolio, and to indicate to students how they may avoid making various mistakes in the portfolio (such as accepting universal premises without looking for obvious counterexamples to the universal claim, or accepting or dismissing a position based on its source rather than the evidence offered in its support). At least one homework focuses on identifying assumptions; another on distinguishing valid from invalid argument forms; another on finding and clarifying ambiguity in arguments; and another on spotting errors in statistical reasoning. The homework assignments that I give—most of which are drawn from exercises in whichever textbook I am currently using—allow students to practice a new skill in relative isolation from other skills covered in the course. And each examination that I give likewise focuses on a limited range of skills. For example, skills relevant to deductive reasoning are treated on a single examination, and skills relating to inductive generalization are treated on another. However, although for pedagogical purposes the exams and homework assignments artificially isolate the reasoning skills that I try to teach, the portfolio assignment helps students synthesize the various skills taught in the course, requiring as it does the display of a variety of skills in the assessment of a single argument. For example, for argumentative discourses that students choose to display the type of reasoning named in Groups I and II, students must discern the main argument of each discourse, must articulate the relevant assumptions of the argument, must clarify any ambiguous or misleading language, and must explain their assessment of that argument.

There are two major advantages to the portfolio. First, it forces students to regard critical thinking skills as both transferable to, and therefore useful in, their everyday reasoning. Each piece of written discourse included by a student in his or her portfolio demonstrates that student's skill in identifying a type of reasoning used in everyday discourse—the use, say, of *modus ponens* or appeal to *ad hominem* considerations, or the use of *post hoc* inferences. The written assessments of items chosen for Groups I and II require skills that are far more general, such as identifying important assumptions of the argument; checking for and articulating ambiguities; being able to decide whether the premises are acceptable or not and, if not, being able to state what might make them acceptable; reconstructing the argument so that it is fully "displayed"; and finally, assessing the argument's soundness.

For the students, a second major advantage of the portfolio is that it allows them to demonstrate their skills in the best possible light since *they* choose the subject that provides the context of assessment. (I have found that students typically submit items that are considerably more challenging than anything found in their textbooks.) The portfolio assignment avoids the problem of the instructor selecting a "long" example on a topic that will be unfamiliar to (a number of) the students. Many critical thinking texts and instructors employ examples drawn from national political debates, but most of my students have little interest and even less knowledge about national and international affairs. However, my students do provide a large number of examples concerning local and campus political life, issues quite familiar to them. Students with a background in agriculture have assessed items concerning regional farm and water policies, topics that I, as the instructor, would never have come across.

For the instructor, use of the portfolio assignment has this advantage: drawing up the list of choices for the assignment forces the instructor to grapple with the issue of which skills are genuinely transferable and which apply to types of reasoning that occur with sufficient frequency in "real-life" that students will actually discover cases. (For example, student responses have convinced me to stop requiring categorical logic as a category within the portfolio.)

Although portfolios are due only at the end of the term, in order to succeed at this assignment, students must get started right away. Students who put off the assembling of their portfolio until the last week of the course invariably do poorly for, at that point, it is difficult even to find twelve appropriate pieces of discourse. Most students who make a habit of collecting potential submissions will eventually begin to discover good items even without actively seeking them. I recommend against an instructor collecting portfolios in stages. Requiring the portfolio in stages blurs the difference between the portfolio and homework: homework is a learning tool in which mistakes are expected, whereas the portfolio is intended—much as an exam does—to provide evidence on the part of the student that skills have been fully mastered.

Two further pedagogical purposes are served by the portfolio. First, it furthers the aim of teaching critical thinking in the "strong sense," where the goal is not merely the acquisition of skills but the inculcation of an appropriate critical attitude and a disposition to employ the skills outside the context of the coursework.[7] True, in the space of a single course, it is difficult to get students consistently to apply new skills to reasoning that they encounter outside the course itself, but trying to find items for the portfolio encourages students to form the habit of critically viewing and assessing the materials that they normally read. Second, student portfolios provide evidence of where course materials have not been clear or where teaching has been weak. When one finds consistent student weakness on specific portfolio items, it is time to rethink presentation of that area. When even the best students have trouble finding items exemplifying a specific type of argumentation, it suggests either a problem with the instructor's presentation or a lack of transferability for associated skills. (My own teaching of straw man and *ad hominem* underwent revision when I found that most students did poorly with them in the portfolio.) When revision of one's teaching of a particular skill does not improve subsequent portfolio presentations, it may be that a particular skill (for example, spotting a straw man) is less transferable than others. Of course, it may take several semesters to ascertain whether it is one's teaching of a particular skill or the skill's general non-transferability that is the source of the problem. My rule of thumb is that when revised presentation and more course time spent on a topic does not pay off in more students correctly finding appropriate items, transferability is minimal and I deemphasize (or eliminate) that topic in the portfolio assignment.

The practice of collecting the portfolios at term's end inevitably delays any course revision to subsequent terms. This drawback can be somewhat mitigated by having sessions toward the semester's end in which students can bring in items they are considering for their portfolios, so that the instructor can spot-check their work, comment on a dozen or so items so that students get a sense of, say, where they are explaining too little in their assessments or are confusing one fallacy with another, and review material that may not have been clear the first time around.

The use of the portfolio assignment has one further good consequence and one drawback. The good consequence is that I receive a steady stream of fresh examples that students find interesting and intelligible. My files now bulge with excellent examples of each skill I cover, drawn from a wide variety of sources. The drawback is that many students actually lower their overall course grade by their portfolio. Grading the portfolio on an objective scale with 100 possible points and a D range of 50-60 points, about 20 percent of the students receive a grade of D or F on their portfolio. Some students who appear average in terms of homework and exams demonstrate that they have actually learned very little. Although the flexibility of the assignment allows students both to focus on their strongest skills—because they can choose not to submit an example of an inference pattern, *modus tollens,* say, if that deductive inference pattern confuses them—and to assess subjects of their own choosing, a single course cannot make critical thinkers out of many students. But for the majority, the portfolio is a useful tool for transferring general skills to everyday contexts.

NOTES

1. John E. McPeck, *Critical Thinking and Education* (New York: St Martin's, 1981), 13.

2. Ibid., 156.

3. Ibid., 92-93.

4. Ibid., 49. McPeck challenges standardized, multiple choice tests of critical thinking abilities, in part, because standardized tests (such as the Cornell and the Watson-Glazer tests) cannot separate reading comprehension and general knowledge from critical thinking. The portfolio approach is compatible with McPeck's demand that tests of critical thinking "be subject-specific in an area (or areas) of the test-taker's experience or preparation."

5. Although restricting it to printed material makes the construction of the portfolio seem a measure only of critical *reading* abilities, as will become clear, the portfolio assignment also requires the display of writing skills as well as skills of logical discernment and organization.

6. Following the classifications in Jerry Cederblom and David W. Paulson, *Critical Reasoning*, various editions (Belmont, CA: Wadsworth, 1982, 1986, 1991).

7. For a survey of what is meant by strong-sense critical thinking, see Arthur B. Millman, "Critical Thinking Attitudes: A Framework for the Issues," *Informal Logic* 10, no. 1 (1988): 45-50.

PART VIII
Teaching Philosophy through History

Chapter 16

The Teaching of Philosophy—
Historically*

John J. McDermott

One does not have to be a Hegelian in order to realize that one of the most significant insights of the last several hundred years is that all human activity takes place in and through an historical matrix. This is not to say that the historical matrix is a sufficient condition for understanding the nature of events or ideas, for that would be to commit a genetic fallacy. It is to say, however, that all events and ideas are webbed fore and aft and that they take their meaning from the surrounding play of ambient events and ideas. In some instances, this can be retroactively significant, as when an event of the twentieth century resuscitates and enhances a prior event. (The Korean War brought the 38th parallel into much bolder relief than its original intention.) I offer here a straightforward form of basic, not vicious, historicism. In the latter, data and facticity disappear entirely while in the former all data are subject to reconstruction given the shift in the context for its understanding.

Given my contention that history is matricial, I offer the following pedagogical suggestions—dramatically appropriate in today's educational process, given the abysmal historical and comparative-culture ignorance into which many of our students have sunk.

First, I believe that a significant and serious portion of the undergraduate curriculum should be devoted to the history of those cultures essential to an understanding of human history and contemporary culture, namely, ancient China, Japan, India, Egypt, meso-America, the Amerindians, and Africa. The curriculum should isolate those ancient cultural positions crucial to the development of Western philosophical thought: their social cosmology (one's place in the world, astral and terrestrial); their views of time and space in the fabric of ordinary life; their moral philosophy; the relations believed to hold between assumption/faith/overbelief and reason/the role of therapy; the attitudes held toward the rites of passage (conception, birth, adolescence, maturity, death, and the attendant institutions, such as marriage); their political structures; their social organization; and their leading figures (those who were charismatically original and pathfinders as well as those who conveyed the essence of the local culture to a wider world). Readings here would include the works of Mencius, Confucius, Lao-tzu, the Rig-Veda, the Bhagavad-Gita, the Norse sagas, material from the Egyptians, and stories from the African past. Speaking for interests philosophical, all of the above material is directly relevant.

Although in our own time, with considerable present-mindedness, we tend to deny it, most of the major themes pertaining to being in the world have been already set out. We need to be aware of these issues and how they were handled in the past. What distinguishes us from the cultural past is significant, precisely because our version is profoundly different from deeply held prior beliefs, particularly in the history of Western civilization (for example, the doctrine of ultimate intelligibility, a finite universe, the doctrine of the cycle, a geocentric galaxy, a single continent, and linguistic and religious monism).

Having presented the student with an overview of the comparative culture characteristics and their philosophical upshot, the next scenario should be the distinctive history of Western philosophy, by which I mean the tradition that begins with Homer, Hesiod and the Pre-Socratics and came to be accompanied by the wisdom of the Jewish Bible. This tradition, with roots in Greece and the Middle East, proceeds through the Roman Empire, Christianity, Byzantium, Islam, Medieval Christendom, the Renaissance, the Scientific Revolution, the Reformation, and the modern period that begins with Descartes in the seventeenth century.

From my perspective, every major philosopher in the Western canon is a creature of a historical matrix, complete with social, political, economic, religious, and scientific drifts of thought, and each under various pressures to accept or to reject regnant, incipient, or counterculture doctrines. Please note that I state "accept" or "reject," for I do not hold that a philosopher is a sycophant of his or her own time. Rather, the time/place is decisive for the direction of the philosopher's thought, *inclusive of technical doctrine*, even if that influence be by way of rejection.

I offer the following cameo versions, which I take to be rock-bottom requirements for giving students an historical understanding of the philosopher in question. In every instance I suggest a detailed biographical introduction to the philosopher.

I. Plato
For understanding Plato, the following is essential:

(a) a grasp of Homer's epics, especially a knowledge of Homeric mythology and his doctrine of hubris.

(b) an understanding of Greek paideia (for example, as found in Werner Jaeger's *Paideia: The Ideals of Greek Culture*[1]), the nature of the agora, and the psychosexual, psychosocial makeup of Greek society.

(c) an understanding of the politics and power of the Temple religions and the dynamics of the shifts in the political process leading to the emergence of the Sophists.

(d) a grasp of pre-Socratic philosophy, especially that of Parmenides.

Without these considerations, at a minimum, Plato is a cipher.

II. Augustine
With respect to Augustine, we must keep in mind that:

(a) in teaching Augustine we face a twin matrix, for his work is unintelligible without Christianity as the backdrop, and Christian doctrine would have been a shambles without the work of Augustine. Further, philosophy from Augustine until the end of the nineteenth century is barely intelligible without an understanding of Christianity, as witness the work of, for example, Descartes, Spinoza, Leibniz, Berkeley, Voltaire, Hegel, Kierkegaard, and Nietzsche.

(b) to study Augustine intelligently, one must know Manicheanism, Plato, Plotinus and the Greek and Roman Stoics.

(c) the philosophy of the High Middle Ages—of Scotus Erigena, Anselm, Bonaventure, Duns Scotus, and even Ockham—requires a knowledge of the thought of Augustine.

III. Thomas Aquinas

Understanding Aquinas requires:

(a) a knowledge of the medieval Augustinian tradition.

(b) a grasp of the Arab/Muslim version of the writings of Plato and Aristotle, especially with regard to the central theme of some 300 years from the eleventh to the fourteenth centuries, namely, the conflict between faith and reason as found, for example, in the writings of Aquinas, Maimonides, Avicenna, Averroes, and Siger of Brabant.

(c) a comparison of the *Summa Theologica* of Aquinas with the *Divine Comedy* of Dante and both of them with the feudalistic structure of medieval society, as well as a further contrast with the architectural aesthetics of the Gothic cathedral. (Throughout all of these comparisons, one faces hierarchy, from the dungeon to the nave to the Rose window, Paradiso, and the *Summum Bonum*.)

IV. Utilitarianism

For understanding this ethical theory I suggest that:

(a) one must examine the eighteenth-century background in the thought of utilitarianism. Relevant material here are the writings of Adam Smith, Ricardo, Malthus, the physiocrats, and the poetry of Alexander Pope. Helpful also is the nineteenth-century Marxist critique of laissez-faire liberalism.

(b) one needs to know the full tradition of British empiricism. Why is it so distinctively different, epistemologically and metaphysically, from that of the continent? (In itself, this is a fascinating philosophical ethnographic question.)

(c) we should consider Bentham and Mill as formal forerunners of American pragmatism and the power and importance of a consequentialist ethics. This material can be contrasted with the deontological ethics of Kant.

V. Nietzsche

Necessary to teaching Nietzsche is:

(a) A knowledge of the themes of Greek tragedy, and the difference between Sophocles and Aeschylus on the one hand and Euripides on the other—a grasp of the conflict between Dionysus and Apollo.

(b) An awareness of nineteenth-century continental bourgeois society, especially in its *allegedly* Christian, democratic, and socialist contentions.

(c) A careful consideration of Romantic music in the nineteenth century, especially the music of Wagner.

VI. William James

In teaching William James, I offer the following suggestions:

(a) First, biography is crucial in the case of James. Seldom has a major philosopher left us so much detail in the integration of his life, work, and the premier activities and currents of thought in his time.[2]

(b) Second, important to understanding James is a discussion of the revolutionary implications of the mid-nineteenth-century development of physiological psychology.

(c) Third, one should examine James's radical attack on both Hegelianism and the associationist psychology of the British empiricists.

(d) Fourth, teaching James requires consideration of his contentions about the "Stream of Consciousness" and its influence on contemporary literature and radical empiricism, the latter foreshadowing modern physics and modern art.

(e) Fifth, significant also is James's anticipation of the transformation of religious thought from an emphasis on doctrine to one on experience. His wide-ranging cultural anthropological sensibility and his deep sensibility for the "sick-soul," the aberrant personality, presages much of our concern in contemporary society.

(f) Finally, we should respect James's cosmological context for all human activity which rivals that of Plato, Aristotle, and Kant. *A Pluralistic Universe*[3] by James is a major effort, based on an intuitive hunch, that has now become a staple in our advanced research into astrophysics and modern cosmology.

So much for a series of brief cameos. They could be duplicated by the dozens. I now turn to a somewhat larger cameo, as an illustration of the philosophical pedagogy that I recommend in this essay. I focus on the sixteenth century for two reasons: it is an explosive and central century if one is to understand the modern world, and its absence from the canonical curriculum of the history of Western philosophy is a pedagogical scandal. The reasons for this absence are twofold: the period does not have a canonical figure, for most histories skip from Aristotle (384-322 BC) to Descartes (AD 1596-1650) or, if more sophisticated, from Aquinas to Descartes.

The fact, however, is that in the sixteenth century—often omitted as a pedagogical leper—the die is cast for an understanding of the modern Euro-American western world. Below I offer one way to teach this period of cultural and philosophical history.

The thought and assumptions of the medieval period did not simply come to an end. Rather, they were slowly transformed by the Renaissance and abruptly challenged by the Reformation and the Scientific Revolution.

The Renaissance differs from the Reformation and the Scientific Revolution in that it was not inspired by an event nor even by a series of events. It is better described as a change in mood, attitude, and cultural style. It began in Italy as early as the fifteenth century and remained vibrant in seventeenth-century Holland and England. Literally, the term "renaissance" means rebirth, and the Renaissance is often referred to as a rebirth of learning after the alleged intellectual doldrums of the medieval period. These claims are patent and offensive nonsense, for medieval civilization was laced with learning, and surely the medieval world of Giotto, Dante, Chaucer, and the Gothic cathedral (of the fourteenth century) deserves fairer interpretive fate. Actually, the meaning of the Renaissance is twofold: first, it means a rebirth of classical or secular learning, especially that traceable to ancient Rome, and second, it means an intense and new concentration on the meaning of the individual. These developments are the source of much of the magnificent painting and sculpture of the Renaissance and are expressed in the work of Michelangelo, Da Vinci and, later, Rembrandt. The Renaissance, known also as the age of "humanism," remains a glittering cultural diamond, poised between the end of medieval civilization and the beginning of modern civilization, which features the rise of the nation-state and the Industrial Revolution.

Even a cursory survey of the fascinating figures and events of the fifteenth and especially the sixteenth century would prove to be virtually interminable. Hence, I will focus on the main intellectual concerns of these centuries, which were in essence an attack on the unitary principles undergirding medieval culture, promulgated and intensely protected by the Church. As late as the fifteenth century, European thought held to the existence of one continent, one true religion, and one finite ordered universe with the earth as its stable center. These medieval cartographical, theological, and cosmological assumptions came apart at the seams in the tumultuous sixteenth century. In 1507 the Waldseemüller map presented the earth in two distinct hemispheres. Following the voyage reports of Amerigo Vespucci, a fourth part—America—was added to the map that had once contained only Europe, Asia, and Africa. The gravity of this event is revealed in the name awarded the new hemisphere, for it was called a *Mundus Novus*, a new world. And "world" it was, for previously the earth had been perceived as a single, unified continent surrounded by water. The implications of the "New World" for medieval consciousness were far reaching. Who were the people of this new land? Were they descendants of Adam? Does the Bible account for them? If there is a "New World," does that not mean that European civilization is an old world? The ramifications of these and other questions were to be worked out in the experiences of the sixteenth- and seventeenth-century Dutch, Spanish, English, and French colonists. During the Renaissance, however, it was clear that the medieval unitary version of geography had received a severe and lasting setback.

In the midst of the turmoil brought on by the discoveries of the explorers, an event took place that was to rend the ostensibly seamless garment of Christendom. In 1517 Martin Luther, critical of the Church, posted his theses on the castle door at Wittenberg

and the Protestant Reformation began. The Church underestimated the theological power of Luther's position and grievously
underestimated his political support. Soon a host of religious
thinkers competed with Luther in opposing the Church, or better,
the "Roman Catholic Church," soon to be its distinctive name.
Among these reformers was the gifted theologian and dialectician
John Calvin. The corruption characteristic of the Church in the
Renaissance, coupled with northern European resentment of the
excessive taxation levied by Rome, brought on a major and irrep-
arable schism. The second unitary assumption of medieval consciousness—that of one true religion—was shattered. By the middle of the sixteenth century, Europe had to acknowledge two
geographical "worlds" and two Christian religions, Roman Ca-
tholicism and Protestantism, the latter further divided by the
creation of multiple sects. Modern pluralism was born in the sixteenth century.

As if these two changes were not sufficiently staggering, the
sixteenth century brought forward still another revolution in
thought—this one of such a magnitude that it can rightly be called
the intellectual watershed of modern history. Despite their bold
philosophical contentions about the infinite God, Judaism, Christianity, and Islam each accepted the finite world bequeathed by
the cosmology of the Greeks, especially as promulgated by Aristotle. The orthodox religious establishment of western Europe,
including the Protestant Reformers, was ill-prepared for the year
1543, when Nicholas Copernicus, a Polish astronomer, published
The Revolution of the Heavenly Spheres, a work that was to spell the
end of the Aristotelian-Ptolemaic geocentric cosmology. Although
this treatise of Copernicus was not sufficient to prove heliocentrism, the subsequent researches of Galileo and Johannes Kepler
soon provided verification. The third unitary assumption of medieval consciousness was now challenged: the earth moves, and
with that movement, the great hierarchical system of metaphors
and beliefs, so exquisitely portrayed by Dante, now found itself in
mortal jeopardy.

The controversy surrounding the heliocentric theory of Copernicus was to become one of the most fascinating and complex in

European intellectual history; in time it would involve the Roman Catholic Church, the Inquisition, and the persons of Galileo, Cusanus, Melancthon, Bruno, and finally Newton. In this ferment, the thinker who is the most intriguing is René Descartes, for it is he who most directly responds to the implications of the Copernican revolution.

One of the casualties of Copernicanism was the Aristotelian doctrine of natural place, whereby everything that exists, celestial or terrestrial, has its proper place in the rational science. The most important implication of this doctrine was that the earth was the center of the universe and, concomitantly, that human life, as the center of the earth, was central to cosmic life. Copernicanism rendered the earth as but a satellite, moving both around the sun and on its own axis. The crisis was clear: if stability and physical centrality were essential for metaphysical importance, the post-Copernican version of human life rendered us trite, trivial, dwarfed, and inconsequential. The English poet John Donne says it best in his "Anatomy of the World":

> . . . new Philosophy calls all in doubt,
> The Element of fire is quite put out;
> The Sun is lost, and the earth, and no man's wit
> Can well direct him where to look for it
> And freely men confess that this world's spent,
> When in the Planets, and the Firmament
> They seek so many new; then see that this
> Is crumbled out again to his Atomies.
> 'Til all in pieces, all coherence gone;
> All just supply, and all Relation:
> Prince, Subject, Father, Son, are things forgot,
> For every man alone thinks he hath got
> To be a Phoenix, and that then can be
> None of that kind, of which he is, but he.[4]

Or perhaps you prefer the plaintive remark of Pascal: "The eternal silence of these infinite spaces frightens me." Whether it be Donne or Pascal or whoever, a crisis in the meaning of the human self had erupted in the late sixteenth century. In my view, the crucial difference between Aristotelianism and Copernicanism traces to the doctrine of place. In the Aristotelian perspective, everything had a natural place, and the human organism was not an exception. Copernicanism dealt a devastating blow to this domestic version of the cosmos by casting deep doubt on the fixed character of the planets. For Aristotle, the importance of human life was inextricably tied to the importance of the planet Earth as nothing less than the physical center of the cosmos. The eradication of that centrality by Copernicanism forebode a deep disquiet about the ontological status of human life. The period between Copernicanism and the twentieth century witnessed an effort at temporary repair by Newtonian physics. But the die was cast, and the full implications of Copernicanism finally arrived in our century, sustained by quantum mechanics, a new cosmology, and the socially derived collapse of religious, political, and ideological eschatologies. In a word, the deepest contemporary ontological problem is that of *Heimlösigkeit*, homelessness. The vast, limitless, perhaps infinite universe does not award us a place. The planet Earth is a node in the midst of cosmic unintelligibility. According to Aristotle, who we are is where we are. But with the overturning of Aristotle's geocentric cosmology, the claim of a natural place and a fixed center is rejected. If that rejection holds, we are now no one, for we are nowhere: we do not know the extent of the cosmos or, for that matter, whether it has any periphery at all and, consequently, we cannot know our place.

It is in the context of this dramatic situation that we consider one aspect of the philosophy of René Descartes, who is the founder of modern philosophy and the transitional figure between ancient and modern consciousness. Descartes was clearly sympathetic with Copernicanism, as we see in his early work *Le Monde* (which he had to suppress after the condemnation of Galileo). The implications of Copernicanism acted as a specter behind all of the works of Descartes. If heliocentrism is true, then the Aristotelian doctrine of natural place is wrecked. Further, if the earth is not the center of the universe, then human life cannot count on physical centrality for the source of its epistemic certitude.

In a series of bold and ingenious methodological and philosophical moves, Descartes sets out to re-anchor the possibility of human certitude. He proceeds in the following way: It is conceivable that God does not exist. In that God is the guarantor of our sense experience, it is also conceivable that I am deluded as to the existence of the physical world, including my body. What is not conceivable, however, is that I, as a thinking being, do not exist, for, as Descartes states (in what is to become one of the most famous of all philosophical phrases), *cogito ergo sum*—in that I think, I exist. In the Fourth Part of the "Discourse Concerning Method," Descartes writes:

> But immediately afterward I noticed that, while I thus wished to think that everything was false, it was necessary that I who was thinking be something. And noting that this truth, *I think, therefore I am*, was so firm and so assured that all the most extravagant suppositions of the skeptics were not capable of disturbing it, I judged that I could receive it, without scruple, as the first principle of the philosophy I was seeking.[5]

The philosophy Descartes sought was one in which the foundation was not subject to doubt and, especially, not subject to the foibles and snares of sense experience. To that end, he opposes Aristotle and the Scholastics such as Thomas Aquinas, by holding that the *res cogitans*, the thinking thing, the human mind, has no need of the physical world, the *res extensa*, for its existence. The *res cogitans* is a complete substance and, as such, is self-guaranteeing of its existence and its knowledge. The thinking self comes equipped with innate ideas of such power that they are able to reconstruct the existence of God and of the material world, with indubitability. To achieve this power, however, Descartes began a tradition known as psychophysical dualism, in which the mind and body were regarded as separate substances. This dualism shattered the experiential unity of the human self and caused serious disarray in the behavioral sciences until the middle of the nineteenth century and the birth of experimental psychology, which focused on the organic continuity of mind and body.

Nonetheless, Descartes bequeathed also an intriguing possibility, namely, that the human mind has innate powers that are independent of sense experience and of the physical place that the mind occupies at any given time. Further, with Plato, he holds that we can know infinitely more than we do, even to knowing the ultimate principles of reality, equivalent to the knowledge of perfect being. This is a heady claim, but we should not forget that Descartes was the father of modern mathematics. As we of the twentieth century know, modern mathematics creates physics and physics creates versions of nature never imagined heretofore. Looked at from a traditional view, Pascal was right—infinite space does terrify us. In the philosophy of Descartes, however, even infinite space is but a local box, potentially transcended by the power of the human mind.

I have offered you a raison d'être for the teaching of Introduction to Philosophy, historically. On behalf of that mission, I have presented several short cameos and one slightly larger cameo as pedagogical examples for my method, approach, and position. Were there space, I would present a full-blown course on how to introduce students to philosophy. In conscience, I have to say that teaching Introduction to Philosophy by the historical method is better served than by the use of contemporary articles in philosophy journals. Having taught philosophy for forty-five years, my experience is that students do not learn very much if they are exposed only to a contemporary recondite debate, when they know nothing of the historical background and nothing as to why the issue is grave, given the historical background.

No matter the ancient text or problem, it is easy to extrapolate the contemporary significance. To reverse the procedure is to leave the student in an intellectual and historical vacuum. Following Robert Boyle, nature may not abhor a vacuum, but students do. It is our obligation to fill their cups to overflowing, so that they can chart their way through the roiling seas of mystery and unintelligibility, and opt for possibility.

NOTES

*A version of the paper that forms this chapter was offered as an invited colloquium presentation at the Pacific Division meeting of the American Philosophical Association in March 1986.

1. Werner Jaeger, *Paideia: The Ideals of Greek Culture*, vols. I-III, trans. Gilbert Highet (New York: Oxford University Press), 1943-45.

2. *The Correspondence of William James*, vols. 1-5, ed. Ignas K. Skrupskelis and Elizabeth M. Berkeley, gen. ed. John J. McDermott (Charlottesville, Va: University of Virginia Press), 1992-1997.

3. *The Works of William James*, ed. Frederick Burkhardt (Cambridge, MA: Harvard University Press, 1977).

4. John Donne, *The Complete Poetry and Selected Prose of John Donne* (New York: The Modern Library, 1941), 191.

5. René Descartes, "Discourse Concerning Method," *The Essential Writings*, trans. John J. Blom (New York: Harper Torchbooks, 1977), 134.

PART IX
Teaching Kant/ Teaching Hegel

Chapter 17

A User-Friendly Copernican Revolution

Merold Westphal

When I present the course designed to prepare our graduate teaching fellows to teach our Theories of Human Knowledge course, I urge them to include Kant and to use *The Critique of Pure Reason*. This is not a matter of misery loving company. It is, rather, a matter of having found a way of looking forward to teaching Kant to undergraduates rather than dreading it. I take the usual running start. At the center of Kant's first *Critique* is the question, How are synthetic a priori (SAP) judgments possible? Since undergraduates are generally innocent of Quinean objections, it is fairly easy to explain the distinction between analytic and synthetic propositions. Nor is it too difficult to draw the distinction between a priori and empirical knowledge. It is only a small step to put these together and to specify what a synthetic a priori proposition would be. Since we have usually just finished reading Hume, I try to show that Hume's problem with inductive inference is best understood in terms of the SAP character of the principle it presupposes, the assumption that the future will be like the past.

I find this standard reference to Hume helpful, but not very. For at this point my students are comprehending but comatose. They know what a synthetic a priori proposition is, but, in their strange diction, they could care less. I doubt it. For if there is any sure way of distinguishing an undergraduate from an analytic

162

philosopher, it is that the former has no passion for propositions.

But, of course, we have not gotten to Kant's point, his very distinctive account of how SAP propositions are possible. Here the problem is different, and here the fun begins. It is anything but easy to explain what Kant means when he says that the forms and categories are conditions of possible experience. Whether or not one imbues these phrases with sound and fury, they signify nothing to the students. The problem is not that their "naive realism" is so strong that they reject Kantian idealism out of hand and will not give it a day in court. The problem is that they cannot sufficiently understand what Kant is saying to see how it actually is a challenge to their realistic assumptions and, thus, exciting, or dangerous, or liberating. It is like someone saying, "Your money or your life" in a totally foreign language. My experience is that students will remain comatose until they can see what Kant is really up to. They need translation.

To this end I abandon Kantian language and resort to a very homely analogy. I ask my students how I can know before I turn on the TV to watch the evening news that Dan Rather's tie will be various shades of gray, noting that this is a synthetic proposition that I claim to know a priori. Almost invariably some student, entirely oblivious to the problematic character of inductive inference that we have just worked through so carefully, will give an inductive answer entirely foreign to Kant's thinking. Dan Rather has been wearing gray ties all week, so I infer that he will wear a gray one tonight.

Rather than go back through Hume, I simply insist that I have not been watching the news lately and have no idea what color ties Dan Rather has been wearing; but I know for sure that tonight, whether his tie is striped, polka dot, paisley, or whatever, it will be shades of gray, and I know this before I turn on the TV. Silence. Then, suddenly, some student will solve the puzzle. "You're watching on a black and white TV set."

Indeed I am. And now it is possible to give meaning to the previously meaningless phrase, "condition of possible experience." The TV set is a receiving apparatus which simultaneously (1) makes it possible for me to see Dan Rather's tie at all, since I am miles away from it and (2) makes it impossible for me to see it as it really is, since it does not convey color. (Obviously I need to be ready to answer the question, "But what if tonight his tie actually is gray?")

Then I say, of course, that Kant views the human mind as a receiving apparatus of just this sort, one that simultaneously enables and disables human understanding. From here it is fairly easy to explain the distinction between appearances and things in themselves, and how, though it is easy to talk about there being two worlds (and two ties), it is less misleading to speak of one world (and one tie) perceived in two different ways (in the studio—a perspective Kant reserves for a divine, creative intellect—and on TV). It is easy to show, in this context, how science is possible, but only as a theory of phenomena; how metaphysics is impossible as a theory of things in themselves; and, as a special case of the latter point, how the proofs for the existence of God are in trouble.

But I regularly find that whether I go through these issues very quickly or in considerable detail, there is a big difference between these explanations and the earlier ones about the analytic/synthetic and empirical/a priori distinctions. Although the students may be puzzled as to why Kant would want to think of the mind as such a strange receiving apparatus, they understand the import of such a thought. They recognize how Kantian idealism is an alternative (challenge? threat?) to their commonsense realism and how this has radical implications for both science and religion. They are no longer comatose.

Much of the history of philosophy for the last two hundred years has been a series of footnotes to Kant. Whether we are talking about ideology critique, "the Present Age," perspectivism and interpretation, horizon and lifeworld, the hermeneutical circle, the social construction of reality, language games, paradigms of normal science, conceptual schemes, or the pragmatic a priori, much post-Kantian thought rests on some historicized version or other of this Copernican Revolution. I try to strike while the iron is hot and open the door to historicized Kantianism by the use of a second example, fully as homely as the first.

Kant has an essentially ahistorical view of the a priori. He thinks that space, time, substance, causality, and so forth belong to human experience in the same way at all times and in all places. He thinks we are all the same brand of TV, composed of the same components and wired in the same way. But suppose I am a racist. My racism turns me into a receiving apparatus to whom persons of certain groups can appear only in certain ways, regardless of what they may be in themselves. Before meeting such persons or bothering to observe anything about them, I "know" that they are intellectually and morally inferior to me; and, at least so long as my racism stays in place, my experience will only confirm these beliefs, and remain impotent to challenge them.

The historical character of my racist a priori stems from the fact that I have been socialized into a particular human culture or subculture. And this means that it differs from the Kantian model in two important ways. First, it is not universally shared. I may be seeing the world in black and white (pun intended), while other viewers are seeing it in living color. Second, I can both learn and unlearn this a priori. I can replace old components with new ones; I can be rewired. And yet, the basic point remains the same. The very structures that make experience possible force the world to appear in this way and preclude it from appearing in that. It is but a short step from here to Heidegger's notion of technology as more a way of seeing things than a way of doing things. In relation to issues as pressing and as contemporary as racism and technology, it becomes both possible and necessary to ask moral questions about our knowledge and about the socialization processes by which it and a corresponding world are in important respects constructed.

Sometimes I supplement my TV and racism analogies with a third one, and talk about the fact that it is a computer's program that determines what output any given input will generate, though I usually find that it does little work not already accomplished by the first two. But perhaps it provides a measure of reinforcement. The first advantage of these models, horrifying as they may be to the Kantian purist, is that while Kant's own lan-

guage sends the message, "You don't know what I'm talking
about," which turns out to be a self-fulfilling prophecy, talk about
television, racism, and computers tells the student that the very
unfamiliar point of Kant's weird language can be understood in
terms of very familiar aspects of their everyday world. The second
advantage is that they make it surprisingly easy to show that
Kant's central idea is neither vacuous nor innocent, but full of
interesting implications for that everyday world.

I am always delighted when I get to spend an entire semester
reading the *Critique of Pure Reason* with students. But most often I
find myself doing Kant as part of a larger story, meaning that I
have limited time to devote to him. If, for example, I am doing a
Hegel to Nietzsche course, I may provide some Kantian background by presenting my Dan-Rather-and-the-racist version of
Kant in a lecture or two without any reading assignments.

If, on the other hand, I am doing a Descartes to Kant course, or
a theories of knowledge course, it is important to me that students
actually read Kant. I have had no luck at all with the *Prolegomena*,
but I find that I can do a lot of Kant with a relatively small amount
of the *Critique*. Normally we read the two *Prefaces*, the *Introduction*,
and the *Transcendental Aesthetic*. The last mentioned section is the
most difficult, but it is easier than almost everything that comes
after it, and with the help of my homely illustrations, it becomes
approachable.

The contrast introduced there between a divine, creative intellect and a human, receptive understanding opens the door to important themes in classical philosophical theology, both to classical
and contemporary theories of the finitude of human understanding and to contemporary ideal-observer theories of truth, such as
those of Peirce and Habermas, in which a counterfactual human
community takes the place of God as the standard of truth and the
real.

One could, I suppose, try to work from the Kantian forms and
categories as the conditions of the possibility and impossibility of
experience to an exposition of Derrida's *différance* as a quasi-
transcendental condition of both the possibility and impossibility
of presence. But so far I have not tried. There is such a thing as
pushing one's luck too far.

Chapter 18

Charting Kant

James P. Cadello

For the past six years, I have been using the chart that follows when teaching Kant. This chart is developed from a version sketched for me by Manfred Kuehn, of Purdue University.

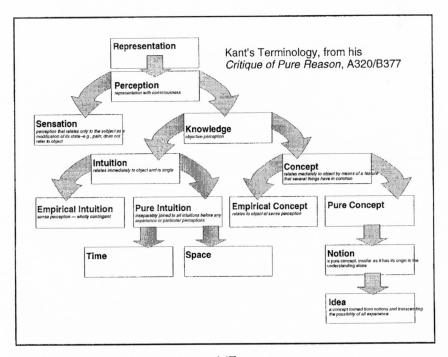

I have found the chart invaluable for both introductory-level and advanced undergraduate classes in which we are studying Kant. It visually represents relationships among many of the concepts central to Kant's *Critique of Pure Reason* and *Prolegomena to Any Future Metaphysics*, and is based on Kant's *Critique of Pure Reason*, page A320/B377. When using the chart, it is important to note—and make clear to the student—that the chart depicts only relationships among concepts, and not how one concept is derived from another.

The chart provides in visual form a cursory outline of Kant's entire system (as presented in the first *Critique* and the *Prolegomena*). Since many of my students are primarily visual learners, this proves to be of immense assistance in facilitating their comprehension of the general contours of Kant's thought. I would like to highlight the two most general ways I use the chart to help explicate Kant in the classroom.

First, the chart helps me develop the cardinal distinctions made by Kant. Because they are not as exacting as the philosopher we are reading, students—even better ones—often have a difficult time understanding a text with the result that they often fail to grasp essential distinctions. This can be especially true when students read Kant. The chart, which I require all students to have in hand during all of the sessions during which we are discussing Kant, alleviates much of this problem by showing if/when terms are related and if/when they are not, and by displaying these relationships and points of contact in a form that can be glanced at all at once. In our discussions of Kant, the students have all of the basic terms and relationships in front of them as a continual reference. When confusion arises in our discussion, I refer the students to the chart and can almost always direct them to some point on the chart that will help clarify the issue in question. (I will give a couple of examples later.)

Of course, the problem is to get students to see that although Kant takes terminological and conceptual distinctions and connections, he intends each term and concept to represent a phenomenon (or phenomena) to be grasped as a component of an integrated, unified, whole process. If this point is not emphasized enough, one of the dangers of the chart is that students will come to see Kant as breaking up the unity of consciousness into abstracted little bits. But this tendency can be avoided if students are reminded, again and again, that Kant is not identifying "pieces" that make up a collection called "consciousness"; rather, he is identifying the conditions and components of consciousness.

Let me give a couple of specific examples of how the distinctions made by Kant can be visually depicted on the chart and, as such, more readily understood by students. Take Kant's distinction between knowledge and sensation. Though both are forms of perception according to Kant, the chart shows they are separate and distinct from one another. The chart makes it clear that they are two *kinds* of perception, in fact, that they are *the* two kinds of perception. It can also be explained/shown that because sensation does not refer to an object, but is merely a modification of the subject's state, it is "irreducible": it has no objective conditions and cannot be plumbed more deeply. For this reason, the chart/Kant has nothing more to say about this issue. Knowledge, on the other hand, can be shown to be radically or categorically distinct from sensation because it is, by definition, objective. We can therefore investigate its conditions and components, which is exactly what Kant does and what the chart depicts. I have found that once this distinction is made clear to students they can begin to ask some pretty sophisticated questions (for undergraduates reading Kant for the first time) about the character of Kant's investigation: Is this a genuine distinction? What is an object? an objective perception? Why doesn't Kant investigate more deeply the conditions of sensation? And, most encouragingly —because it leads to a discussion of the various levels on which Kant's views can be analyzed—what does Kant think are the conditions of knowledge?

The second valuable feature of the chart is that it visually depicts the levels of Kant's system. The chart displays Kant's distinction between intuition and concept and indicates the difference between the pure and empirical forms of each of these. The chart shows that knowledge comprises both an intuitional and a conceptual compo- nent (that is, a "sensory" and a "theoretical" dimension); both of these are components and necessary conditions of objective knowledge. Likewise, intuition can be explained/shown by the chart as having two components, the empirical and the pure (that is, the "content" and "form" of intuition). Anyone familiar with Kant can, with a quick view of the chart, see where there is a relation among terms and when there is not, and explicate the character of that relationship.

A few warnings about the chart. Again, to iterate what I said at the beginning, this chart shows only the relationships among concepts and is not an attempt to show how they are derived. This is of essential importance. As can be seen from the two examples I have given, the lines indicating relationships do not all function in the same way. For example, sensation and knowledge are two *kinds* of perception, not two necessary component features of perception. However, intuition and concept are two *necessary component features* of objective knowledge, not two kinds of objective knowledge. Clearly, then, the chart is not sufficiently finely grained to exhibit these intricate points. One must still have a solid grasp of Kant to explicate the nature of the relationship among the concepts at issue.

For this reason, the chart is no easy shortcut for learning or teaching Kant. Nor is it, as I always warn my students, a substitute for carefully reading Kant. However, although Kant remains for me one of the most difficult philosophers to teach, using the chart enables me to generate in students a much greater understanding of and interest in Kant, even if they are reading Kant for the first time. Furthermore, I have found that in subsequent discussions of Kant (whether these discussions are part of the same course or part of a different course taken at a later date) most students reach a higher degree of understanding and sophistication with respect to Kant than do students who are not introduced to the chart when they first encounter the philosophy of Kant. Indeed, the chart is by far the most useful instrument I have found for teaching Kant to undergraduates.

Chapter 19

On Teaching Hegel: Problems and Possibilities

John McCumber

I. The Difficulty of Teaching Hegel

One reason Hegel is difficult for Americans to understand is that he did not write in English, but in a highly idiosyncratic German. This would not be a problem if good translations were easy to obtain, but for several reasons they have not been. The early choices of both texts and translators were disastrous. In 1873, for example, there appeared a version of Hegel's smaller *Logic*, translated by the Oxford professor William Wallace.[1] Wallace took the whole point of the book to be to "witness to the belief" in the ultimate identity of philosophy and religion.[2] The result was the presentation of Hegel as a sort of evangelistic philosophical theologian. Except for the exuberance of Wallace's creation, it bore a more than passing resemblance to F. H. Bradley—but scant likeness to Hegel himself. J. Sibree, translating a text of the *Lectures on the Philosophy of History* that Hegel himself never wrote (it was put together after his death by his pupils and son), produced yet another theologized travesty.[3] It was only with the appearance of such works as A. V. Miller's translation of the larger *Science of Logic*, in 1969, and of the *Phenomenology of Spirit* ten years later[4] that this situation began to be remedied.

Today's students of Hegel, then, are luckier than their teachers. Professors who studied Hegel in translation during their own graduate education, if that was more than a couple of decades ago, were basically studying caricatures. But even newer translations are problematic, for, like a poet, Hegel remains largely untranslatable. He often plays on words, for example, or uses them with etymological meanings. Thus, the expounder of his *Logic* is likely to have no problem with its first three headings (or, as Hegel calls them, "moments"): *Sein, Nichts, Werden.* They can be rendered by "being," "nothing," and "becoming." But at the fourth, there is trouble: Hegel uses *Dasein*, not with its colloquial meaning of "to be in existence," but in accordance with its etymology. Constructed out of *da*, meaning "here" or "there," and *sein*, "being," the word, for Hegel, means "being in an indeterminate location." This concept, as the awkwardness of my formulation attests, can hardly be rendered in English with the same economy as the original.

Farther on in the *Logic*—in its all-important section on "Contradiction"—we find Hegel saying that opposition *geht zugrunde*, "goes to ground"—a bad but important pun.[5] On the one hand, in the dynamic of contestation that makes up "contradiction" for Hegel, the opponents eventually die away: they "go to ground" like hunted animals. But this process also, for Hegel, reveals the common "ground" within which the contestation took place. What the pun conveys, then, is that, for Hegel, contestation most importantly produces not winners and losers, but common ground. And how can we grasp this doctrine unless we are aware of the puns that convey it?

Hegel's writings are bound not only to the language in which he wrote them but also to the culture in which he lived. He was no bloodless philosopher of the Absolute, but a thinker actively engaged in highly concrete reflections on history and his own time—the fore-runner of Feuerbach and Marx. Hegel *engagé* is doubtless more attractive than the hermetic theologician many of us learned about. But he is more difficult to understand.

Students from the Anglo-Saxon world, for example, are naturally interested in Hegel's view of empiricism and are normally puzzled, if not irritated, by the quick and thoughtless dismissal of it in the

Logic.[6] But it turns out that "empiricism" in Hegel's time had a very special meaning. A group of politicians had formed an "empiricist" caucus in the Bavarian parliament. They sounded like respectable empiricists in that they held that all knowledge came from "experience." But there the resemblance (and the respectability) ended, because by "experience" they merely meant whatever it is that one gains by hanging around for many years. Their "empiricism" thus worked out to the view that only long-standing members of the inner circle should have power. Hegel was openly, and rightly, contemptuous of it.[7] But his contempt lends an unfortunate coloration to his treatments of philosophical empiricism, with which his thought has more affinities than he himself was perhaps aware.[8]

Hegel's situatedness within his own culture thus makes it difficult to understand him in terms of our own. Other examples could be given. Religion, for example, played a very public role in Hegel's Germany, providing, among other things, theological justification for the Kaiser himself. It was not easily ignored (as American intellectuals tend to do), much less ridiculed (*à la* the French). So German nonbelievers tended to twist religion, rather than break with it ("God exists, but only in our minds" was a standard gloss on Kant). If Hegel (whose views on the existence of God remain mysterious to this day) was no lover of such obfuscation, he was also no stranger to it.

It is also true that in some respects Hegel was far outside his own culture. For the idiosyncracies of his German are not always merely stylistic: they often amount to startling and fundamental linguistic revisions. This, too, makes understanding and teaching him burdensome. Consider, for example, his views on "truth." Hegel is fond of proclaiming that he is presenting the truth, indeed the "absolute" truth. Students and professors, reading such claims, feel they have the right to an argument or two. And so it is disheartening to open Hegel and find nothing, or almost nothing, that remotely resembles even a simple "if P then Q." It is one thing not to like arguments; Richard Rorty does not.[9] But Rorty also does not like truth. Hegel claims not only to like truth but also to have it, and without benefit of argument. What gives? Rampant dogmatism?

It turns out that Hegel's concept of truth is in fact more akin to what the philosophical tradition has called "beauty" than to what we call "truth."[10] In its Aristotelian formulation, "beauty" (*to kalon*) has to do with order and size. The heavens, for example, are extremely *kalon* because they are remarkably large and notably well-ordered. A city-state is smaller and more rambunctious, so it has a lesser degree of *kalon*. And so on. Hegel reconceptualizes this Aristotelian notion, first, as harmony of diversity: what gets ordered is not merely a number of units, but a set of entities that are diverse in nature. (By this standard, the heavens are not very *kalon* at all, because all the stars are alike.) Then Hegel dynamizes it so that it applies mainly to the human realm. "Diverse" entities are not merely entities that differ from one another, but are individuals or groups that actively increase their differences until they become not merely "different" from each other, but opposed to each other. Hegelian "truth" is then the reconciliation of opposites.

Expressed philosophically, this reconciliation takes the form of a single discourse that mediates among other discourses by redefining their terms, so that they can talk to one another (and produce common ground). The series of redefinitions Hegel comes up with is constructed, not argued for. Its standards and criteria have little to do with the truth of sentences or propositions, the kind with which Anglo-Saxon philosophy is almost exclusively concerned. So Hegel's use of "truth" is not merely idiosyncratic, but inevitably misleading; he ought to have behaved differently. But he didn't.[11]

Diagnoses of the provinciality of American college students are by now commonplace, and most of these diagnoses are deeply provincial themselves. Still, that does not make them false. One wonders how American collegians can be brought to cope with someone who was, paradoxically, both deeply identified with and removed from his own far-off place and long-ago time. Hegel would seem to be teachable only by those who have immersed themselves in his culture and epoch, on the one hand, and also in his own unique texts, on the other. And if he can be taught only *by* that very small minority of American philosophers who call themselves Hegel scholars, it is also likely that Hegel can be taught only *to* the tiny and prima facie deranged band of graduate students who would like to join their number. But Hegel is too important to be left to Hegel scholars, at least not without tragic consequences. Such is not the case for many thinkers. It has been said of Plotinus that there are perhaps a couple of dozen people, at most, who can make some sense out of his immensely difficult texts, texts that show a similar combination of rootedness in an alien culture and highly original departures from that culture. It is surely unfortunate that Plotinus is not more widely read and taught, but hardly tragic. Why so with Hegel?

II. The Value of Teaching Hegel

Though rooted in an alien culture, Hegel is central to our own—certainly, at least, to our own philosophical culture, which you cannot study without running up against him. This is partly because we share a philosophical world with French and German thinkers who, without exception, have been weaned on Hegel. It is not an exaggeration, for example, to say that the very different philosophical projects of both Sartre and Gadamer arise out of an effort to reconcile Hegel and Heidegger. Hegel's influence on Marx, Habermas, and (through Kojève) on the French in general is too well known to need documentation. The writings of all these thinkers are shot through with Hegelian expressions and Hegelian ideas, even when they reject them. Is it too much to say that without an understanding of Hegel we Anglo-Saxons can understand only each other?

Indeed, without Hegel, even the origins of analytical philosophy become incomprehensible. For did not analytical philosophy begin with Russell and Moore's rejection of what they thought was Hegelianism?[12] And if my reading is right, and what they rejected—British Hegelianism—was no more than a caricature, then it is arguable that Moore and Russell's rejection of Bradley and others was in fact a *return* to Hegel, albeit one accompanied by Russellian logic and its very different conception of truth.

But quite independently of the viabililiy of Hegel's project—I believe that, correctly understood, it is more viable now than it was even in Hegel's time—it turns out that Hegel is central to our self-understanding as philosophers. We cannot teach undergraduates what contemporary philosophy is, even in the English-speaking world, without teaching them how it came about; and we cannot teach them how it came about without teaching them about Hegel. When we add to this philosophical centrality Hegel's influence on the studies of literature, of history, of politics, of religion, and so on, it is tempting indeed to press on and teach Hegel in spite of the problems.

There is another dimension to Hegel's relevance. Just as Hegel was situated in his own time and culture while still being highly original, so he is important to ours while posing significant challenges to it—precisely because his way of doing things differs so deeply from our own. An example of this emerges from consideration of Hegel's view of truth. It is an important, even a defining, characteristic of our philosophical culture that two beliefs about truth be accepted: that truth is a property of certain sentences or propositions, and that it is the only (or paramount) goal of rational inquiry. This conjunction, which I call "assertionism," is not often stated, perhaps because it is so basic. One who does state it, with characteristic lucidity, is Quine. In every edition of his *Methods of Logic* from 1959 through 1982, the first sentence runs as follows:

> Logic, like any science, has as its business the pursuit of truth. What is true are certain statements; and the pursuit of truth is the endeavour to sort out the true statements from the others, which are false.[13]

Quine apparently takes the conjunction of these two very different ideas—that what is true are certain statements, and that such truth is the goal of all science—to be trivially true. Hegel, however, challenges us to question it, and leads us to wonder if perhaps other goals than assertionistic truth are formulable for rational inquiry.

So Hegel's originality enables him to challenge us, and our students, about some very fundamental axioms of our culture. To appreciate the challenges that Hegel poses is not to suppose that he was right, either in the details or in the overall cast of his thought. But it is to take him seriously, and it is to teach him.

III. How to Teach Hegel

How can we see that Hegel is productively taught? One approach might be to abjure teaching Hegel directly, but still teach about him, by teaching the history of Hegel reception and interpretation. Unlike Hegel himself, some of those philosophers who tried to understand him critically and to think creatively in his wake have managed to make themselves relatively clear. (Whether they actually understood Hegel is, of course, another story.)

Because it is creative and usually critical of Hegel, Hegel reception differs from the more strictly scholarly enterprise of explaining Hegel on his own terms. For one thing, the major figures in Hegel reception are somewhat fewer—the most complete bibliography of Hegel scholarship has over 10,000 entries—and, generally, they are much better known. Few Hegel scholars compare in reputation with Kierkegaard, Marx, Bradley, Dewey, Royce, Foucault, Derrida, Habermas, and the like. A course that presented their varying interpretations of Hegel would convey something of his thought and influence without deluding students into thinking that they had actually studied, let alone mastered, Hegel himself.

Texts exist for such a course. The writings of Hegel's earliest critics, the "Young Hegelians," are available in an excellent translation edited by Lawrence S. Stepelevich.[14] The story of the Young Hegelians has also been ably told in a number of secondary works, such as Karl Löwith's *From Hegel to Nietzsche*[15] and John R. Toews's *Hegelianism*.[16] Kierkegaard gives his own critical understanding of Hegel in the *Concluding Unscientific Postscript*.[17]

Hegel's relation to the birth of analytical philosophy in England has been explored in Peter Hylton's *Russell, Idealism, and the Emergence of Analytic Philosophy*,[18] and Karl Popper's egregious *The Open Society and Its Enemies*[19] can be read against its demolition by Walter Kaufmann's *Hegel: A Reinterpretation*.[20] In America, the nature of Pragmatism's appropriation of Hegel is suggested by Josiah Royce's *Lectures on German Idealism*;[21] a more recent example is "Why Hegel Now" by Richard J. Bernstein.[22]

French Hegel reception dates from Alexandre Kojève's *Introduction to the Reading of Hegel*.[23] Jean Hyppolite's *Studies on Marx and Hegel*[24] is exemplary. The overall story is told in Judith Butler's

Subjects of Desire and by Vincent Descombes' *Modern French Philosophy.*[25] In Germany, the somewhat tormented relation between Hegel and Heidegger is explored in Dennis Schmidt's *The Ubiquity of the Finite*, and Hegel's relation to Habermas is most subtly rendered by Habermas himself in his "Labor and Interaction: Remarks on Hegel's Jena Philosophy of Mind."[26]

So we could put a course together that begins with some typically knotty and elusive text of Hegel's, such as the unfathomable Preface to the *Phenomenology of Spirit* or the many layered Introduction to his *Lectures on Aesthetics.*[27] Without going too deeply into the mysteries of those texts, we would move to the history of Hegel reception. We could first consider the reactions of the Young Hegelians, as they turned Hegel from a mumbling lecturer into a resource for daring social criticism. The second phase of the course could concentrate on the English-speaking world. It would begin with a glance at Hegel's mutation into the "theological witness" of British Hegelianism, followed by an entertaining excursus into Popper and Kaufmann. This phase would end with a discussion of Hegel as the builder of concrete community that the pragmatists took him to be. The third, "continental" phase of the course would consider Heidegger's Hegel, the "completer of metaphysics." This would lead to Habermas's restoration of the Young Hegelian approach. Since contemporary French philosophy rivals Hegel in the difficulty of its comprehension, the course should probably end with Sartre or Hyppolite.

Such a course would be difficult to teach, but not, I think, nearly so much as teaching Hegel himself. Rather, such a course would convey the manifold influences of Hegel, without depriving the student of the one truly valuable thing anyone is sure to take away from any serious attempt to read Hegel's own texts: a proper mystification.

NOTES

1. G. W. F. Hegel, *The Logic of Hegel*, from *The Encyclopaedia of the Philosophical Sciences*, 2nd ed., trans. William Wallace (Oxford: Oxford University Press, 1892).

2. Hegel, *The Logic of Hegel*, xxv.

3. G. W. F. Hegel, *Lectures on the Philosophy of History*, trans. J. Sibree (New York: Dover, 1956).

4. G. W. F. Hegel, *Hegel's Science of Logic*, trans. A. V. Miller (London: Allen & Unwin, 1969); Hegel's *Phenomenology of Spirit*, trans. A. V. Miller (Oxford: Oxford University Press, 1979).

5. G. W. F. Hegel, *Wissenschaft der Logik*, vol. 2, ed. Georg Lasson (Hamburg: Meiner, 1934), 50.

6. Hegel, *The Logic of Hegel*, 76-82.

7. Cf. G. W. F. Hegel, *Hegel: The Letters*, trans. and ed. Clark Butler and Christine Seiler (Bloomington, IN: University of Indiana Press, 1984), 133-37.

8. Cf. John McCumber, *The Company of Words: Hegel, Language, and Systematic Philosophy* (Evanston, IL: Northwestern University Press, 1993).

9. Cf. Richard Rorty, *Philosophy and the Mirror of Nature* (Princeton: Princeton University Press, 1979).

10. Cf. McCumber, *The Company of Words*, 33-118.

11. What entitles Hegel to his revision is, perhaps, that the reconciliation of discursive oppositions, like the traditional philosophical concept of truth, designates the goal of inquiry. It is what Hegel himself is aiming at.

12. Cf. Peter Hylton, "Hegel and Analytic Philosophy," in *The Cambridge Companion to Hegel*, ed. Frederick C. Beiser (Cambridge: Cambridge University Press, 1993), 445-85.

13. W. V. Quine, *Methods of Logic*, 2nd ed. and subsequently (Cambridge, MA:Harvard University Press, 1959). For a more recent affirmation of assertionism by Quine, see p. 77 of his *Pursuit of Truth* (Cambridge, MA: Harvard University Press, 1990) in conjunction with, of course, the title article of the book.

14. Lawrence S. Stepelevich, ed., *The Young Hegelians* (Cambridge: Cambridge University Press, 1983).

15. Karl Löwith, *From Hegel to Nietzsche*, trans. David E. Green (Garden City, NY: Anchor Books, 1967).

16. John R. Toews, *Hegelianism* (Cambridge: Cambridge University Press, 1980).

17. Søren Kierkegaard, *Concluding Unscientific Postscript*, trans. David Swenson and Walter Lowrie (Princeton: Princeton University Press, 1968).

18. Peter Hylton, *Russell, Idealism, and the Emergence of Analytic Philosophy* (Oxford: Oxford University Press, 1990).

19. Karl Popper, *The Open Society and Its Enemies*, rev. ed. (Princeton: Princeton University Press, rev. ed. 1950).

20. Walter Kaufmann, *Hegel: A Reinterpretation* (Garden City, NY:

Anchor Books, 1966).

21. Josiah Royce, *Lectures on German Idealism* (New Haven, CT: Yale University Press, 1964).

22. Richard J. Bernstein, "Why Hegel Now?" *Review of Metaphysics* 31 (1977): 227-31.

23. Alexandre Kojève, *Introduction to the Reading of Hegel*, trans. James Nichols (New York: Basic Books, 1969).

24. Jean Hyppolite, *Studies on Marx and Hegel*, trans. J. O'Neill (New York: Basic Books, 1969).

25. Judith Butler, *Subjects of Desire* (New York: Columbia University Press, 1987); and Vincent Descombes, *Modern French Philosophy* (Cambridge: Cambridge University Press, 1980).

26. Jürgen Habermas, "Labor and Interaction: Remarks on Hegel's Jena Philosophy of Mind," in Habermas, *Theory and Practice*, trans. John Viertel (Boston: Beacon Press, 1973); and Dennis Schmidt, *The Ubiquity of the Finite* (Cambridge, MA: MIT Press, 1988).

27. G. W. F. Hegel, *Aesthetics*, 2 vols. with consecutive pagination, trans. T. M. Knox (Oxford: Oxford University Press, 1975).

BIBLIOGRAPHY

Bernstein, Richard J. "Why Hegel Now?" *Review of Metaphysics* 31 (1977): 227-31.

Butler, Judith. *Subjects of Desire* (New York: Columbia University Press, 1987).

Descombes, Vincent. *Modern French Philosophy* (Cambridge: Cambridge University Press, 1980).

Habermas, Jürgen. "Labor and Interaction: Remarks on Hegel's Jena Philosophy of Mind." In *Theory and Practice*, trans. by John Viertel (Boston: Beacon Press, 1973).

Hegel, G. W. F. *Hegel's Science of Logic.* Trans. by A. V. Miller (London: Allen & Unwin, 1969).

———. *Hegel: The Letters.* Ed. and Trans. by Clark Butler and Christine Seiler (Bloomington: University of Indiana Press, 1984).

———. *The Logic of Hegel.* 2nd ed. Trans. from *The Encyclopaedia of the Philosophical Sciences* by William Wallace (Oxford: Oxford University Press, 2nd. ed., 1892).

———. *Wissenschaft der Logik.* Ed. by Georg Lasson (Hamburg: Meiner, 1934), 2 vols.

Hylton, Peter. "Hegel and Analytic Philosophy." In Frederick C. Beiser, ed.

The Cambridge Companion to Hegel (Cambridge: Cambridge University Press, 1993).

————. *Russell, Idealism, and the Emergence of Analytic Philosophy* (Oxford: Oxford University Press, 1990).

Hyppolite, Jean. *Studies on Marx and Hegel*. Trans. by J. O'Neill (New York: Basic Books, 1969).

Kaufmann, Walter. *Hegel: A Reinterpretation* (Garden City, NY: Anchor Books, 1966).

Kierkegaard, Søren. *Concluding Unscientific Postscript*. Trans. by David Swenson and Walter Lowrie (Princeton: Princeton University Press, 1968).

Kojève, Alexandre. *Introduction to the Reading of Hegel*. Trans. by James Nichols (New York: Basic Books, 1969).

Löwith, Karl. *From Hegel to Nietzsche*. Trans. by David E. Green (Garden City, NY: Anchor Books, 1967).

McCumber, John. *The Company of Words: Hegel, Language, and Systematic Philosophy* (Evanston, IL: Northwestern University Press, 1993).

Popper, Karl. *The Open Society and Its Enemies*. Rev. ed. (Princeton: Princeton University Press, 1950).

Quine, W. V. *Methods of Logic*. 2nd ed. (Cambridge, MA: Harvard University Press, 1959).

Rorty, Richard. *Philosophy and the Mirror of Nature* (Princeton: Princeton University Press, 1979).

Royce, Josiah. *Lectures on German Idealism* (New Haven, CT: Yale University Press, 1964).

Schmidt, Dennis. *The Ubiquity of the Finite* (Cambridge, MA: MIT Press, 1988).

Stepelevich, Lawrence S., ed. *The Young Hegelians* (Cambridge: Cambridge University Press, 1983).

Toews, John R. *Hegelianism* (Cambridge: Cambridge University Press, 1980).

Chapter 20

Hegel and Family Values

Merold Westphal

Hegel's theory of the state is significant not only for its importance in understanding Marx but also for its place in the communitarian tradition that currently challenges the regnant liberalism of our social order. I find that two strategic moves are helpful, even indispensable, in teaching the *Philosophy of Right*.

The first is to call attention to the strange meaning Hegel gives to the term "state." Although he does not entirely separate it from the government, which he calls "the political state," he does not identify the two either. In fact, most of the government functions that represent the regulation of civil society, that is, a capitalist economy, he discusses as a part of civil society. So my first move is to try to get students, whose natural instinct is to assume that writers, from whatever time or place, mean the same thing by a given term, to feel their distance from Hegel. I try to get them worried about what is left over to refer to as "the state" when most of what we think of as government gets assigned to civil society.

One possible answer is that Weber's distinction between politics and administration solves the puzzle, that Hegel treats government-as-administration as part of civil society and government-as-policy-formation as the state. This is not entirely wrong, and there is a good deal of textual support for it. But it is not very helpful, for it tends to distract attention from the fact that Weber subsumes these two activities together as functions of the state, suggesting the difference between the higher and lower levels of government, whereas Hegel fixes a much greater gulf between them in terms of the difference between civil society and the state, which he presents as based on wholly different principles. My aim in referring to Weber is to show how different is Hegel's view and to try to reinstate the original anxiety about the difference between Hegel's assumptions and our own.

My second strategic move is to focus on the role Hegel's theory of the family plays in his theory of the state. He regularly insists that both family and state, unlike civil society, are not contractual relations. Thus the family, or more specifically marriage, is the microcosmic model of the state in its radical difference from civil society.

By looking at the three characteristics Hegel finds to be central to contractual relations, we follow a *via negativa* in relation to both marriage and the state. One of these characteristics is immediately problematic. Hegel sees contractual relations as contingent in the sense of optional, while insisting that both marriage and citizenship are necessary. Students naturally challenge the notion that marriage is not optional, just as they challenge the patriarchal assumptions that accompany Hegel's account of marriage. I invite them to test whether the other components of the theory are essentially or only accidentally linked to these features.

It is the other two characteristics of contractual relations that do the interesting work. The first of these is its abstract character. In contract, I relate to another person as the owner of property, including labor power and money; I do not relate to that person in his or her concrete totality, but only to one characteristic—ability and willingness to buy or sell—abstracted from all the rest of who he or she is. Students are usually willing to follow Hegel's suggestion that marriage is not a contractual arrangement for the exchange of services, sexual and otherwise, but a relation to the totality of another person's being. One needs to explore the following:

- What are the implications of the idea that the state is a relation among whole, concrete persons and not among select characteristics abstracted from that wholeness?
- What can it mean to say that as a citizen I have rights and duties,

privileges and responsibilities *as a whole person and not just as a laborer and consumer*?

The final characteristic of contractual relations is their self-centered motivation. A contract is an "I'll-scratch-your-back-if-you'll-scratch-mine" affair. Each party is in it for what he or she will get out of it. Hegel claims that marriage is a transcendence of this individualism, that it is the creation of a We that is not just the sum of two I's, because, alongside their concern for their individual prosperity, the welfare and flourishing of the We becomes the goal of each I. Of course, in a business partnership, the partners want the company to flourish, but only as a means to their private ends. Hegel's claim is that in marriage the concern of each party for "our" well-being is not instrumental in this way because "we" have become the identity of each. In addition to being who I myself am, I have also become who We are. My identity has been altered in marriage. Hegel thinks, of course, that this is nothing radically new. I have always been who We are with reference to the family in which I was born, for example. Contrary to atomistic theories of selfhood, I have always been more than who I myself am. By making me part of a different family, marriage alters, to repeat, my identity. That is why divorce is not experienced as the dissolving of a certain kind of business partnership, but as something far more fundamental.

It is especially in this sense that Hegel speaks of marriage as a double liberation. Like all modes of family life, it reorients my self-consciousness by raising me above self-centeredness to participation in something that is both larger than myself and, at the same time, an essential part of my identity. The other liberation is the elevation of sexual life beyond the level of nature to that of spirit. Sex becomes more than (but not less than) a matter of biological reproduction and physical pleasure. It takes on a kind of sacramental character as the physical enactment of a spiritual relation.

By making marriage his prime model of the state, Hegel claims that political freedom has this same double character: (1) in the state we rise from individual life to communal life, and (2) in the state our economic life, the political analogue to sexuality, is raised from the realm of nature to spirit. He makes it clear that the basis of this larger community is not kinship, that this is not a tribal theory of political life. It is based on law rather than natural affection for one's own.

This view of things raises a whole host of interesting questions:

- What is the view of freedom that underlies this view, and how does it relate to our everyday assumptions about freedom?
- If this community is not based on kinship, but still belongs to my identity, what is its nature? Is such a community possible on a secular basis? If so, how? If not, how can its religious basis avoid a sectarian lapse into tribalism?
- What would be the transformation of economic life that corresponds to the transformation of sexual life already discussed? Is a theory at least something like this necessary if singing about "brotherhood from sea to shining sea" is to be more than empty patriotic self-congratulation (and self-deception)? How does this notion relate to the popular idea that the state is primarily the nonviolent forum for war between competing economic interests?

My whole strategy in focusing on the "family values" ingredient in Hegel's theory of the state is to generate the kind of questions I have just listed in italics. I find the advantages of this approach to include the following:

(1) It provides an opportunity to reflect philosophically on family life in general and marriage in particular, something all too rare in our usual curricula.

(2) It helps to bring a highly "metaphysical" and, at first, rather intimidating text into direct contact with contemporary political experience.

(3) By presenting an understanding of political life noticeably at odds, for the most part, with contemporary theory and practice, it provides both a stimulus and some conceptual tools for reflecting on what are the strengths and weaknesses of that theory and practice. Students experience the alchemy by which a disciplined entry into the text of a distant writer becomes reflection about the reader's life and lifeworld.

There is nothing new about this last point. Such an experience is, I suspect, a very standard goal in the teaching of philosophy. My point is simply that the strategy I have found most helpful for achieving it in relation to Hegel's political theory is to pay detailed attention to the similarities between family and state and their mutual difference from civil society in the *Philosophy of Right*.

I have developed this reading of Hegel's political theory in an essay entitled, "Hegel's Radical Idealism: Family and State as Ethical Communities." It provides a more detailed textual support for the strategy I have sketched here and is to be found in my book, *Hegel, Freedom, and Modernity*.[1]

NOTES

1. Merold Westphal, *Hegel, Freedom, and Modernity* (New York: State University of New York Press, 1992).

PART X
Teaching Existentialism/
Teaching Continental Philosophy

Chapter 21

Teaching Existentialism

Eugene Kelly

A professor may approach the teaching of existentialism with some trepidation. Existentialism contains a moral appeal to the individual person to look at his or her life in a new and unfamiliar way and to rethink the commitments that have hitherto defined that person's life. It is not simply that the doctrines of existentialism, where they exist at all, are obscure, elusive, and dependent upon metaphor; they seem too personal to deal with in the usual classroom setting. Nonetheless, it may be that to teach existentialism we must, and in this paper I will discuss four means of access to the material: by a critical reading of texts by existentialists, by a study in the history of ideas, by a study of the phenomenology of the human being, and by a study of the literary texts that existentialists have produced. I will add to this list a fifth possibility in section 4 of this paper.

I. Two Simple Approaches

One method that skirts the problem of teaching something that, by its nature, defies reduction to doctrines is to treat the works of persons commonly called existentialists as texts (that is, apart from their time, place, and occasion) and merely as objects for interpretation, criticism, and, perhaps, deconstruction. Alternatively, existentialism can be treated as a historical phenomenon and understood as a phase in the history of ideas. This second approach, probably the one taken most frequently, is useful in two ways. First, it supplies a content for teaching; after all, we must give exams. Second, it allows us to present existentialism as an ordered sequence of ideas concerning the "human situation." Major existentialist figures can be treated as persons in crisis, living intellectually through some critical phase of that situation. One textbook useful for a course on this model is F. H. Heinemann's *Existentialism and the Modern Predicament*,[1] the title of which illustrates the historical context of existentialism. Of course, the age of existentialism may still be our own, and teachers can point out its predicaments and crises to their students. Heinemann sketches the major historical existentialists in separate chapters under rubrics that express the essential character of that thinker's encounter with intellectual crisis: Heroic Defiance (Heidegger); The Philosophy of Detachment (Jaspers); and the Mystical Anarchist (Berdyaev). Another book suitable for this approach to the subject is H. J. Blackham's *Six Existentialist Thinkers*,[2] a classic of exposition, and Walter Kaufmann's *Existentialism from Dostoyevsky to Sartre*,[3] a collection of primary texts. Anyone who presents existentialism as a historical phenomenon with a distinct set of issues that constitute its concern ought to consider not only the nineteenth-century thinkers who shared these concerns but also the postexistentialist writers, including Sartre himself, who reject some of the social and political implications of the philosophical positions developed in *Being and Nothingness*. Even during Sartre's lifetime, existentialism seems to have passed rather quickly from a cult into irrelevance, and it may be useful to reflect, in class, on the social and historical situations that may have led intellectuals away from it. De Beauvoir's memoir of her relationship with Sartre[4] is surely helpful in that regard, as also are Sartre's discussions of his career on a videotape that is available under the title of *Sartre par lui-même*.[5]

II. Teaching Existentialism through a
Focus on Phenomenology

A more authentic way of teaching existentialism than these two methods is to approach existentialism as Sartre himself did, by a study of the phenomenology of Husserl and Heidegger; after all,

Sartre subtitles *Being and Nothingness* "An Essay on Phenomenological Ontology."

One advantage of doing this is that it can turn the difference between Continental and Anglo-American philosophy to pedagogical advantage. Anglo-American philosophy supports a critical study of linguistic structures as part of a strategy for achieving conceptual clarity. It assumes the givens of immediate experience as the foundation of all linguistic structures (and, for some of the representatives of this tradition, as the elements to which these structures can be reduced). The Continental tradition—of which phenomenology is part—is primarily a reflection upon experience as such and attempts to disengage from experience the elements of sense-data or "perspectives," emotions, and other meanings that are thought to make lin-guistic structures possible. These latter elements are in Husserl's ter-minology "essences."

This phenomenological project, though weighed down with tech-nical vocabulary and notoriously difficult to execute, is nonetheless not essentially beyond the reach of undergraduates. To reflect upon, and to describe with care, one's apprehension of objects involves taking a special standpoint for viewing oneself. This is not what is usually called self-consciousness, such as when I become aware of myself writing this paper, but rather the stance of observing oneself as one experiences things and situations. Ludwig Landgrebe, of whom I was briefly a student in Cologne over twenty years ago, would often distribute to his seminar students copies of some of Husserl's unpublished manuscripts in which Husserl would "exhibit" his apprehension of, say, the notes of a scale, or the colors on a panel, reflecting all the while on the epistemological and methodological aspects of what he was doing. Now I occasionally ask my own students to observe themselves moving their fingers, and encourage them to distinguish between what they think they know about the biological and physiological bases for such actions and what is in fact experienced in the action itself. Such efforts can be a salutary exercise for budding existentialists. Further on in the course, one may have one's students try to reflect more broadly upon some of the key categories of the existentialist vocabulary and how they may be lived out. Robert C. Solomon's anthology,

Phenomenology and Existentialism,[6] which could serve very well as the primary source for an undergraduate course in this topic, contains selections in which several of these categories are analyzed phenomenologically: there are passages on the ego by Husserl, Sartre, and Heidegger; on intersubjectivity and the Other by those writers and by Marcel and Merleau-Ponty; and on freedom and responsibility by Camus and de Beauvoir. Each of these selections may be treated, at least initially, as apperceptive reflections upon experience and as thought-experiments, rather than as philosophical position papers. They each attempt, as phenomenologists would say, to "bring to givenness" underlying elements of our experience. Terms such as "ego," "self," "freedom," and "the Other" refer to highly subjective phenomena that students may encounter only unreflectively within themselves. One may have a sense of oneself as morally responsible for the outcome of some action without having asked oneself not what the basis for such moral respon-sibility may be, but how this responsibility is experienced as such. Similarly, one may think oneself to be free in some sense without having reflected not on how freedom is possible, but on how it is actualized in choice. Solomon's book has the advantage of encourag-ing a kind of introspective journey whose object is the exploration of the human way of existing.

To recommend teaching existentialism in this way is not to deny the importance of logical analysis; it is indeed worthwhile to consider that existentialism may consist in a misuse of the verb "to be" or that such Heideggerian blather as his untranslatable "das Nichts nichtet" is devoid of sense.[7] But the kind of criticism that the existentialist texts of Heidegger's kind seek must be based upon an exploration of the lived apprehension of those aspects of experience that his often obscure idioms refer to obliquely, and which existentialists wish, in their texts, to exhibit phenomenologically. If existentialism is "the thinking of the existing subject about his existence as he 'exists' his existence,"[8] then it is surely not illegiti-mate to try to reexperience in reflection the sense of one's own self-hood. One hopes students will discover in this attempt different levels of reflection and different standpoints one may take upon them. It is, of course, more difficult to gauge students' success in reflections of this kind than their success in the process of the interpretation and criticism of texts. If having students engage in this sort of reflection awakens in them a habit of introspection and self-reflection the noisy world outside tends to smother, something worthwhile, I think, will have been achieved.

III. Teaching Existentialism via the Literary Works Produced by Existentialists

Teaching existentialism through the works of literature that have been created by persons we count as existentialists allows an extensive choice of bibliographical materials. Not only are the choices very large but the important works are also sufficiently short to allow the instructor to order paperback editions of individual works rather than an anthology that contains only excerpted material. As a general study to accompany the readings of sources, I find Hazel E. Barnes's book, *The Literature of Possibility*[9] to be still the best introduction to this literature. It offers sensitive readings of the texts and possesses considerable philosophical acumen. Let us begin with Sartre, for many of his works are an attempt to exhibit aspects of experience revealed in phenomenological reflection by means of imaginary situations.

Sartre's short story "The Wall" requires us to reflect carefully upon what our students—and perhaps we ourselves with any fidelity—rarely can bring to givenness imaginatively, namely a situation that confronts us with our inevitable death in the very near future. Perhaps the most prominent difficulty here is sympathetically reexperiencing the effects such a situation would have on our feeling of our body. Only if one can induce extremely powerful emotions in oneself by imaginative reenactment of such a situation could such a transformation in one's sense of one's own body be apprehended. Pablo's body "feels like a vermin" pressing against him, and he perspires profusely even though it is quite cold. What must that be like? "The Childhood of a Boss," also by Sartre and contained in the collection of stories entitled *The Wall*,[10] is a study of "bad faith." His one-act play *No Exit* can be used as a vehicle for an exploration of such categories of Sartre's phenomenology as temporality and the Other. The study of situations depicted in existentialist literature offers brief, penetrating means of access to the existentialist worldview.

Camus's play *Caligula* can be used to analyze the phenomenon of absurdity.[11] This phenomenon is, in fact, very difficult to perceive with any clarity, and most people take the world for granted in its general features. In *Caligula*, the emperor Caligula, like Nietzsche's madman, alone of all those about him, has discovered that something is wrong with the world, and he follows up the logic of what that new knowledge implies. The madman grasps that God is dead, and Caligula grasps that "men die, and they are unhappy." How strange what these madmen find, when they escape from the cave of everydayness!

Simone de Beauvoir's *All Men Are Mortal* forces us to reconsider whether we really desire what we all immediately think we desire, namely, to live forever.[12] De Beauvoir's imaginary immortal man, Fosca, soon discovers that he shares nothing with the mortal men and women around him, for the meanings they give to their lives are all predicated upon the assumption that they will die someday. Since Fosca can never die, de Beauvoir suggests, he cannot live a life at all. For one can be committed to a cause or to a person—what else is it to live a life?—only if one can risk one's life or at least some of one's finite number of hours for it.

Every hero must have a villain, and existentialist heroes are no exception. Their villains are characterized variously as "inauthentic" persons, as persons in "bad faith," as members of the "Serious World" (Sartre), as persons living solely as "public" persons, as persons living on what Kierkegaard calls the "aesthetical" level or even as Nietzsche's typical Christian. Of course, we, as teachers, are by no means required to treat our authors' heroes' villains as villains; we are not mere narrators. Perhaps, indeed, we may even come to express a liking for these villains, if only we learn to uncover the partiality and, perhaps, unfairness of our authors' treatment of them.

IV. The Critique of Existentialism

Allowing the representative of the "Serious World" to speak back to the existentialist is, I think, infrequent in criticisms of existentialism.

Such criticism is important pedagogically, for the existentialist writers display such talent as writers and such passion as persons that it is difficult for young students not to be swept up in sympathy for their philosophy. Robert G. Olson's book, *An Introduction to Existentialism*,[13] stands firmly in the pragmatic tradition in its critique of existentialism, and an introductory course in existentialism should give his work—especially his criticisms of freedom, authenticity, and the Other—a careful hearing. In a similar vein, we might allow the social sciences to speak out critically against existentialism, and answer the existentialist challenge that scientific/rationalist analysis of human origins and behavior belies the truth of human freedom. This leads to the fourth approach to teaching existentialism that I would like to discuss, namely, teaching existentialism as a humanistic perspective—in contrast to a scientific one—from which to view human beings and their lives.

The "humanistic" perspective examines the human individual from the "inside," and attempts to introspect the lived, personal existence of human individuals, whereas the "scientific" perspective examines the human species from the outside, as it were, as an object of detached, quantitative inquiry. The spatial metaphors of "inside" and "outside" are just that; they are not to be taken literally, but are used to call attention to the direction of approach to the nature of man. The former considers mankind as it presents itself to the observations of the biologist, psychologist, or ethologist. The latter directs itself upon mankind apperceptively and attempts to grasp human existences in their uniqueness. The contrast between these two perspectives is explored in an anthology a colleague and I created for use in introductory philosophy, *The Fundamental Questions*.[14] The readings relevant to existentialism, introduced by a discussion of these ideas and distinctions, consist of two groups of authors. On the one hand, there are selections from Richard Dawkins on the origins of human biology, from B. F. Skinner on the idea of a science of man, from Sigmund Freud on the structure of the human psyche, and from Konrad Lorenz on the implications of ethology for the study of human behavior. The authors in this group, guided by the scientist's care for observable evidence, make human beings an object of dispassionate scrutiny and examine their behavior from the outside, as it were. They are not at all loath to extend their views about animal behavior into the human sphere, for they consider man to be but an extension of the animal realm. They grant, of course, that our species displays some unique complexities, such as language and thought. But they believe that we can say everything that is significant about a human being without recourse to the vague and mysterious concepts that occupy the existentialists.

The second group of writers I shall refer to as "humanists"; they include Sartre, Heidegger, and Camus. Instead of regarding humans as the proper objects of dispassionate scrutiny, these authors reflect upon the ways human beings live through personal crises of meaning and value. They hold that science cannot answer questions concerning the significance of human life because the scientist has no means of dealing with the interior space carved out by consciousness. Dawkins's remark that Darwinianism can answer sensibly questions concerning the meaning of life would be greeted by them with incredulity. After all, the "humanist" would argue, whatever our origins, the meaning of life—of *my* life—can only be revealed and affirmed in actions in which I affirm a meaning *for* myself: this process of self-definition escapes the "laws of behavior" striven after by biologists, psychologists, and ethologists. Whether one's experience of this inner space justifies the use of such concepts as the "ego," the "self," or "selfhood" is a question that students might be asked to respond to by writing position papers at the end of their study of the subject.

In sum, we have sketched five approaches to the teaching of existentialism. In the first two, existentialism is taught either as a set of texts for logical analysis or as a phase in this history of ideas; in the third, it is taught as many twentieth-century existentialists themselves approached it, namely through Husserl and their adaptations of his phenomenology; in the fourth, it is taught via a critical study of the literature that has been written by existentialists and, in the fifth, by a contrast drawn between it and the philosophical anthropology that emerges from contemporary biology and social science.

Existentialism can also be taught as an invitation to a personal adventure into the self. We may ask our students to begin a metaprocess in which they reflect upon the categories that condition their being-in-the-world. Just as we try, in our courses in philosophy, to convey to students how difficult thinking is, and how infrequently complete clarity is achieved, so in a course on existentialism we may try to impress on our students how serious and difficult human existence becomes, once we learn to be reflective. Perhaps Kierkegaard is the greatest master of that kind of lesson, but he teaches it behind a cloak of pseudonymous *alter egos*. It is more difficult, and perhaps not even desirable, for the classroom teacher to conceal himself or herself behind the Socratic cloak of ignorance; after all, the teacher is living a life right before the students' eyes.

With this in mind, it might be worthwhile, at the end of a course on existentialism, when students and teacher have come to know one another a bit, for the professor to reveal to students his or her own journeying along the path of self-reflection to the point in life he or she now occupies. Of course, the encounter with existence is essentially individual and cannot be grasped in purely intellectual terms, nor can it be compared in any detail with that of other persons. We can, however, give students some sense of how we have wrestled with our own angels—and, perhaps, devils—as we try to wrest some meaning and value from them. That each of us may finally fail in this contest is no reason to refuse to speak of the efforts we have made.

NOTES

1. F. H. Heinemann, *Existentialism and the Modern Predicament* (New York: Harper and Row, 1953, 1958).

2. H. J. Blackham, *Six Existentialist Thinkers* (London: Routledge & Kegan Paul, 1952).

3. Walter Kaufmann, *Existentialist Thinkers* (New York: Meridian Books, 1956).

4. Simone de Beauvoir, *Adieux: A Farewell to Sartre* (New York: Pantheon Books, 1984).

5. Film by Alexandre Astruc and Michel Contat, 1976; English subtitles.

6. Robert C. Solomon, *Phenomenology and Existentialism* (Lanham, MD: Rowman & Littlefield, 1991; reprint edition).

7. This locution of Heidegger is criticized by Rudolf Carnap as lacking meaning in his "*Überwindung der Metaphysik durch logische Analyse der Sprache,*" *Erkenntis* (Leipzig), Bd. 2, H.4 (1932) 219-41, reprinted in A. J. Ayer, *Logical Positivism* (Glencoe, IL: The Free Press, 1959). I have seen the expression translated into English as "nothing nothings."

8. Will Herberg, in *Four Existentialist Theologians,* ed. Will Herberg (Garden City, NY: Doubleday Anchor, 1958), 3.

9. Hazel E. Barnes, *The Literature of Possibility* (Lincoln: University of Nebraska Press, 1959).

10. Jean Paul Sartre, *The Wall and Other Stories* (New York: New Directions, 1975).

11. Camus, Albert, *Caligula and Three Other Plays.* Translated from the French by Stuart Gilbert (New York: Vintage Books [ca. 1958]).

12. Simone de Beauvoir, *Tous les hommes sont mortels* (Paris: Gallimard, 1946).

13. Robert G. Olsen, *An Introduction to Existentialism* (New York: Dover, 1962).

14. E. Kelly and L. E. Navia, *The Fundamental Questions* (Dubuque, IA: Kendall-Hunt, 1985, 1995).

Chapter 22

Teaching Recent Continental Philosophy

Stephen H. Daniel

Many philosophy programs have for some time offered courses in existentialism that treat Kierkegaard, Nietzsche, Kafka, Camus, and Sartre as representatives of a popular and, for the most part, accessible mentality. In many college curricula, an existentialism course is listed at a sophomore level in order to encourage students with no formal background to consider the possibility of studying philosophy in a way that might have immediate application to their lives. In fact, when these courses were first introduced, they did attract many students who were looking for just the kind of insights that existentialism provided.

However, it was apparent early on that the doctrines of Heidegger and even Sartre could not be understood without some familiarity with phenomenology; it also became apparent that unraveling the intricacies of Hegel, Husserl, or Merleau-Ponty would have curtailed the amount of time instructors would be able to devote to the very writings that had drawn students to the course in the first place. In light of this, some departments opted to develop an upper-division course in phenomenology and existentialism; others split nineteenth-century philosophy off as a separate course. Depending on who taught them, some of these courses were part of a sequence in the history of philosophy, whereas others were more topical, literary, or in the history-of-ideas mode.

The development of continental philosophy, especially since the 1960s, has now made it clear that further work on the curriculum is in order. Though some phenomenology and existentialism instructors have made valiant attempts to keep their students abreast of what has happened in the last forty years, they have generally failed to do justice to recent developments in continental philosophy when they have tried to tack them onto existing courses. For many teachers, it has been easier to yield the study of structuralist psychoanalysis, semiotics, deconstruction, critical theory, philosophical hermeneutics, poststructuralism, and postmodernism to literature or language departments, or to reserve these movements for graduate students, rather than to develop new courses geared to undergraduates.

Resisting such temptations, I set out several years ago to develop a course that would allow students to examine some of the central themes of "postmodern" philosophy. Specifically, I wanted wanted to design a course that showed how continental thinkers in the last half of the twentieth century challenge assumptions and practices that are often equated with philosophy itself. Since these challenges are directed against presuppositions first formulated explicitly in the seventeenth century, they are usually identified as aspects of a broad critique of classical modernity—hence their designation as postmodern. Together, they aim to overturn three fundamental beliefs at the core of modernist thought: (1) of everything we know, we know ourselves first and most clearly; (2) history is the progressive summary of the interactions of autonomous, naturally self-interested individuals; and (3) an objective world of things is knowable only in terms of our representations or narrations. The purpose of my course was to reveal how continental theorists have pursued this effort in vastly different ways. So instead of focusing on a few works by three or four postmodern figures, I selected a broad array of thinkers, movements, and approaches for inclusion in the course. My aim was to examine the central ideas developed by mainly French and German philosophers in the last fifty years within the context of major movements that included structuralist psychoanalysis, deconstruction, neo-Marxist critical theory, semiotics, philosophical hermeneutics, poststructuralism, and postmodernism.

Based on my experience in teaching modern philosophy courses, I chose breadth over depth for two reasons. First, because of the great deal of exchange and commentary that characterize the work of continental thinkers, it is fruitless to consider these thinkers in isolation. Remarks about one another's ideas so fill their texts that the instructor has to spend as much time talking about what is only alluded to in the text (and thus what is not immediately available to the student) as what is in the text. Second, the pedagogic elevation of major figures or works—and the marginalization or exclusion of others—undermines the effort in current continental philosophy to include literary authors, artists, and social theorists. A course limited to a canonical list of works by Derrida, Foucault, Habermas, and Lyotard would ignore their invitations to read sources other than Hegel, Marx, Nietzsche, Freud, and Heidegger. Admittedly, the constraints of ordinary course planning require that *some* selection be made; but by leaving out Lacan, Kristeva, Adorno, Althusser, Gadamer, or Deleuze, we legitimate the narrowing of focus that they and their more well-known counterparts such as Derrida and Foucault reject.

Indeed, in modern philosophy courses, the very students who are unimpressed with exemplars of philosophical orthodoxy such as Descartes or Kant are often the ones who get excited by Condillac or Vico, precisely because these thinkers do not fit easily into rationalist, empiricist, or idealist categories. A course devoted to thinkers who disrupt the principles underlying this nineteenth-century taxonomy would certainly be an odd place to impose another, exclusive model of canonical domination, this time one that marginalizes a Saussure, Althusser, and Baudrillard merely because they do not have name recognition in the United States comparable to Derrida.

However, anyone who confronts recent continental philosophy quickly recognizes that, without the support of secondary sources, it can be an overwhelming experience. Most undergraduates, even the bright ones, become frustrated with some of the texts in ways that far from endear them to any further study in the field. It is a mistake to have students wade through Derrida, Habermas, or Deleuze without already knowing a good bit about what they are up to. For, typically, students will not understand or appreciate the writings of these authors if they are thrown primarily into original sources. The most the instructor can expect of students is a familiarity with the general insights of some of these figures—something often best gleaned from secondary sources. This means emphasizing central themes in the enterprises of selected thinkers: for example, Lacan's structuralist analysis of the unconscious in terms of language, Derrida's critique of logocentrism and doctrine of *différance*, or Habermas's theory that communicative exchange continues the Enlightenment project.

The challenge of a course on how recent movements in continental thought reject classical modernist beliefs (for example, knowledge as representation, and the independence and supposedly nonideological nature of reality and history) lies in a careful selection of accessible yet characteristic readings. Some currently available selections are easy to read but do not capture the spirit or main ideas of the writer. For authors such as Habermas, Derrida, Deleuze, Althusser, and Adorno, it is difficult to find a nice short essay that gives a sense of what the writer espouses. All one can do is to find some evenhanded secondary literature that includes sizable quotes that will lead the curious back to the texts.

When I started teaching the course, I found the most comprehensive collection of primary materials to be *Critical Theory Since 1965*, edited by Hazard Adams and Leroy Searle.[1] This collection includes work from Saussure (on how the meaning of terms is a function of their relation to other terms and not to some extralinguistic referent); Lacan (on how the self is a function of language); Derrida (on how philosophy's effort to identify objects of knowledge is necessarily frustrated); Kristeva (on how the feminine body, like language, threatens the stability of identity and meaning); Jardine (on the difference between American and French feminism); Benjamin (on how history is possible only as an affirmation of discontinuity); Foucault (on how subjectivity is itself a function of historical displacements of power); Althusser (on Marxism as the practice of theorizing); and Deleuze and Guattari (on the material, capitalist conditions of psychoanalysis). To supplement this collection, I prepared a packet of readings that included material from Bataille (on what is necessary for radical heterogeneity);[2] Lukács (on how Marxism is humanistic without being subjectivistic);[3] Adorno (on the Marxist analysis of subjectivity as the negation of the real);[4] Gadamer (on how consciousness is inherently historical and interpretative);[5] Lyotard (on how post-modernism accepts the impossibility of a transcendental theory of reality);[6] Irigaray (on how feminist theories of embodiment undercut attempts to identify truth in terms of stability);[7] and Rorty (on how truth is a function of practices but is not subjective).[8]

In the years since I first offered the course, I have dropped some of these essays in favor of more accessible and representative selections from Adorno (on how the real always exceeds that which can be thought),[9] Derrida (on how the real cannot be thought in oppositional terms),[10] and Baudrillard (on how the real is a function of its representability).[11] Because I could not find a brief overview that brought together the different approaches in current continental thought, I ultimately wrote such a piece myself,[12] the first half of which my students read in the first week of class. For some students, this summary becomes the reference point for situating the various movements and isms in relation to one another.

Some recent anthologies include now standard texts. *The Continental Philosophy Reader*, edited by Richard Kearney and Mara Rainwater,[13] contains selections from Heidegger, Jaspers, Levinas, Lukács, Gramsci, Benjamin, Levi-Strauss, Deleuze, and Irigaray, along with the standard array of works from Saussure, Lacan, Foucault, Lyotard, Derrida, and others. Todd May contributes an informative introduction to his *Twentieth Century Continental Philosophy*,[14] an anthology that includes works by Saussure, Lacan, Horkheimer and Adorno, Gadamer, Lyotard, Foucault, Irigaray, Kristeva, Derrida, and Habermas, as well as Husserl, Heidegger, Sartre, and Ricoeur. *From Modernism to Postmodernism*, edited by Lawrence Cahoone,[15] begins with writings from Descartes and other moderns but adds pieces from Horkheimer and Adorno, Derrida, Foucault, Deleuze, Baudrillard, Irigarary, Lyotard, Jameson, Rorty, and Habermas. Will McNeil and Karen Feldman's edition of *Modern European Philosophy*[16] has selections from these thinkers and others (for example, Nancy and Cixous) who are often left out of other anthologies.

Complementing these primary sources are secondary readings from Richard Kearney's *Modern Movements in European Philosophy*[17] and *Twentieth Century Continental Philosophy*,[18] Simon Critchley and William Schroeder's *Companion to Continental Philosophy*,[19] John Lechte's *Fifty Key Contemporary Thinkers*,[20] David West's *Introduction to Continental Philosophy*,[21] Quentin Skinner's *The Return of Grand Theory in the Human Sciences*,[22] John Sturrock's *Structuralism and Since*,[23] and a wealth of other books and essays.

To make all of this material more accessible, I decided to assemble a compendium of primary sources, supplemented by more than 100 pages of my own introductions, summaries, and commentaries.[24] This collection both introduces students to the field and provides them with representative readings from each of the thinkers we cover. In addition to general background discussions and overviews of significant strategies, movements, and thinkers of current continental philosophy, before each reading I have composed notes that highlight the main points developed by the author of that reading. The readings themselves have been selected either because they capture the spirit or main ideas of the writer and are relatively straightforward or are now considered central in understanding the writer's overall thought. In some cases they are short essays, in others they are selections from longer works.

The collection of materials described above makes two points in particular: First, in arranging thinkers and movements in a specific order and according to determinate groupings, it is clear that, apart from chronology, there are scholarly reasons to associate thinkers in the groupings in which they appear. Second, an argument is presented for regarding as false the widespread assumption that strategies such as deconstruction, poststructuralism, and postmodernism all refer to roughly the same thing. Rather, for both scholarly and pedagogic purposes it is made clear that it is important to differentiate these movements from one another.

I recognize that any effort to provide a taxonomy or schema for these views seems to contradict the spirit of intertextuality and exchange that informs all of them. But for someone who initially confronts current continental philosophy, it is better to get a good sense of a position (even if later found to be in need of qualification) than to think that understanding the view is necessarily complicated by its inherent relations to other positions. Anyone who wants to understand the major ideas of current continental philosophy must thus get clear on the real differences between critical theory, structuralism, psychoanalytic feminism, deconstruction, poststructuralism, postcolonialism, and post-modernism.

It is obvious that with as many different thinkers as my course covers, only a few can receive more than the attention of one seventy-five-minute class session. (Althusser, Derrida, Deleuze, and Foucault are each the focus of two class sessions.) The course is divided into three parts, each of which concludes with an in-class exam. The exams consist of three essay questions distributed a week in advance so that students can consult with one another to prepare what they will write in class without the aid of any notes.

The first part of the course begins with a week on the modernity/postmodernity contrast and thematic background figures (Marx, Freud, and Nietzsche). I then move on to critical theory and the Frankfurt School: Lukács (*History and Class Consciousness*), Horkheimer ("Traditional and Critical Theory"), Benjamin ("Theses on the Philosophy of History"), Adorno (*Negative Dialectics*),

Gadamer ("The Universality of the Hermeneutical Problem," Foreword to the second edition of *Truth and Method*), Habermas ("Reconstruction and Interpretation in the Social Sciences," and "Discourse Ethics"), and Althusser ("Marxism and Humanism," and "From *Capital* to Marx's Philosophy").

The second part of the course covers (a) psychoanalytic structuralism: Saussure (*Course in General Linguistics*), and Lacan ("The Function and Field of Speech and Language," and "The Subversion of the Subject and the Dialectic of Desire"); (b) feminism and psychoanalysis: Irigaray ("The Power of Discourse," and "Sexual Difference") and Kristeva ("Women's Time," *Interviews*); and (c) deconstruction: Levinas ("Substitution"), Derrida ("The End of the Book and the Beginning of Writing," and "Structure, Sign, and Play," "Afterword: Toward an Ethic of Discussion"), and Cixous ("Laugh of the Medusa").

The third part covers (a) poststructuralism: Deleuze (*Difference and Repetition*, "Psychoanalysis and Capitalism"), and Foucault ("Discourse on Language," *History of Sexuality*, vols. 1 & 2); (b) postcolonialism: Spivak (*Critique of Postcolonial Reason*) and Bhabha ("The Other Question"); and (c) postmodernism: Lyotard (*The Postmodern Condition*, "Answering the Question: What Is Postmodernism?") and Baudrillard (*Symbolic Exchange and Death*).

On seeing this list of readings, most instructors will shake their heads saying, "Too much; the students will never be able to keep them straight; and those they do, they won't really understand." Surprisingly, though, students not only differentiate these figures but also appreciate the way the course puts them in touch with a number of people and themes they have heard about somewhere else and about which they are curious to learn more. But the process does place a good deal of responsibility on the instructor to make sure that students have a clear idea about certain readings. Even if only two or three sentences written on the board before class serve as a springboard for discussion, it is important that the students have something concrete to go back to in their notes when they begin to study for their exams.

At least three times during the semester, each student is required to write a two-page summary of the material covered on a particular day. The grade assigned to each summary counts as points added to a test score (A=22 points; B=12 points, C=2 points). Summaries are submitted at the beginning of the class discussion. Because the summaries vary according to student schedules and interest, they tend to spread out throughout the semester, which results in there being at least one or two students in the class who have prepared especially well for any one discussion. By the end of the semester, students are in a good position to decide whether they will write a ten-page research paper in place of taking the third in-class exam.

I have now taught the course seven times, first as an honors class and subsequently as a class open juniors and seniors. Evaluations of the class have been the highest I have ever received. Students say they appreciate the variety of the readings and credit their understanding of this difficult material to being introduced to it in small doses. They admit that the readings are some of the most difficult they have ever encountered. But they take pride in being allowed to struggle with and even understand figures and themes that mystify some of their other teachers.

NOTES

1. *Critical Theory Since 1965,* ed. Hazard Adams and Leroy Searle (Tallahassee: Florida State University Press, 1986).

2. Georges Bataille, *Visions of Excess,* ed. Allan Stoekl (Minneapolis: University of Minnesota Press, 1985), 137-45.

3. Gyorgy Lukács, "The Ideology of Modernism," in *The Meaning of Contemporary Realism* (London: Merlin, 1963).

4. Theodor Adorno, *Negative Dialectics* (New York: Continuum, 1987), 4-15, 26-42, 53-56.

5. Hans-Georg Gadamer, "The Universality of the Hermeneutical Problem," in *The Hermeneutic Tradition,* ed. Gayle Ormiston and Alan Schrift (Albany: State University of New York Press, 1990).

6. Jean-François Lyotard, "The Postmodern Condition," in *After Philosophy: End or Transformation?* ed. Kenneth Baynes, James Bohman,

and Thomas McCarthy (Cambridge, MA: MIT Press, 1987).

7. Luce Irigaray, "Sexual Difference," in *The Irigaray Reader*, ed. Margaret Whitford (Cambridge, MA: Blackwell, 1991).

8. Richard Rorty, "The Contingency of Language," in *Contingency, Irony, and Solidarity* (New York: Cambridge University Press, 1989).

9. Theodor Adorno, "Cultural Criticism and Society," in *Prisms* (Cambridge, MA: MIT Press, 1983).

10. Jacques Derrida, "Deconstruction and the Other," in *Dialogues with Contemporary Continental Thinkers*, ed. Richard Kearney (Dover, NH: Manchester University Press, 1984).

11. Jean Baudrillard, "Simulacra and Simulations," in *Jean Baudrillard: Selected Writings* (Stanford: Stanford University Press, 1988).

12. Stephen H. Daniel, "Postmodernity, Poststructuralism, and the Historiography of Modern Philosophy," *International Philosophical Quarterly* 35 (1995): 255-67.

13. *The Continental Philosophy Reader*, ed. Richard Kearney and Mara Rainwater (New York: Routledge, 1995).

14. Todd May, ed., *Twentieth Century Continental Philosophy*, ed., Todd May (Upper Saddle River, NJ: Prentice Hall, 1997).

15. Lawrence Cahoone, ed., *From Modernism to Postmodernism* (Cambridge, MA: Blackwell, 1995).

16. Will McNeil and Karen Feldman, eds., *Modern European Philosophy* (Cambridge, MA: Blackwell, 1997).

17. Richard Kearney, *Modern Movements in European Philosophy*, 2nd ed. (New York: St. Martin's Press, 1994).

18. Richard Kearney, *Twentieth Century Continental Philosophy*, vol. 8 of *Routledge History of Philosophy* (New York: Routledge, 1994).

19. Simon Critchley and William Schroeder, eds., *A Companion to Continental Philosophy* (Cambridge, MA: Blackwell, 1997).

20. John Lechte, *Fifty Key Contemporary Thinkers* (New York: Routledge, 1994).

21. David West, ed., *Introduction to Continental Philosophy* (Cambridge, MA: Polity, 1996).

22. Quentin Skinner, ed., *The Return of Grand Theory in the Human Sciences* (New York: Cambridge University Press, 1985).

23. John Sturrock, ed., *Structuralism and Since* (New York: Oxford University Press, 1979).

24. *Current Continental Philosophy* (Upper Saddle River, NJ: Prentice Hall, 2004).

PART XI
Teaching Philosophical Explanation

Chapter 23

Teaching 'Inference to the Best Philosophical Explanation'

David B. Martens

I. Introduction

Inference to the best explanation (IBE) is a common form of argument in science and is commonly taught by means of scientific examples in Critical Reasoning courses. However, IBE is also common in philosophical theory and practice, and rightly should be taught to philosophy students by means of philosophical examples.[1]

In this paper I will describe a method for teaching graduate and upper-level undergraduate philosophy students how to recognize, construct, and evaluate inferences to the best philosophical explanation.[2] The method initially provides students with IBE examples that are simplified (to aid comprehension) but specifically philosophical (to motivate attentiveness and application), and subsequently reinforces students' comprehension regularly with examples from course-related readings. I will describe the method in application in an epistemology course but the method is easily adaptable for other sorts of philosophy courses.

II. IBE and the Analysis of Propositional Knowledge

Plato, in the *Theaetetus*, set the curriculum by which the analysis of propositional knowledge still tends to be taught in epistemology courses. In this traditional curriculum, the instructor first introduces Theaetetus's hypothesis that knowledge is merely true belief, without suggesting why the hypothesis might be thought to be plausible.[3] Then the instructor uses a quick Socratic refutation of that hypothesis as a convenient entry to extended discussions of more plausible analyses of knowledge. I suggest that the initial discussion of Theaetetus's hypothesis provides the instructor with an opportunity to introduce students to basic concepts and procedures for recognizing, constructing, and evaluating philosophical IBEs.

As an exercise, the instructor and students can speculatively construct a train of 'explanationist' thought by which Theaetetus might have arrived at and supported his hypothesis that knowledge is merely true belief. The purpose is not actually to defend Theaetetus's hypothesis, so the speculated reasoning need not be ultimately acceptable or even initially plausible.[4] Rather, the purpose of the exercise is pedagogical, so the reasoning and its construction should be simple, systematic, and clear in ways that exhibit and highlight basic concepts and procedures.

What follows below is a script for the exercise. In the script, the speculated reasoning is constructed in a 'play' consisting of a prologue followed by five acts and an epilogue. I invite the reader to imagine herself and her students acting out the 'play' expressively, perhaps with improvised deviations from my script. In each of the five acts of the 'play,' one IBE is constructed. The conclusion of the final IBE is identical with Theaetetus's hypothesis. In each of the five acts, there is a repetitive six-scene structure corresponding to the six repetitive tasks of specifying data, specifying competitor hypotheses, constructing an IBE, evaluating an IBE as to truth-of-premises, evaluating an IBE as to strength-of-inference, and considering how to act on an evaluation of an IBE. In giving 'stage directions' in the script, I will use a small number of formal symbols, as follows: The letters 'P,' 'C,' 'E,' 'H,' and 'B' will represent propositions that are, respectively, premises, conclusions, data (or evidence), hypotheses, and background beliefs.

The script for the exercise now begins.

Prologue

At the class preceding the class at which the exercise is to take place, the instructor prepares students for the exercise by distributing two handouts and briefly reviewing those handouts with students. (A third handout will be distributed later in the exercise.)

The first handout (titled "Inference to the Best Explanation") describes the form of an IBE and provides both a glossary of terms and criteria for evaluating an IBE.[5] Reviewing the handout with students, the instructor emphasizes several points. First, the IBE form has an essential three-premise structure: Premise one (P1) presents the data to be explained; premise two (P2) presents the competitor hypotheses proposed to explain the data; and premise three (P3) claims that one of the competitor hypotheses (the target hypothesis, whose correctness is affirmed in the IBE's conclusion, C) is the best proposed explanation of the data. A purported IBE that does not have all three premises is malformed. Further, with an IBE as with any argument, truth-of-premises and strength-of-inference are two distinct evaluative factors that must be assessed independently of each other. Since IBE is a nondeductive form of argument, strength-of-inference is always a matter of degree. Finally, IBE is a form of *argument*, not a *theory* of explanation and not a method for the *discovery* of hypotheses. IBE is compatible with a wide range of theories of explanation, which might differ widely in their respective accounts of theoretical virtues, that is, characteristics (typically thought to include, for example, explanatory power, simplicity, and coherence) that make a hypothesis a better explanation.[6] And IBE does not require that competitor hypotheses be discovered by any particular method.

The second handout (titled "Data and Hypotheses for IBE Exercise") begins with these instructions to students:

> Using only the data (E1, E2, and E3) and the potential competitor hypotheses (H1 through H9) listed below, construct two inferences to the best explanation (IBEs). First, construct the strongest IBE you can to support the first hypothesis (H1). Second, construct the strongest IBE you can to support the fourth hypothesis (H4). In constructing your IBEs, you may choose to

use all or only some of the data and all or only some of the potential competitor hypotheses listed below. In evaluating the IBEs you construct, you may use the auxiliary hypothesis (HA) and the background beliefs (B1, B2, and B3) listed below. Be prepared to discuss your IBEs next class!

The second handout then gives all the elements to be used in the exercise: three fictional but possible cases, three pieces of data, three background beliefs, one potential auxiliary hypothesis, and nine potential competitor hypotheses.[7]

Act One

Scene One.

The instructor begins the exercise by introducing two pieces of data, that is, propositions already believed to be true, but for which an explanation is sought. Referring to the second handout, the instructor introduces the data by describing two fictional but possible cases, asking students for their intuitions about the cases, and posing why-questions about the cases.

> **First case:** Adam, who did not finish school, regularly buys and drinks moonshine whisky. Adam has never heard of wood alcohol and so has no beliefs about it. In particular, Adam does not have a belief that wood alcohol in moonshine whisky is poisonous, and he does not have a belief that it is nonpoisonous. It is true, though, that wood alcohol is poisonous.

The instructor has students vote "yes" or "no" on the question of whether, given the case as described and taking the word "ignorant" in its ordinary sense, they would say that Adam is ignorant of the poisonousness of wood alcohol in moonshine whisky. (The case is simple and uncontroversial, so the vote should be a unanimous "yes."[8])

> **First datum (E1):**[9] In the circumstances of the first case, Adam is ignorant of the poisonousness of wood alcohol.

The instructor poses the question, "Why is Adam ignorant of the poisonousness of wood alcohol in the circumstances of the first case?" The question expresses a desire for an explanation.[10]

> **Second case:** Beth, a physician, has heard of wood alcohol but does not believe that it is nonpoisonous. She believes that wood

alcohol in moonshine whisky is poisonous. And it is true that wood alcohol is poisonous.

The instructor has students vote "yes" or "no" on the question of whether, given the case as described and taking the word "ignorant" in its ordinary sense, they would say that Beth is ignorant of the poisonousness of wood alcohol in moonshine whisky. (The case is simple and uncontroversial, so the vote should be a unanimous "no.")

> **Second datum (E2):** In the circumstances of the second case, Beth is not ignorant of the poisonousness of wood alcohol.

The instructor poses the why-question, "Why is Beth not ignorant of the poisonousness of wood alcohol, in the circumstances of the second case?" The question expresses a desire for an explanation.

Scene Two.
The instructor introduces two competing hypotheses to explain the data and to offer answers to the why-questions.

> **First hypothesis (H1):** True belief is logically necessary for knowledge.

> **Second hypothesis (H2):** Neither truth nor belief is logically necessary for knowledge.

If the first hypothesis is correct, then a correct answer to the why-questions about Adam and Beth is to say, "Because true belief is logically necessary for knowledge." If the second hypothesis is correct, then a correct answer is to say, "Because neither truth nor belief is logically necessary for knowledge."[11]

Scene Three.
The instructor and students together construct their first IBE from elements already provided. This IBE is an argument to support the first hypothesis (as the IBE's target hypothesis) on the grounds that it is the best explanation for the data about Adam and Beth. The task of constructing the first IBE is mechanical, since students already have the IBE form on the first handout. The IBE looks like this.

> **First IBE:**

> (P1)   These data are to be explained:

(E1)   In the circumstances of the first case, Adam is igno-
        rant of the poisonousness of wood alcohol.
(E2)   In the circumstances of the second case, Beth is not
        ignorant of the poisonousness of wood alcohol.
(P2)   These competitor hypotheses are proposed to explain
        the data (E1 and E2):
(H1)   True belief is logically necessary for knowledge.
(H2)   Neither truth nor belief is logically necessary for
        knowledge.
(P3)   With respect to the data (E1 and E2), the first hypoth-
        esis (H1) has theoretical virtues to a higher degree
        overall than any alternative competitor hypothesis
        (H2) has.
(C)   So (probably), the first hypothesis (H1) is correct; that
        is, true belief is logically necessary for knowledge.

Scene Four.

The instructor and students together evaluate the first IBE as to
truth-of-premises.

There should be no question that the first two premises are
true, since the data and the hypotheses were largely stipulated by
the instructor.[12] Premise three is also true, though students likely
will need help to see that it is true. The instructor focuses on explanatory power as the overridingly important theoretical virtue
in this instance and reasons as follows. The hypothesis that true
belief is logically necessary for knowledge (H1) has some, limited
explanatory power with respect to the data about Adam's ignorance (E1) and Beth's nonignorance (E2). On the other hand, the
alternative hypothesis that neither truth nor belief is logically
necessary for knowledge (H2) has no explanatory power at all
with respect to the data. So, other things being equal, the target
hypothesis (H1) has theoretical virtues to a higher degree overall
than any alternative competitor hypothesis (H2) has with respect
to the data. That is, premise three is true.

The instructor helps students to see that the first hypothesis
has some limited explanatory power with respect to the data and
that the second hypothesis has none. The instructor emphasizes
two points: First, an important component of the explanatory
power of a hypothesis with respect to certain data is the extent to

which those data are deductively or nondeductively inferable from that hypothesis, perhaps with the assistance of background beliefs and auxiliary hypotheses. Second, in the present instance, the data (E1 and E2) are inferable to a greater extent from the first hypothesis (H1) than from the second hypothesis (H2).

In making the points just mentioned, the instructor uses the handouts as aids. On the second handout are the following background beliefs and auxiliary hypothesis.

> **First background belief (B1):** In the circumstances of the first case, Adam does not have a belief that wood alcohol is nonpoisonous and he does not have a belief that it is poisonous, but it is true that wood alcohol is poisonous.

> **Second background belief (B2):** In the circumstances of the second case, Beth does not believe that wood alcohol is nonpoisonous, but instead believes that it is poisonous; and it is true that wood alcohol is poisonous.

> **Auxiliary hypothesis (HA):** To be ignorant of a truth is to lack knowledge of it, that is, not to know of it whether it is true or not.

These two background beliefs (B1 and B2) reflect the stipulated descriptions of the first and second cases and this auxiliary hypothesis (HA) reflects standard dictionary definitions of the word "ignorance." From these facts it should be clear to students that the background beliefs and the auxiliary hypothesis are all plausible, and that they do not derive their plausibility from the competing hypotheses (H1 and H2) in the IBE.

As an additional aid, the instructor now distributes a third handout (titled "Inferring Data from Hypotheses"), which shows how the individual data used in the exercise are or are not inferable, as the case may be, from the various hypotheses used in the exercise. Adam's ignorance (E1) is inferable from the hypothesis that true belief is logically necessary for knowledge (H1), with the assistance of the background belief about how things are with truth and belief in Adam's circumstances in the first case (B1) and the auxiliary hypothesis about the nature of ignorance (HA). However, even with the assistance of the background beliefs and the auxiliary hypothesis, Beth's nonignorance (E2) is not inferable from the first hypothesis and none of the data are inferable from the second hypothesis (H2). In other words, the second hypothesis (H2, that neither truth nor belief is logically necessary for knowledge) is an irrelevant hypothesis while the first hypothesis (H1, that true belief is logically necessary for knowledge) is a relevant hypothesis that has some, limited explanatory power with respect to the data about Adam's ignorance (E1) and Beth's nonignorance (E2). So, the target hypothesis has greater explanatory power than any alternative competitor hypothesis has with respect to the data. So, other things being equal, the target hypothesis (H1) has theoretical virtues to a higher degree overall than any alternative competitor hypothesis (H2) has with respect to the data (E1 and E2). That is, premise three is true.

Scene Five.
The instructor and students together evaluate the first IBE as to strength-of-inference.

Notwithstanding the truth of the premises, the inference from the premises to the conclusion of the IBE clearly is too weak for the argument to be acceptable. The instructor helps students to see the weakness of the inference by pointing out the following factors. For one thing, even though the target hypothesis has more explanatory power than its sole competitor has with respect to the data, the target hypothesis does not account for all or even most of the data and so is not a very powerful explanation of the data. Furthermore, the argument mentions only a limited number and variety of data. Finally, the target hypothesis faces only one alternative competitor hypothesis in the argument, so the competition is not very vigorous.

Scene Six.
The instructor and students explore whether a more acceptable IBE might support the hypothesis that true belief is logically necessary for knowledge (H1), by increasing the vigor of the competition faced by the target hypothesis. Act two pursues this.

Act Two

Scene One.
The data in act two are the same as in act one.

Scene Two.

The competitor hypotheses in act two are those in act one, plus a third competitor hypothesis that the instructor now introduces.

Third hypothesis (H3): Belief is logically necessary for knowledge, but truth is not.

If the third hypothesis is correct, then a correct answer to the why-questions about Adam and Beth is: "Because belief is logically necessary for knowledge, but truth is not."

Scene Three.

The instructor and students together construct, from elements already provided, a second IBE to support the first hypothesis.

Second IBE:

(P1)	These data are to be explained:
(E1)	In the circumstances of the first case, Adam is ignorant of the poisonousness of wood alcohol.
(E2)	In the circumstances of the second case, Beth is not ignorant of the poisonousness of wood alcohol.
(P2)	These competitor hypotheses are proposed to explain the data (E1 and E2):
(H1)	True belief is logically necessary for knowledge.
(H2)	Neither truth nor belief is logically necessary for knowledge.
(H3)	Belief is logically necessary for knowledge, but truth is not.
(P3)	With respect to the data (E1 and E2), the first hypothesis (H1) has theoretical virtues to a higher degree overall than any alternative competitor hypothesis (H2 or H3) has.
(C)	So (probably), the first hypothesis (H1) is correct; that is, true belief is logically necessary for knowledge.

Scene Four.

The instructor and students together evaluate the second IBE as to truth-of-premises.

There should be no question that the first two premises are true, since the data and the hypotheses were largely stipulated by the instructor. However, premise three is false, though students likely will need help to see that it is false. The instructor focuses on explanatory power and simplicity as the two most important theoretical virtues in this instance and reasons as follows. The hypothesis that true belief is logically necessary for knowledge (H1) and the hypothesis that belief is logically necessary for knowledge but truth is not (H3) have the same significant but limited degree of explanatory power with respect to the data about Adam's ignorance (E1) and Beth's nonignorance (E2). (The alternative hypothesis that neither truth nor belief is logically necessary for knowledge, H2, has no explanatory power at all with respect to the data.) However, the third hypothesis (H3) is simpler than the first hypothesis (H1). So, other things being equal, there is an alternative competitor hypothesis (H3) that has theoretical virtues to a higher degree overall than the target hypothesis (H1) has with respect to the data (E1 and E2). So, premise three is false.

The instructor helps students to see that the first and the third hypotheses have the same limited explanatory power with respect to the data, and that the second hypothesis has none at all. Referring again to the third handout, the instructor points out that the explanatory powers of the hypothesis that true belief is logically necessary for knowledge (H1) and of the hypothesis that neither truth nor belief is logically necessary for knowledge (H2) have not changed since the first IBE. Adam's ignorance (E1) is inferable from the hypothesis that belief is logically necessary for knowledge but truth is not (H3), with the assistance of the background belief about how things are with truth and belief in Adam's circumstances in the first case (B1) and the auxiliary hypothesis about the nature of ignorance (HA). However, Beth's nonignorance (E2) is not inferable from the third hypothesis, even with the assistance of the background beliefs and the auxiliary hypothesis. In other words, the second hypothesis (H2, that neither truth nor belief is logically necessary for knowledge) is an irrelevant hypothesis while the first hypothesis (H1, that true belief is logically necessary for knowledge) and the third hypothesis (H3, that belief is logically necessary for knowledge but truth is not) are relevant hypotheses each having the same limited explanatory power with respect to the data about Adam's ignorance (E1) and Beth's nonignorance (E2).

The instructor helps students to see that the third hypothesis has the competitive advantage that it is simpler than the first hypothesis, in the following sense: Both hypotheses 'postulate entities,' that is, each imputes one or more distinguishable logically necessary conditions to knowledge. But the third hypothesis imputes only one logically necessary condition (belief) to knowledge, while the first hypothesis imputes two (truth, belief). So, the third hypothesis 'postulates entities' more parsimoniously than the first hypothesis does. (Another way of putting the point is to say that the first hypothesis requires knowledge to be logically more complex than the third hypothesis requires knowledge to be.)

Since there is an alternative competitor hypothesis (H3) that has theoretical virtues to a higher degree overall than the target hypothesis (H1) has with respect to the data (E1 and E2), premise three is false. Since there is a false premise, the argument is not acceptable.

Scene Five.
The instructor and students together evaluate the second IBE as to strength-of-inference, first noncomparatively and then comparatively.

Compounding the injury caused by the falsehood of premise three, the inference from the premises to the conclusion of the IBE clearly is too weak for the argument to be acceptable. The instructor helps students to see the weakness of the inference by pointing out the following factors. For one thing, even though no alternative competitor has more explanatory power than the target hypothesis does with respect to the data, the target hypothesis does not account for all or even most of the data and so is not a very powerful explanation of the data. Furthermore, the argument mentions only a limited number and variety of data. Finally, the target hypothesis faces only two alternative competitor hypotheses in the argument, so the competition is not very vigorous, though it is more vigorous than the competition in the first IBE.

The instructor shows students that the inference in second IBE is stronger than the inference in the first IBE. While the data are the same in the two IBEs and the explanatory power of each target hypothesis with respect to its data is the same, the vigor of the competition in the second IBE is greater than the vigor of the competition in the first IBE.

Scene Six.

The instructor and the students wonder together whether the hypothesis that true belief is logically necessary for knowledge (H1) ought to be abandoned in favor of the hypothesis that belief is logically necessary for knowledge but truth is not (H3). Act three pursues this suggestion.

Act Three

Scene One.

The data in act three are the same as in act two.

Scene Two.

The competitor hypotheses in act three are the same as in act two.

Scene Three.

The instructor and students together construct a third IBE from elements already provided. The third IBE differs from the second IBE only in that the first and the third hypotheses have exchanged places in the third premise and in the conclusion. That is, the target hypothesis supported by the third IBE is the third hypothesis.

Third IBE:
- (P1) These data are to be explained:
- (E1) In the circumstances of the first case, Adam is ignorant of the poisonousness of wood alcohol.
- (E2) In the circumstances of the second case, Beth is not ignorant of the poisonousness of wood alcohol.
- (P2) These competitor hypotheses are proposed to explain the data:
- (H1) True belief is logically necessary for knowledge.
- (H2) Neither truth nor belief is logically necessary for knowledge.
- (H3) Belief is logically necessary for knowledge, but truth is not.
- (P3) With respect to the data (E1 and E2), the third hypothesis (H3) has theoretical virtues to a higher de-

gree overall than any alternative competitor hypothesis (H1 or H2) has.

(C)   So (probably), the third hypothesis (H3) is correct: that is, belief is logically necessary for knowledge, but truth is not.

Scene Four.

The instructor and students together evaluate the third IBE as to truth-of-premises.

There should be no question that all three premises are true. Premises one and two are true, since the data and the hypotheses were largely stipulated by the instructor. Premise three is also true, for reasons already described (in scene four of act two). That is, the first hypothesis has explanatory power to the same significant but limited degree as the third hypothesis, and each has more explanatory power than the second hypothesis has with respect to the data. However, the third hypothesis is simpler than the first hypothesis. So, the target hypothesis (H3, that belief is logically necessary for knowledge but truth is not) has theoretical virtues to a higher degree overall than any alternative competitor hypothesis (H1 and H2) has with respect to the data about Adam's ignorance (E1) and Beth's nonignorance (E2).

Scene Five.

The instructor and students together evaluate the third IBE as to strength-of-inference, first noncomparatively and then comparatively.

Notwithstanding the truth of the premises, the inference from the premises to the conclusion of the IBE is too weak for the argument to be acceptable. The instructor helps students to see the weakness of the inference by pointing out the following: For one thing, even though the target hypothesis has theoretical virtues to a higher degree overall than either of its competitors has with respect to the data, the target hypothesis does not account for all or even most of the data and so is not a very powerful explanation of the data. Furthermore, the argument mentions only a limited number and variety of data. Finally, the competition to which the argument subjects the target hypothesis is not very vigorous, though it is more vigorous than the competition in the first IBE.

The instructor shows students that the inference in the third IBE has essentially the same strength as the inference in the second IBE. The data are the same in both, the explanatory power of each target hypothesis with respect to its data is the same, and the vigor of the competitions in the two IBEs is the same.[13]

The instructor shows students that the inference in the third IBE is stronger than the inference in the first IBE. While the data are the same in the two IBEs and the explanatory power of each target hypothesis with respect to its data is the same, the vigor of the competition in the third IBE is greater than the vigor of the competition in the first IBE.

Scene six. The instructor and students together wonder how an advocate of the hypothesis that true belief is logically necessary for knowledge (H1) might proceed in the face of the third IBE. The instructor suggests that one might well look for additional data, specifically to justify the greater complexity of that hypothesis in comparison with the alternative hypothesis that belief is logically necessary for knowledge but truth is not (H3). Act four pursues this suggestion.

Act Four

Scene One.

The data in act four include those in act three, plus a third datum that the instructor now introduces. The instructor introduces the third datum by describing a third fictional but possible case, asking students for their intuitions about the case, and posing a why-question about the case.

> **Third case:** Chris, who did not finish school, makes and sells moonshine whisky. Chris has heard of wood alcohol, but she does not believe that it is poisonous. She honestly believes that wood alcohol in moonshine whisky is nonpoisonous. What Chris believes is not true, for wood alcohol is poisonous.

The instructor has students vote "yes" or "no" on the question of whether, given the case as described and taking the word "ignorant" in its ordinary sense, they would say that Chris is ignorant of the poisonousness of wood alcohol in the circumstances of the third case. The case is simple and uncontroversial, so the vote should be a unanimous "yes."

> **Third datum (E3):** In the circumstances of the third case, Chris is ignorant of the poisonousness of wood alcohol.

The instructor poses the why-question, "Why is Chris ignorant of the poisonousness of wood alcohol, in the circumstances of the third case?" The question expresses a desire for an explanation.

Scene Two.
The competitor hypotheses in act four are the same as those in act three.

Scene Three.
The instructor and students together construct a fourth IBE from elements already provided. The target hypothesis supported by the fourth IBE is the first hypothesis. The IBE looks like this.

> **Fourth IBE:**
>
> | (P1) | These data are to be explained: |
> |---|---|
> | (E1) | In the circumstances of the first case, Adam is ignorant of the poisonousness of wood alcohol. |
> | (E2) | In the circumstances of the second case, Beth is not ignorant of the poisonousness of wood alcohol. |
> | (E3) | In the circumstances of the third case, Chris is ignorant of the poisonousness of wood alcohol. |
> | (P2) | These competitor hypotheses are proposed to explain the data (E1, E2, and E3): |
> | (H1) | True belief is logically necessary for knowledge. |
> | (H2) | Neither truth nor belief is logically necessary for knowledge. |
> | (H3) | Belief is logically necessary for knowledge, but truth is not. |
> | (P3) | With respect to the data (E1, E2, and E3), the first hypothesis (H1) has theoretical virtues to a higher degree overall than any alternative competitor hypothesis (H2 or H3) has. |
> | (C) | So (probably), the first hypothesis (H1) is correct; that is, true belief is logically necessary for knowledge. |

Scene Four.
The instructor and students together evaluate the fourth IBE as to truth-of-premises.

There should be no question that the first two premises are true, since the data and the hypotheses were largely stipulated by the instructor. Premise three is also true, though students likely will need help to see that it is true. The instructor focuses on explanatory power and simplicity as the two most important theoretical virtues in this instance and reasons as follows. With respect to the data about Adam's ignorance (E1), Beth's nonignorance (E2), and Chris's ignorance (E3), the hypothesis that true belief is logically necessary for knowledge (H1) has greater explanatory power than the alternative hypothesis that belief is logically necessary for knowledge but truth is not (H3). (The alternative hypothesis that neither truth nor belief is logically necessary for knowledge, H2, has no explanatory power at all with respect to the data.) It is true that the third hypothesis (H3) is simpler than the first hypothesis (H1). However, explanatory power trumps simplicity in this instance. So, other things being equal, the target hypothesis (H1) has theoretical virtues to a higher degree overall than any alternative competitor hypothesis (H2 or H3) has with respect to the data (E1, E2, and E3). So, premise three is true.

The instructor helps students to see that the first hypothesis has greater explanatory power than either the second or the third hypothesis has with respect to the data. The instructor uses the handouts as aids. On the second handout is the following background belief.

> **Third background belief (B3):** In the circumstances of the third case, Chris does not believe that wood alcohol is poisonous; rather, she believes that it is nonpoisonous; but wood alcohol is poisonous.

This background belief (B3) reflects the stipulated description of the third case. From this fact it should be clear to students that this background belief, like the two other background beliefs (B1 and B2) and the auxiliary hypothesis (HA) introduced previously (in scene four of act one), is plausible and does not derive its plausibility from the competing hypotheses (H1, H2, and H3) in the IBE. Referring again to the third handout, the instructor shows students that, with the assistance of the three background beliefs and the auxiliary hypothesis, more of the data are inferable from the third hypothesis than are inferable from either the second or the third hypothesis.[14]

The instructor helps students to see that the greater explanatory power of the first hypothesis trumps the greater simplicity of the third hypothesis. Both hypotheses 'postulate entities,' that is, each imputes one or more distinguishable logically necessary conditions to knowledge. But the third hypothesis imputes only one logically necessary condition (belief) to knowledge, while the first hypothesis imputes two (truth, belief). So, the third hypothesis 'postulates entities' more parsimoniously than the first hypothesis does. Nevertheless, by imputing more logically necessary conditions to knowledge than the third hypothesis imputes, the first hypothesis is able to explain more of the data than the third hypothesis can explain. So, the greater complexity of the first hypothesis is reasonable. So, other things being equal, the target hypothesis (H1) has theoretical virtues to a higher degree overall than any alternative competitor hypothesis (H2 or H3) has with respect to the data (E1, E2, and E3). So, premise three is true.

Scene Five.
The class evaluates the fourth IBE as to strength-of-inference, first noncomparatively and then comparatively.

Notwithstanding the truth of the premises, the inference from the premises to the conclusion of the IBE is too weak for the argument to be acceptable. The instructor helps students to see the weakness of the inference by pointing out the following factors. For one thing, even though the target hypothesis has theoretical virtues to a higher degree overall than either of its competitors has with respect to the data, the target hypothesis does not account for all the data (Beth's nonignorance, E2, remains unexplained) and so is not an optimally powerful explanation of the data. Furthermore, the argument mentions only a limited number and variety of data, though it does mention more data than the first and third IBEs. Finally, the competition to which the argument subjects the target hypothesis is not very vigorous, though it is more vigorous than the competition in the first IBE.

The instructor shows students that the inference in the fourth IBE is stronger than the inference in the third IBE. The data in the fourth IBE are more numerous and more varied than the data in the third IBE, and the target hypothesis (H1) in the fourth IBE explains its data (E1, E2, and E3) to a greater extent than the target hypothesis (H3) in the third IBE explains its data (E1 and E2).

Scene Six.
The instructor and students explore how an advocate of the first hypothesis might try to strengthen the case made for that hypothesis by the fourth IBE. Noting that it is problematic for the first hypothesis that the second datum (E2, Beth's nonignorance) remains unexplained, the instructor suggests two approaches that might be tried by an advocate of the first hypothesis. One approach is to try to strengthen the fourth IBE by discarding the second datum from the first premise, on the ad hoc hypothesis that intuitions about the second case are faulty. However, the ad hoc hypothesis increases the complexity of the first hypothesis without yielding any compensating increase in genuine explanatory power. So, the first approach does not succeed in strengthening the fourth IBE. Another approach is to add complexity to the first hypothesis in some other, non-ad-hoc way, to generate sufficient additional genuine explanatory power to account for the second datum. Act five pursues the latter approach.

Act Five

Scene One.
The data in act five are the same as those in act four.

Scene Two.
The competitor hypotheses in act five are six new hypotheses that the instructor now introduces.

> **Fourth hypothesis (H4):** True belief is logically necessary and sufficient for knowledge.
> **Fifth hypothesis (H5):** True belief is logically necessary but not sufficient for knowledge.
> **Sixth hypothesis (H6):** Neither truth nor belief is logically necessary for knowledge, but belief is logically sufficient.
> **Seventh hypothesis (H7):** Neither truth nor belief is logically necessary for knowledge, and belief is not logically sufficient.
> **Eighth hypothesis (H8):** Belief is logically necessary and suffi-

cient for knowledge, but truth is not logically necessary.
Ninth hypothesis (H9): Belief is logically necessary but not sufficient for knowledge, and truth is not logically necessary.

If the fourth hypothesis is correct, then a correct answer to the why-questions about Adam, Beth, and Chris is: "Because true belief is logically necessary and sufficient for knowledge." And so on, with the necessary changes, for the fifth through ninth hypotheses.

The instructor notes that the old hypotheses are embedded in the new hypotheses, in the following sense. H1 (that true belief is logically necessary for knowledge) is deducible from H4 and also from H5. H2 (that neither truth nor belief is logically necessary for knowledge) is deducible from H6 and also from H7. H3 (that belief is logically necessary for knowledge, but truth is not) is deducible from H8 and also from H9.

Scene Three.
The instructor and students together construct a fifth IBE from elements already provided. The target hypothesis supported by the fifth IBE is the fourth hypothesis, as follows:

Fifth IBE:

(P1)   These data are to be explained:

(E1)   In the circumstances of the first case, Adam is ignorant of the poisonousness of wood alcohol.

(E2)   In the circumstances of the second case, Beth is not ignorant of the poisonousness of wood alcohol.

(E3)   In the circumstances of the third case, Chris is ignorant of the poisonousness of wood alcohol.

(P2)   These competitor hypotheses are proposed to explain the data (E1, E2, and E3):

(H4)   True belief is logically necessary and sufficient for knowledge.

(H5)   True belief is logically necessary but not sufficient for knowledge.

(H6)   Neither truth nor belief is logically necessary for knowledge, but belief is logically sufficient.

(H7)   Neither truth nor belief is logically necessary for knowledge, and belief is not logically sufficient.

(H8)   Belief is logically necessary and sufficient for knowledge, but truth is not logically necessary.

(H9)   Belief is logically necessary but not sufficient for knowledge, and truth is not logically necessary.

(P3)   With respect to the data (E1, E2, and E3), the fourth hypothesis (H4) has theoretical virtues to a higher degree overall than any alternative competitor hypothesis (H5 through H9) has.

(C)   So (probably), the fourth hypothesis (H4) is correct; that is, true belief is logically necessary and sufficient for knowledge.

Scene Four.

The instructor and students together evaluate the fifth IBE as to truth-of-premises.

There should be no question that the first two premises are true, since the data and the hypotheses were stipulated by the instructor. Premise three is also true, though students likely will need help to see that it is true. The instructor focuses on explanatory power as the overridingly important theoretical virtue in this instance and reasons as follows. Only the hypothesis that true belief is logically necessary and sufficient for knowledge (H4) has optimal explanatory power with respect to the data about Adam's ignorance (E1), Beth's nonignorance (E2), and Chris's ignorance (E3), since it is only from that competitor hypothesis that all the data are inferable. So, other things being equal, the target hypothesis (H4) has theoretical virtues to a higher degree overall than any alternative competitor hypothesis (H5 through H9) has with respect to the data (E1, E2, and E3). That is, premise three is true.

The instructor helps students to see that only the fourth hypothesis has optimal explanatory power with respect to the data. Referring again to the third handout, the instructor shows students how the data are or are not inferable from the various competitor hypotheses. With the assistance of the three background beliefs (B1, B2, and B2) and the auxiliary hypothesis (HA) introduced previously, all of the data are inferable from the fourth hypothesis, and some but not all of the data are inferable from each of the other competitor hypotheses except the seventh hypothesis, which is an irrelevant hypothesis.

The instructor points out that the sixth and eighth hypotheses are each incompatible with the datum of Chris's ignorance (E3).[15] In other words, the third case, which generates the intuitions reported in that datum, is a counterexample to the sixth hypothesis and to the eighth hypothesis.

Scene Five.
The instructor and students together evaluate the fifth IBE as to strength-of-inference, first noncomparatively and then comparatively; and then they reassess the fourth IBE.

Notwithstanding the truth of the premises, the inference from the premises to the conclusion of the fifth IBE is too weak for the argument to be acceptable. The instructor helps students to see the weakness of the inference by pointing out the following factors. For one thing, the argument mentions only a limited number and variety of data, though it does mention more data than the first and third IBEs. Furthermore, the competition to which the argument subjects the target hypothesis is not very vigorous, though it is more vigorous than the competition in the first, third, and fourth IBEs.

The instructor shows students that the inference in the fifth IBE is stronger than the inference in the fourth IBE, as the latter was previously assessed (in scene five of act four). For one thing, the target hypothesis (H4) in the fifth IBE explains its data (E1, E2, and E3) to a greater extent than the target hypothesis (H1) in the fourth IBE explains its data (E1, E2, and E3). Furthermore, the vigor of the competition in the fifth IBE is greater than the vigor of the competition in the fourth IBE.

The instructor points out that, since the first hypothesis (H1) is deducible from the target hypothesis (H4) of the fifth IBE, that IBE supports the first hypothesis by supporting its target hypothesis. Since the inference in the fifth IBE is stronger than the inference in the fourth IBE (as previously assessed) while the premises in both IBEs are all true, it appears that the first hypothesis is supported more strongly by the fifth IBE than by the fourth IBE.

The instructor shows students that the fifth IBE requires reassessment of the fourth IBE, because the fifth IBE exhibits a theoretical virtue of the first hypothesis that was not taken into account when the fourth IBE was previously assessed. That virtue is coherence. The fifth IBE shows that the first hypothesis (H1), to a higher degree than any of its competitors (H2 and H3) in the fourth IBE, coheres with the best more-inclusive explanatory hypothesis.[16] The fourth IBE must now be reassessed, both as to truth-of-premises and as to strength-of-inference. By exhibiting a theoretical virtue of the first hypothesis that was not taken into account when the fourth IBE was previously assessed, the fifth IBE gives additional support for the truth of premise three of the fourth IBE. But the fifth IBE also increases the strength of the inference in the fourth IBE in two ways. First, since the competitor hypotheses from the fourth IBE are multiply embedded in the competitor hypotheses in the fifth IBE, the vigor of the competition in the fourth IBE is indirectly increased by the competition in the fifth IBE. Moreover, since the more-inclusive hypothesis (H4) in which the first hypothesis is embedded is an optimal explanation of the data (E1, E2, and E3) in the fourth IBE, the explanatory power of the first hypothesis with respect to that data is indirectly increased.

Scene six.
The instructor and students now conclude the exercise.

Epilogue

In the exercise just concluded, students practiced identifying and constructing IBEs using an explicit IBE argument-form. Students also practiced evaluating IBEs using explicit criteria for evaluating an IBE as to truth-of-premises and (both noncomparatively and comparatively) as to strength-of-inference. All the IBEs were relatively simple and basic concepts and procedures were exhibited clearly and highlighted. All the IBEs were specifically philosophical and relevant to the content of the epistemology course.

The conclusion of the final IBE was Theaetetus's hypothesis that knowledge is merely true opinion. So, at the end of the exercise, students are ready to rejoin the traditional curriculum in their studies of the development of the analysis of knowledge. From Socrates' rejection of Theaetetus's hypothesis, through Gettier's rejection of the justified-true-belief analysis, to the growing contemporary proliferation of analyses and repudiations of analysis, the instructor and students will find many opportunities to recognize, construct, and evaluate IBEs in their epistemology course. The instructor will regularly use these opportunities to reinforce students' comprehension of the concepts and procedures learned in the exercise.

III. Conclusion

Much more could be said about IBE and about explanation, in particular, about such meta-epistemological issues as the nature of explanation and of inference to the best explanation, and about the justification of inference to the best explanation and of explanationism—probably obligatory additional topics in an epistemology course emphasizing explanationist methods. However, it has not been my purpose in this paper to defend any views about such issues or about how to teach them. My only purpose here has been to describe a method for teaching graduate and upper-level undergraduate philosophy students how to recognize, construct, and evaluate inferences to the best philosophical explanation.*

NOTES

* I am grateful for assistance from Jody Graham, Eric Marcus, Francis Remedios, Michael Watkins, and especially Tziporah Kasachkoff.
    1. For discussions of IBE and of explanationism in philosophy, and further references, see R. Fumerton, "Inference to the Best Explanation," in J. Dancy and E. Sosa, eds., *A Companion to Epistemology* (Oxford: Blackwell, 1992), pp. 207–209; W. G. Lycan, "Explanationism," in T. Honderich, ed., *The Oxford Companion to Philosophy* (Oxford: Oxford University Press, 1995), p. 263; W. G. Lycan, "Explanation and Epistemology," in P. K. Moser, ed., *The Oxford Handbook of Epistemology* (Oxford: Oxford University Press, 2002), pp. 408–33; P. K. Moser, D. H. Mulder, and J. D. Trout, *The Theory of Knowledge* (Oxford: Oxford University Press, 1998); and J. Vogel, "Inference to the Best Explanation," in *Routledge Encyclopedia of Philosophy Online:* http://www.rep.routledge.com/philosophy/cgi-bin/article.cgi?it=P025>((accessed 31 Dec 2002).

2. The method assumes that students have some: necessary/sufficient conditions, deductive/nondeductive arguments, validity/strength vs. soundnes of arguments, necessary vs. contingent propositions, logically necessary/sufficient conditions vs. contingently necessary/sufficient conditions. For ideas about teaching IBE to lower-level undergraduate students, see J. Eflin, "Teaching 'Inference to the Best Explanation,'" *Teaching Philosophy*, vol. 17 (1994), pp. 151–60; and E. Sober, *Core Questions in Philosophy*, 3rd ed. (Upper Saddle River, NJ: Prentice Hall, 2001).

3. I will venture to assert that knowledge is true opinion." (*Theaetetus* 187b, trans. B. Jowett, in P. K. Moser and A. vander Nat, eds., *Human Knowledge*, 3rd ed. [Oxford: Oxford University Press, 2003], p. 48.)

4. See C. Sartwell, "Why Knowledge Is Merely True Belief," *The Journal of Philosophy*, vol. 89 (1992), pp. 167–80.

5. The glossary gives a brief account for each of these: background belief; counterexample to a hypothesis; data; hypothesis (ad hoc, auxiliary, competitor, relevant, target); theoretical virtues (explanatory power, simplicity, coherence).

6. For a survey of theories of explanation, and further references, see J. Woodward, "Explanation," in P. Machamer and M. Silberstein, eds., *The Blackwell Guide to the Philosophy of Science* (Oxford: Blackwell, 2002), pp. 37–54.

7. Except for the five IBEs constructed in the exercise, the second handout contains every exhibit in acts one through five that has a run-in and boldfaced heading ending with a colon, for example, "**First case:**," "**Second datum (E2):**," "**Third hypothesis (H3):**," and so on.

8. If any students do vote "no," the instructor should summarily disqualify all "no" votes and declare (with tongue clearly in cheek and with clear actual respect for students and their opinions) that anyone who voted "no" either did not understand the question or was being perverse. Discussion of this action should be deferred until scene four of act one.

9. On the second handout, this datum is given as follows: "The first datum (E1) is whatever your answer is to the question 'In the circumstances of the first case, is Adam ignorant of the poisonousness of wood alcohol?' ('yes, he is,' or 'no, he is not')." Subsequent data (E2, E3) are given the same way on the handout, with the necessary changes.

10. "Explanations are answers to the question 'why?'" (E. Nagel, *The Structure of Science* [New York: Harcourt, Brace & World, 1961], p. 15) See also S. Bromberger, "Why-Questions," in R. G. Colodny, ed., *Mind and Cosmos* (Pittsburgh PA: University of Pittsburgh Press, 1966), pp. 86–111. The question now posed by the instructor is merely rhetorical because the class is only going through the motions of a methodological exercise.

11. Note that neither H1 nor H2 has the form of a nomological law,

neither hypothesis is a scientific hypothesis, and neither hypothesis offers a scientific explanation of the data. Rather, H1 and H2 are philosophical hypotheses that give philosophical explanations of the data.

12. If students do challenge the first premise on the grounds that their votes about Adam and Beth were not unanimous, the instructor should take the opportunity to discuss the concept of an ad hoc hypothesis. The instructor's earlier declaration (that anyone who voted contrary to the instructor's expectations either did not understand the question or was being perverse) functions now as an ad hoc hypothesis to protect the target hypothesis. The instructor should explain that ad hoc hypotheses weaken an IBE, since they increase the complexity of the target hypothesis without increasing its explanatory power. The instructor should nevertheless continue, with all due respect and only for the purposes of the exercise, to maintain the ad hoc hypothesis in this instance.

13. It is not relevant here that the target hypothesis in the third IBE (H3) is simpler than the target hypothesis in the second IBE (H1), since H3 and H1 do not compete in their respective roles as target hypotheses of different IBEs. H3 and H1 do compete in their roles as alternative competitor hypotheses mentioned in the third premise of the second IBE, and they similarly compete in the third IBE. H3's greater simplicity gives it an advantage over H1 in both competitions. That advantage ensures the falsehood of the third premise in the second IBE and the truth of the third premise in the third IBE.

14. E1 is inferable from H1 via B1 and HA, and E3 is inferable from H1 via B3 and HA. E1 is also inferable from H3 via B1 and HA. But, even with the assistance of the background beliefs and the auxiliary hypothesis, E3 is not inferable from H3. As well, no data are inferable from H2, and E2 is not inferable from any competitor hypothesis.

15. The falsehood of H6 and of H8 is inferable from E3 via B3 and HA. Each of the other four competitor hypotheses in the fifth IBE is compatible with all the data, though H7 is irrelevant.

16. Note that a hypothesis in which H1 is embedded (H4) prevails against its (H4's) explanatory competitors (H5 through H9) in the fifth IBE. On the other hand, none of the hypotheses in which H1's competitors (H2 and H3) in the fourth IBE are embedded (H5 through H9) prevails against its (H5's through H9's, as the case may be) competitors in the fifth IBE.

PART XII
Teaching Philosophy of Gender

Chapter 24

Teaching Gender Issues—Philosophically*

Celia Wolf-Devine

Many disciplines deal with issues to which gender differences are relevant. Sociologists study family structures, lawyers try to figure out whether laws that treat women and men differently are constitutional, and medicine and health care address problems having to do with reproduction. But courses that take gender as their central focus are most often taught in Women's Studies programs or English departments. Those teaching such courses are, generally speaking, not philosophically trained, and have often been accused (with at least some justice) of being too rhetorical and political in their approach, with the result that some philosophers have come to regard the field of gender studies as intellectually unserious. Philosophers who do offer courses that focus on gender issues usually do so under the heading of applied ethics, a state of affairs I regard as unfortunate because gender issues, like many other issues in applied ethics, are also concerned with broader theoretical issues such as the relative roles of reason and emotion in moral judgment, central questions in metaphysics and social philosophy, and even philosophy of religion.

Since Socrates, philosophers have always been interested in studying and analyzing contested concepts, concepts whose employment engages deep differences of outlook and evaluation.

'Male' and 'female' (much like 'justice') are two prime examples of such concepts. Those who take them to be mere social constructions and those who regard them as categories in a broadly Kantian sense (organizing and structuring the way we perceive the world in deep ways) agree that sex and gender categories are central to our self-understanding. (I shall use 'sex' to refer to biological facts and 'gender' to refer to what a given cultural tradition makes of these facts.)

The deepest philosophical issue about sex and gender concerns the question of the moral importance of our existence as bodily creatures. Should we view our physical, animal nature—including sex differences and our characteristic mode of reproduction—as a prison from which we must be liberated or a source of biologically grounded norms to which we must conform our behavior in order to live virtuous and happy lives.

In the first part of this essay, I explain the way I structure my course on Philosophy of Sex and Gender, showing how such issues connect with broader philosophical issues. In the second part I address the pedagogical issues that arise in teaching a course on sex and gender issues, suggesting ways to structure such a course and create an atmosphere that is as open, as relaxed and as conducive to dialogue as possible. My remarks draw on my experience in the classroom—I have taught a course on Philosophy of Sex and Gender for a number of years—and on what I have learned from my struggle to put together an anthology on sex and gender that would fairly represent the various outlooks at work in our current debates and pitch the introductory materials and study questions in an even-handed way.[1]

Part I: Philosophy and Gender Issues

The question of the cognitive role of emotions arises particularly strongly in this area where emotions are strong, complicated, and sometimes in tension with what the person making moral judgments regards as the requirements of rationality. For example, a man might be rationally convinced that bisexuality is the ideal form of sexuality and thus wish to embrace it, but be quite unable to conjure up the appropriate emotional and physical responses to other men. Or a woman might be rationally convinced that her womanliness does not depend on having children but still feel incomplete without a child and succumb, on that account, to what is sometimes called "baby fever."

No doubt, there are some cases where we would be inclined to trust reason over emotion, as, say, when we discount feelings of repugnance to interracial sex (if we have such feelings) on the grounds that we can find no rational justification for them. But there are also cases where we would be inclined to trust our emotions despite our believing them to be in conflict with reason—as would be the case, for example, were we to trust our spontaneous revulsion toward having sex with orangutans (if we have such revulsion), even, that is, were we persuaded by Peter Singer's arguments that it is irrational to regard having sex with a member of another species as morally wrong.[2] Are the deep feelings people have about sex/gender issues only obstacles to clear thought, to be screened out so far as possible? Or should we regard them as revelatory of deep truths about ourselves as sexual creatures? I begin the course with a discussion of these sorts of questions.

Consideration of the proper roles of emotion and reason leads naturally to the question of whether there is any validity to the stereotypical judgment that men are more rational than women and women are more emotional than men. In turn, this question points one in the direction of the most pervasive question in the study of sex-and-gender: the status of male-female differences. Some people find the difference between the sexes a matter of mere "plumbing,"[3] not linked in any deep way with who we are, like the color of our eyes or (more controversially) our skin color. Others, such as Mary Daly,[4] attribute cosmic importance to the difference.

Thinking about what it is to be male or female clearly involves thinking about some traditional metaphysical issues. For example, the phenomenon of transsexualism raises interesting questions about the relationship between mind and body. How are we to make sense of the claim, made by some transsexuals, that they have always felt that they were in the wrong type of body—that despite the fact that their bodies were male (or female), their souls were female (or male)?

Ethical questions about sex, reproduction and family structure quickly involve us in thinking about social philosophy. To enable students to understand how their thinking about sex, reproduction and family is affected by their background assumptions about social philosophy, I give them some readings on liberalism and communitarianism (listed below). I also connect these with Carol Gilligan's concepts of the masculine and feminine "voice" in ethics,[5] arguing that liberal individualism is a social philosophy expressive of the "masculine voice," while the feminine voice as defined by Gilligan has strong affinities with communitarianism, and encouraging students to think about the connections between ethical theory and social philosophy along these lines.[6]

Finally, issues in philosophy of religion also come into play when reflecting about gender issues. Whether we come to these issues from a naturalistic or a theistic perspective makes a difference in a number of different ways. It is not just a matter of whether one takes certain behaviors to be enjoined or forbidden by God, or whether God should be understood through gendered concepts such as "Father" or "Mother" (important though these questions are). Human beings characteristically experience a tension between their animality and their humanity, and associate their humanity especially with their moral and spiritual aspirations. And sex is one area of our lives in which we can experience this sort of tension particularly acutely.

Part II

Goals of the Course
At the start of the class I make it clear that I expect students will disagree both with each other and with me on many issues, and that I anticipate that this will still be the case at the end of the class, but that I hope that whatever views they emerge with, they will at least have learned to understand those who disagree with them, and to seek common ground with them. Not all differences necessarily prove unreconcilable, of course; often one can convince others by offering them arguments or reasons that had not

occurred to them before, challenging them through questioning, or showing that their presuppositions actually lead to a conclusion different from the one that they assert.

Course Structure and Readings

The course I teach is structured along the lines indicated above. I begin with the methodological issue of the proper roles of reason and emotion in thinking about gender issues. I have students read the following: selections from D. H. Lawrence's "A Propos of Lady Chatterly's Lover,"[7] which defends the importance of the emotions rooted in the body for understanding sexuality, and selections from Janet Radcliffe Richards' *The Skeptical Feminist*[8] which defends the importance of reason in thinking about gender issues, and criticizes the antirationalist stance taken by some feminists. If one wants to go into these issues more deeply, one might look at Genevieve Lloyd's *The Man of Reason*,[9] and Janet Moulton's "A Paradigm of Philosophy."[10]

I begin with the story of a transsexual, and have my students read selections from Jan Morris's autobiography, *My Conundrum*,[11] a reading that raises interesting questions about the differences and connections between sex and gender. We then look at the traditionalist position on the relationship between sex and gender, reading a selection by Anthony Mastroeni, S. J., who argues that, on philosophical grounds, it is impossible to have a gender different from the sex of one's body,[12] and a selection from Stephen Clark's *Man and Woman in Christ*[13] in which Clark points out certain culturally universal sex role patterns, arguing that these are in some sense natural or rooted in human nature. Students then read two essays by cultural radicals who regard gender as a social construction not rooted in biology: Suzanne Kessler and Wendy McKenna's *Gender: an Ethnomethodological Approach*[14] which emphasizes the role of social construction of gender in the most radical way, and Richard Wasserstrom's *Philosophy and Social Issues*[15] which argues that an ideal society would be one in which people's sex was of no more importance for how they were treated—in both personal life and in society—than the color of their eyes. We conclude with a selection from Mary Midgley and Judith Hughes' *Women's Choices: Philosophical Problems Facing*

Feminism,[16] (in which it is argued that although biology does indeed influence our behavior, there is still room for freedom of action), and Roger Scruton's "Sex and Gender"[17] in which Scruton argues for gender as a social construction but one that we cannot and should not eliminate.

Since the topic of sex naturally leads to a discussion of the sexual interaction of two or more persons, the natural progression is to a discussion of the some of the various issues that arise when people interact sexually. I begin this section by describing four different world views (paganism, Manicheanism, naturalism and the Jewish/Christian worldview) that underlie the way we think about particular issues of sexual morality. Though the readings in this section do not fall into neat categories, they nonetheless give students a sense of the multiplicity of views that different people have towards sex. Among these readings are Bertrand Russell's *Marriage and Morals,*[18] which is a good example of naturalism; Andrea Dworkin's *Intercourse*[19] which provides a rather gut-wrenching account of sexual penetration as inherently degrading; Thomas Nagel's "Sexual Perversion,"[20] Richard Mohr's "Why Sex is Private: Gays and the Police," which argues for the importance of sexual privacy while leaving open the possibility for multiple partners and public sex in designated "gay cruising" zones;[21] and Richard Connell's "A Defense of Humanae Vitae," which offers a very traditional biologistic natural law argument for the importance of being open to reproduction in sexual activity.[22]

We conclude this section of the course by looking at differences between gay and lesbian culture to help students reflect on the differences between male and female sexuality and homosexuality. We read a chapter of Richard Rodriquez's *Days of Obligation*[23] which focuses on Castro Street gay culture, and a section from Arlene Stein's, *Sex and Sensibility: Stories of a Lesbian Generation,* which discusses the difference between "old gay" lesbian culture (identified as based on desire) and the "new gay" culture (prevalent in the 1970s and 1980s) which recommends itself as a choice to all women for reasons that are political, namely, as an extension of one's commitment to feminism.[24] The very last reading in the unit is "The ladder of eros" from Diotima's speech to

Socrates in the Symposium, which emphasizes the spiritual dimension of eros.

Since one of the most important issues that arises from the sexual interaction between men and women is the possibility of reproduction, the class then turns to a discussion of contraception, abortion, and some of the new reproductive technologies. I have students read the following: Sally Tisdale's article "We Do Abortions Here," about life in an abortion clinic,[25] Thomson's "A Defense of Abortion,"[26] and my own essay "Abortion and the Feminine Voice."[27] Although contraception is not a hot topic in the news these days, discussing it brings out certain important issues with broader ramifications. How closely is the meaning of sexual intercourse connected with reproduction? Should the body be regarded as a machine to be modified to suit the purposes of its "owner," or should we try to be guided by the body's immanent norms? Can a sharp line be drawn between contraception and abortion (IUD's, for example, function as abortifacients), and does widely available contraception lead to more or fewer abortions? Related readings here are Rosemary Radford Ruether's article, "Birth Control and the Ideals of Marital Sexuality,"[28] and a piece by Cormac Burke entitled "Marriage and Contraception."[29] On surrogate mothering, we read a selection from John Roberston's *Children of Choice*[30] which presents a utilitarian defense of surrogacy, and two opponents of surrogate mothering: Jean Bethke Elshtain, who presents a communitarian feminist critique of surrogacy in "Technology as Destiny,"[31] and Hilde and James Lindemann Nelson's essay "Cutting Motherhood in Two."[32]

Our discussion of reproduction leads naturally to a discussion of family structure. We focus on the arguments for and against the traditional family. Relevant readings on this topic may be drawn from the following: Donald Hatcher, "Why It Is Immoral to Be a Housewife," in which an existential critique of the family is presented and arguments made by Simone de Beauvoir are summarized[33] and a selection from Sandra Bartky's, *Femininity and Domination*[34] in which Bartky argues from a Marxist perspective that women are disempowered in the traditional family by the exploitation of their 'emotional labor.' We then turn to Susan Moller

Okin's critique of the traditional division of labor in families in her *Justice, Gender and the Family*.[35] As background to understanding her claim that the traditional family is unjust to women, we read short selections from John Rawls' *Theory of Justice*[36] and from Michael Sandel's communitarian critique of Rawls on the family from his *Liberalism and the Limits of Justice*.[37] Responses to these criticisms of the traditional family are taken from Phyllis Schlafly's, *Power of the Positive Woman*,[38] Sylvia Hewlett's book *When the Bough Breaks*,[39] and another essay by Jean Bethke Elshtain entitled "Feminists Against the Family."[40]

Turning to the political arena, we look at two important political movements in the Twentieth Century—the feminist movement and the gay- and lesbian-rights movement. I use concrete issues such as sexual harassment, affirmative action for women, and same sex marriage to illustrate the theoretical issues, such as (in the case of same sex marriage) whether or not heterosexuality ought to be viewed as normative and (in the case of feminist projects) whether feminism is a movement for fairness or merely the political pursuit of women's interests (and if the latter, whether all women are to be viewed as having the same interests).

Readings for this section of the course are: Timothy Murphy's "Homosex/Ethics,"[41] which argues that there are no morally significant differences between homosex and heterosex; Michael Novak's "Men Without Women,"[42] which argues that there are important benefits to individuals and to society as a whole that are obtainable only by the struggle of learning to know and live with the other sex; Alison Jaggar's classic essay "Political Philosophies of Women's Liberation,"[43] which defines four different types of feminism, and Juli Loesch Wiley's article "Reweaving Society," which advocates a communitarian sort of feminism which she calls "social feminism."[44] On sexual harassment, students read a chapter from Catharine MacKinnon's *Feminism Unmodified*,[45] and a chapter from Katie Roiphe's book *The Morning After: Sex, Fear and Feminism*.[46] On affirmative action, I use Laura Purdy's piece, "In Defense of Hiring Apparently Less Qualified Women,"[47] and Louis Katzner's essay "Is the Favoring of Women and Blacks in Employment and Educational Opportunities Justified?"[48] On same sex marriage, students read Robert George's "Same Sex Marriage and Moral Neutrality,"[49] and David Coolidge's "The Question of Marriage."[50] I also use several essays from Andrew Sullivan's book on same sex marriage,[51] as well as his own essay entitled "The Conservative Case for Same Sex Marriage," from *Virtually Normal.*[52]

The course ends with discussion of the way in which gender concepts have been applied to a reality transcending the merely human. Thinking about ultimate reality through gendered concepts is not limited to theistic religions of course (consider, for example, the *yang* and the *yin* in Taoism), but in my class I focus on the following questions: "Is God properly described as 'Father?'" "Does the practice of calling God 'Father' sanction patriarchy, suggesting, perhaps that we should call God 'Mother' or something gender-neutral instead?" The readings I assign in connection with the question of gender and ultimate reality are: a selection from Mircea Eliade's *The Sacred and the Profane: the Nature of Religion,*[53] in which Eliade discusses sky gods (conceived as male) and earth goddesses; the first three chapters of *Genesis,* Carol Christ's "Why Women Need the Goddess,"[54] Juli Loesch Wiley's essays "On the Fatherhood of God," and "Is 'God the Mother' Just as Good." which defend calling God "Father,"[55] and a selection from *She Who Is* by Elizabeth Johnson.[56] I also include Rosemary Ruether's "Ecofeminism: Symbolic and Social Connections of the Oppression of Women and the Domination of Nature,"[57] Edith Black's commentary on Genesis,[58] a selection from Susanne Heine's *Christianity and the Goddesses,*[59] a piece entitled "Traditional Judaism and Feminine Spirituality" by Tamar Frankiel[60] and Richard Davis' "Making Inclusive Language Inclusive: A Christian Gay Man's View."[61]

Depending on time, class size, and student interest, I think it is valuable to have some discussion of the ways that different cultures view sex and gender and the extent to which these views diverge from our own (though, of course, to be accurate, there is no one view that can be said to be "our" view). I teach a small advanced class, so I have interested students do presentations on other religions at the end.

Some Suggestions for Better Teaching

Students are not only entitled to hear what opposing parties have to say for their positions but also respond best when offered both sides of an issue before being asked to make up their own minds. So if one is putting together a set of readings, one should be careful not to 'wall out' one's opponents. In discussing gender issues, for example, one should not simply assume that gender differences are socially constructed rather than natural and then proceed to raise the question of how this construction occurs.

1. Get a sense of where your students are 'coming from'

In planning a class on sex and gender issues, one should begin by thinking about one's own students' social and cultural background and the pedagogical problems this might present for the teacher who wants to encourage reflection on what are likely to be emotionally-laden issues. I devote the first day of class largely to asking students the following sorts of questions:

(a) Do they feel comfortable expressing their views on gender issues to other students not only outside of class but also in class?

(b) Are there perspectives on gender issues that the students feel they have not been exposed to (and would like exposure to)?

(c) What topics are they most interested in?

Although I teach at a Catholic school, sometimes I have been surprised to find students saying that they find that people with traditional Christian views feel inhibited about expressing them. There is no easy solution to this problem, but it helps if you lay out clearly and calmly the reasons that have been given for more traditional positions and the arguments with which one might defend them. Then, seeing their opinions treated with respect, students will feel included and may venture to contribute their own ideas more. (Many freshman orientation sessions involve sensitizing students to racial and gender issues, sometimes in a way that puts emotional pressure on students to act and think in ways that have become associated with 'political correctness.'

Instructors should familiarize themselves with the orientation programs in their colleges and should be aware that students may, as a result of their orientation experience, be unwilling to express their real feelings for fear of being thought to be 'bad' people.)

Many students who have previously taken courses on sex and gender will have taken them through Women's Studies programs, so again, it helps to be aware of the approach taken in such courses at one's school, since this will affect the expectations students bring to the class. Sometimes such courses give students the impression that gender issues are the territory of women and that men have no right to have opinions about them, and it is important to counteract this right at the start, by making all students feel welcome, and communicating to male students that I am genuinely interested in their perspective on the issues. For gender-related issues have important effects on men, albeit effects that (typically) differ from those experienced by women. Men, for example, often experience feelings of powerlessness, anger and guilt in the wake of an abortion, and I find that opening up the question of whether fathers should have a say in the woman's choice to abort always triggers a lively and thoughtful discussion.

I do not distribute a full syllabus at the start of the course because I want first to get a sense of where the students in that particular class 'are coming from.' Instead, at the end of the first class session, I have the students in the class write down the questions that they would like to have answered during the course.[62] It is only after the midterm—by which time the students have written two short papers, one in which they take and defend a position on the question of whether Jan Morris was a man or a woman, both before and after surgery,[63] and one that indicates which of the four worldviews discussed in the Sexuality section of the course most closely approximates their own—that I hand out the syllabus for the rest of the course in detail. Depending on the eagerness and willingness of students to do presentations or engage in class debates, I schedule those in, devoting three or four 1 and 1/4 hour sessions to them.

2. Respect the Consciences of All Students

It is particularly important to allow students the freedom of conscience to hold their own opinions about gender issues because they have in all likelihood been subjected already to strong emotional pressure to conform to certain views (be they religious or "politically correct") and a philosophy course should provide a clear space in which to think out their own views. All too often they are paralyzed by the fear of offending anyone and want to give everybody what they want. So they fear to form their own opinions clearly at all. One thing that helps is to draw a clear distinction between what it means to form an opinion (which is good) and how this is different from going around indiscriminately expressing one's opinions in wounding ways (which is not good). Trying to placate everyone lest you be thought to be a bad person is a habit of mind that stifles philosophical reflection. For example, questions like what sort of family is best for children, or whether a male to female transsexual has in fact become a woman, should be answered on the basis of evidence and philosophical reflection, and not on the basis of whether or not someone will feel offended if we were to assert that some form of family other than the one they are living in would be more in the interests of children, or question the claim of the postoperative transsexual to be a woman.[64]

I make it clear that I will proceed on the assumption that all my students are basically well-intentioned, even if in need of assistance in sorting out and thinking about the issues under discussion. In discussing issues such as sexual harassment, for example, one should try not to focus on egregious examples of male misconduct, but rather get students to talk constructively about how men and women can communicate better about their preferences and intentions. It may be desirable to have students initially discuss what they think constitutes sexual harassment in same sex groups,[65] and then have them share with the entire class what they concluded in their groups. Structuring discussions this way helps bring to the surface all sorts of—sometimes unacknowledged—cultural expectations (for example, that in regard to sexual matters men should be a bit persistent and women should not say yes too quickly). Making views, expectations, and habits of thought explicit helps both men and women students achieve some distance from their own perspective and so helps towards alleviating what could otherwise become too adversarial a discussion about appropriate sexual behavior.

3. Be Careful about Labels; Discourage Crude or Inflammatory Language

Using labels to describe the various positions that people may take on gender issues is almost always misleading (and sometimes insulting). For example, "liberal" and "conservative" are virtually useless. Especially, one should be careful not to present favored and disfavored views using value-loaded language by referring, for example, to favored views as "progressive" and disfavored ones as "reactionary," or by referring to defenders of certain gender roles as "sexists" or to feminists as "women's libbers." As much as possible, one should strive in the classroom to use descriptions of positions that those holding them would accept, and encourage students to do the same.

Furthermore, avoiding in oneself and discouraging in others the use of graphic, crude, or inflammatory language will help keep the emotional temperature of the classroom down. Even when some of the readings employ words like "fuck" (as Andrea Dworkin does), it is not good to permit their use in the classroom. On the other hand, it is not good to retreat into highly abstract language about "persons" and "relationships" while overlooking the concrete physical reality of sex. Although one may think, as I do, that Camille Paglia,[66] goes too far in the direction of making explicit the dark, irrational and atavistic side of sexuality (such as fantasies of vaginas with teeth, for example), omitting the atavistic and primal side of sexuality is not a good idea if one wants students to acquire a balanced perspective of the full spectrum of different views about sex that people actually have. In discussing abortion, likewise, it is essential to appreciate the physical facts—in particular the facts about fetal development and the concrete details about how abortions are performed—in order to responsibly engage in moral reflection about it.

4. Encourage Students to Explore Moderate Positions

In order to encourage nuanced thinking and because there are almost always more than two alternative possible positions that an intelligent person might take on any particular controversial issue, students ought to be weaned away from thinking that every question admits of only a yes or no answer. On the abortion issue, for example, there are clearly positions other than just "pro-life" and "pro-choice" that one can take. Indeed, any number of compromise positions between these two extremes is possible, and if one separates clearly questions about morality and questions about what the law should be, then the number of different positions that one might plausibly argue for regarding the permissibility of abortion becomes even greater. Students, however, should be discouraged from too quickly just "splitting the difference" on every issue and trying to satisfy everyone as this often results in incoherent thinking.

5. Get Students to Think Concretely about the Implications of Views

One technique for getting students to integrate what they are reading into their everyday lives is to get them to imagine in concrete detail just what it would be like to live in a society where some writer's ideal society were realized, how living in such a society would be different from the way they lead their current lives,[67] and whether they would like to live in such a society. I use this technique to help them think more clearly about Okin's ideal of a genderless society, or Wasserstrom's nonsexist society.

Techniques for Structuring Discussion

In my class on Sex and Gender, as in all my classes, I use a combination of lecture and discussion. To encourage discussion, I do the following:

First, for all the assigned readings, I hand out, in advance of the assignment, two types of study questions—those that direct students to the most important points in the text so that they can be sure to focus on what is important, and those that require them to do one of the following: connect the reading with their own lives, indicate how one of the authors of a different, previous, reading assignment might respond to the salient points made by

the author of the current reading, take and defend a position regarding a particular issue discussed in the reading, or formulate a
thoughtful question about the issue under discussion in the current reading.

Second, I often use the following technique: I divide students
into groups of between 4 and 6 people, designating one student in
the group as the 'spokesperson.' I give each group a question or
set of questions that it is to discuss and then report its answer(s)
back to the class. I usually allow students to group themselves
with others sitting near them, but sometimes vary this by having
students count themselves off consecutively and then have all the
1's sit together, all the 2's sit together, all the 3's, and so on. This
has the advantage of breaking up 'cliques' of students who already know each other and might be less likely to work seriously
as a discussion group. As mentioned above, occasionally I set up
the groups segregated by sex. I allow each group 10-15 minutes,
but monitor the groups so that I can shorten the time if they are
finished beforehand or extend it if the students find they need
more time. I give members of the groups the following instructions:

(a) *Students in each group are to try to come to agreement concerning the answer to the question put to the group, but if at the
end of the allotted time members are still in disagreement, the
group should present both majority and minority reports. The
spokesperson sketches the 'majority' answer, but students who
disagree with that answer are encouraged to speak in their own
voices explaining why they disagree. (This helps the instructor
know what some individual students think and allows reference
back to what they said at some later point.)*

(b) *Members of each group should be careful not to come to an
agreement too quickly. If they find they all do quickly agree on
some position, then someone in the group should adopt the position of "devil's advocate" and try to counter the arguments
made in favor of the agreed-upon view.*

(c) *Groups that present later than others are encouraged to refer
back to what earlier ones have said or compare their ideas with
those already voiced.*

Although it is often preferable to have students defend views that they actually hold (since people have a hard time defending a position in a debate if they don't agree with it), I suggest that for especially sensitive topics, it is best to form debate groups by having the students in the class count off by twos with the 1's assigned to take the 'pro' side and the 2's the 'con' side. This sometimes helps both to distance the debating students from their own feelings on the topic (that is, if they are assigned a position other than their own) and to avoid students' taking personally the arguments for positions that run counter to their own (since every student in the class knows that the positions argued for are ones that have been 'assigned').

Distinguish Clearly between Moral and Legal Questions

Distinguishing between moral and legal questions and recognizing that the issues of legality and morality can, at least sometimes, be separated, often helps students more easily to engage in dialogue with those who disagree with them. They need to realize, for example, that a person could think homosexuality is morally all right and still believe that the law should not recognize same sex unions, and that the question of what the law should be on abortion is in part a prudential judgment about what Americans will be prepared to accept. Thus, students who disagree on the morality of a given sexual issue might still be able to agree about what the law should be—a fact that might bring opposing parties closer together.

Help Students Make Sense of Their Feelings

The problem of integrating emotional responses and rational reflection is especially hard when sexual issues are under discussion. Abortion and gay and lesbian issues usually trigger strong emotional responses, but 'gut' feelings can crop up as well during discussion of many other gender issues. (One striking example of this occurred the semester I had predominantly male students in my class. In discussing the case of a male to female transsexual, one male student who was trying very hard to be tolerant and

accepting of the person's choice, suddenly blurted out "Do whatever you want, man, but don't cut it off!")

When discussing homosexuality, one must be especially careful that students who have feelings of repulsion toward such
practices not express them in raw terms since it is not at all unlikely that some of the students in the class are gay or lesbian. But
of course the instructor should encourage students not merely to
become aware of their feelings (which they usually are, in any
case) but to think about why they have the feelings they do. Students should be encouraged to take a hard look at what it is about
the acts in question that they find disturbing.

One useful exercise when treating sensitive topics of a sexual
nature—it works especially well for the question of the morality
of abortion—is to ask students to explain, leaving their own opinions aside, what they think the strongest arguments are on both
sides, writing the arguments on the board as students give them.
Next ask the students to try to enter into the way that the people
on each side feel and try to understand why they feel so strongly.

NOTES

*I would like to thank Phil Devine for his help at every stage of the
writing of this chapter.

1. Philip Devine and Celia Wolf-Devine, eds., *Sex and Gender: A Spectrum of Views*, (Belmont, CA: Wadsworth, 2002).

All materials referenced in this chapter that are reprinted in *Sex and
Gender: A Spectrum of Views* are marked with an asterisk (*) in the endnotes.

2. Singer defends bestiality in his review of Midas Dekkers' *Dearest Pet:
On Bestiality*, trans. Paul Vincent (Verso, 2000), published online at:
www.nerve.com (March 2001).

3. This expression is used by Shulamith Firestone in *The Dialectic of Sex*
(New York: Bantam) 1971.

4. Mary Daly not only holds that the difference between the sexes is
cosmically important but also that the male sex is 'inherently evil.' See
Mary Daly, *Outercourse* (Boston, MA: Beacon Press, 1992).

5. *In a Different Voice* (Cambridge, Mass: Harvard University Press,
1982).

6. The whole notion of "masculine voice" and "feminine voice" in ethics is, I realize, highly controversial, and has been questioned from a number of different directions. The anthology edited by Eva Feder Kittay and Diana Meyers, *Women and Moral Theory* (Totowa, N.J.: Rowman & Littlefield, 1987) contains a number of interesting essays that bear on the issues in dispute. Some psychologists have found Gilligan's results hard to replicate and have questioned the representativeness of her sample. George Sher has argued that the distinction is merely a matter of emphasis and not a radical difference of kind since all major ethical theories contain some aspects of both. Some feminists have opposed the notion on the grounds that it threatens to return women to traditional gender roles based on a sort of biologistic understanding of male-female differences. But for the 'masculine voice'/'feminine voice' distinction to be important, it need be neither biologically based nor total.

7. Published with *Lady Chatterly's Lover* (Cambridge, England: Cambridge University Press, 1993).*

8. Boston, MA: Routledge and Kegan Paul, 1982.*

9. Minneapolis: University of Minnesota Press, 1984.

10. In S. Harding and J. Hintakka, eds., *Discovering Reality* (Dordrecht, Holland: Reidel, 1983).

11. New York: Harcourt Brace Jovanovich, Inc., 1974.*

12. Mastroeni's essay, "The Extended Principle of Totality—A Possible Justification for Transsexual Surgery," is excerpted from his dissertation: *A Moral Evaluation of Surgical Sex Reassignment.**

13. Ann Arbor: Servant Books, 1980.*

14. New York: John Wiley and Sons, 1978.*

15. Notre Dame: University of Notre Dame Press, 1980.*

16. New York: St. Martin's Press, 1983.*

17. Roger Scruton, *Sexual Desire: A Moral Philosophy of the Erotic* (New York: Free Press, 1986).*

18. London, England: Horace Liveright, Inc., 1929 & 1953.*

19. New York: Free Press, 1987. *

20. *Journal of Philosophy*, LXVI, Jan. 1969.*

21. *Public Affairs Quarterly*, vol. 1, April 1987; 57-81.*

22. *Laval Theologique et Philosophique*, vol. 26, fall 1970: 57-87.*

23. New York: Viking Penguin 1992.*

24. Berkeley, CA: University of California Press, 1997.

25. *Harpers Magazine*, October 1987.*

26. *Philosophy and Public Affairs* (fall, 1971): 47-66. Princeton University Press.*

27. "Abortion and the Feminine Voice,"originally published in *Public Affairs Quarterly*, July 1989. Reprinted in: James E. White, ed., *Contemporary Moral Issues*, 6th ed., (Belmont, CA: Wadsworth/Thompson, 2000).*

28. From *Contraception and Holiness* (New York: Herder & Herder, 1964).*

29. From *Covenanted Happiness* (Princeton: Specter, 1999).*

30. Princeton, NJ: Princeton University Press, 1994.*

31. *The Progressive*,* June 1989, vol. 53, no. 6: 19.

32. *Hypatia*,* vol. 4, no. 3, 1989.

33. *Journal of Value Inquiry*, vol. 23, 1989: 59-68.*

34. New York: Routledge, 1990.*

35. New York: Basic Books, Inc., 1989.*

36. Cambridge, Mass: Harvard University Press, 1971.*

37. Cambridge: Cambridge University Press, 1992.*

38. New Rochelle, New York: Arlington House, 1977.*

39. New York: Basic Books, 1991.*

40. *The Nation*, November 1979.*

41. *Journal of Homosexuality*, 27, 1994.*

42. *Human Life Review*, vol. 5, no.1, 1994.*

43. Sharon Bishop, ed., *Philosophy and Women* (Belmont, CA: Wadsworth, 1979).*

44. *Social Justice Review*, July-August 1987: 122-24.*

45. *Feminism Unmodified* (Cambridge, MA: Harvard University Press, 1987).*

46. Boston, MA: Little Brown Co., 1993.*

47. *Journal of Social Philosophy*, vol. 15, summer 1984.*

48. Joel Feinberg and Hyman Gross, eds., *Philosophy of Law*, ed.,* (Belmont, CA: Wadsworth, 1980).

49. In Christopher Wolfe, ed., *Homosexuality and American Public Life* (Dallas, Texas: Spence, 1999).*

50. Ibid.*

51. Andrew Sullivan, ed., *Same Sex Marriage: Pro and Con* (New York: Vintage Books, 1997).

52. (New York: Alfred A. Knopf, 1995).*

53. San Diego: Harcourt Brace Jovanovich, 1959 and 1987.*

54. From Carol Christ and Judith Plaskow, eds., *Womanspirit Rising* (San Francisco, CA: Harper Books, 1979).

55. Part of this appeared in the *New Oxford Review* (Dec.1984) and is newly published in *Sex and Gender: A Spectrum of Views*, op. cit. 369-71.*

56. New York: Crossroad, 1992.*

57. From Carol Adams, ed., *Ecofeminism and the Sacred* (New York: Continuum Publishing Company, 1993).*

58. *In Sex and Gender: A Spectrum of Views.**

59. London: SCM Press, 1988.*

60. From *The Voice of Sarah* (San Francisco: Harper Collins) 1990.*

61. Davis's essay was rewritten for *Sex and Gender*, op. cit.

62. I keep these questions, and often use one or more of them as essay questions for the midterm.

63. *My Conundrum* (New York: Harcourt Brace Jovanovich, Inc. 1974).*

64. The way in which philosophical reflection can come into conflict with emotional and political pressures was brought home to us during the copyediting phase of our book. The copy editor informed us that it was Wadsworth's policy to refer to postoperative transsexuals using pronouns corresponding to their chosen gender, and not, more ambiguously as "he/she" (as we had done), because they (the transsexuals) found the latter offensive. This was something of a problem, since the philosophical question we wanted students to ponder was whether the transsexual whose story we were reprinting had in fact become a woman after the hormonal and surgical treatments, so we did not want to beg the question either way.

65. I focus on harassment between peers, and do not go into legal issues, though some instructors may wish to do so.

66. See *Sexual Personae* (New Haven: Yale University Press, 1990).

67. Even granting that it is hard for those whose imaginations were formed in the world as it is to imagine a different world, the exercise can still be valuable for its potential to lead student to become more self-conscious about the ways that gender shapes their lives—their dress, their hobbies, their hopes and dreams, and their conception of who they are.

PART XIII
Looking at What We Do in the Classroom

Chapter 25

Uncovering the "Hidden Curriculum": A Laboratory Course in Philosophy of Education

Anthony Weston

My Philosophy of Education course stands in the grand Socratic tradition: its aim is to draw out and critically examine the presuppositions of education, especially education as we know it. I do so, however, by enacting alternative educational methods—methods whose presuppositions are different, sometimes radically different, from the presuppositions of education as we know it. The usual presuppositions emerge as it were in *silhouette*.

Weeks 1-3: Opening the Questions

Week 1 begins with a standard lecture. I speak for all but five minutes of the period, inviting questions from the class only at the end. The topic is an introduction to classical philosophies of education, from Plato to Rousseau.

The next session we sit in a circle and discuss the lecture style. Students report that they usually experience lecturing as boring and alienating. I insist that they figure out *why*. Lecturing, they answer, conveys the message that the lecturer is an authority on a subject about which the students are essentially ignorant and have nothing to offer. This message is resented by students even when it is accepted as true (and often, of course, it is not true).

The same message also reinforces and legitimizes us as lecturers. Having the "space" of the classroom free to ourselves, filling the room with our voices alone, free of challenge, ratifies our own sense of authority and power. Correspondingly, we render the students passive, as if they themselves have nothing to contribute, a passivity that is, perhaps, reinforced by the conception of knowledge usually at play in the lecture style, namely, as finished. Indeed, especially if the lecture is well-organized and clear—that is, precisely if it is a good lecture by the usual standards—the twists and turns of the development of the knowledge being presented are laid out so that the final result seems only fitting and natural. The uncertainty, struggle, and incompleteness that characterize students' own work, and in fact characterize *all* intellectual work, are seldom present. One can, of course, try to present one's subject as an open-ended and ongoing search for knowledge. But that intention tends to be defeated and undercut by the very mode of presentation—and again, paradoxically, *especially* if the lecture is a good one.

The class begins to explore how a sense of the teacher's authority may even be reflected in the structure of the classroom. For example, all of the chairs face forward, which may discourage communication among the students and convey the message that the teacher stands apart from the students and relates to them only en masse. Think of the usual lecture hall, with chairs fixed in long semicircular rows, facing a microphone-equipped podium at center.

The reading for week 2 is the first part of Robert Paul Wolff's *The Ideal of the University*,[1] which sets out four different models of the university and tries to show how profoundly they affect the shape and the rationale of the curriculum. As students enter the room, I ask them to form groups of four or five. Each group is to decide what sort of curricular requirements, if any, their ideal university would have, and then to explain *why*. Later I bring each group some poster paper and markers and ask them to draw a poster representing their mutually agreed upon ideal university, in particular rationalizing its distribution requirements to incoming students (I post a sample of their own institution's attempt to do the same). These posters are then taped up around the room, and class ends with students viewing each other's work.

"Tuning out" in group work is difficult when concrete outcomes are required in specific time frames. Each group has to discuss various curricular options, come to agree on a specific curriculum, decide on the best way to present it to their classmates, and post the results, all in the space of about seventy minutes. In this way, students actually begin to gain a sense of how the university's curricular requirements became what they are: an inclusive compromise between competing interests. Because the students' conceptions of and interests in education vary so greatly, they naturally resort to compromise and, therefore, in the end arrive at something very like what they already have, including the disliked core requirements. This proves to be eye-opening.

This style is intended to contrast sharply with the lecture session. In group work, knowledge is not something "conveyed" to students by the teacher. It is striking to a number of students that they can have an extremely engaging and profitable class (clarifying the readings and provoking their interest in a new range of questions) in which the instructor is almost completely absent. My role is confined to structuring the questions and providing materials.

At the beginning of week 3, I enter the room accompanied by a colleague whom I introduce as a law-school professor. Then I excuse myself. The "law-school professor" immediately launches into an interrogation of students randomly selected from the class list. After about ten minutes, he calls on a prearranged "plant" in the class. He or she objects to the style of the class, especially since it seems radically at odds with the reading for that class session, in which Wolff criticizes the grading system on the grounds that it fosters competition and anxiety.[2] Another "plant" chimes in for support. The "law-school professor" then fakes annoyance, announces that since the class does not appreciate his method, he does not intend to stay, and packs up and stalks out.

The result is a teacherless class. The students, not surprisingly, just leave. Without a teacher, it seems that students do not see the point of having a class at all (which is why my more recent and simpler route to the same end is simply not to show up at all). But in fact their leaving becomes the focus of a productive discussion. In our next session, we ask the same questions we discussed in previous weeks. What assumptions about teaching and learning does their leaving reflect? Is it actually true that learning always requires a teacher? I remind them that there are contributions they could have made without me, since at the end of the previous class they were explicitly invited to help shape the next part of the course. Now they see that this was quite deliberate. I had even suggested that they go to the library and look for articles. Why did they not take up this invitation when they had the chance?

This week actually proves to be a turning point of the course. Some serious self-questioning about motives and assumptions usually follows. Many students do not like the passivity they seemed to show this week, and it stays with them as a provocation.

Weeks 4-8: Variations

The main writing assignments for this course are one-page commentaries, due at the end of each week, analyzing the week's events. An initial handout outlines the questions the commentaries should address: For each way in which the classroom has been organized, what is knowledge? What is learning? Who is active? Who is in control? Who is reactive, and how? Each week students exchange commentaries, comment on each others' work, and suggest grades.

Week 4 opens with a workshop on grading, using the student commentaries from previous weeks. The guidesheet for the commentaries, distributed on the first day of class, outlines the questions the commentaries should answer. We now talk about those elusive and hard-to-describe qualities of intelligence, clarity, insight, and so on. Then I hand out two sample commentaries from the week before (names removed) and ask the class to read and grade them as usual. One is a nicely written commentary, typed with no errors, but making little headway on the basic questions being asked; the other is badly written, with many grammatical errors, but is truly suggestive at several points. Students' grades tend to vary, but the majority tend to grade the first kind of paper fairly high and the second low. I explain why my own grades go in the opposite direction: the second essay's insights, though not clearly formulated, may nonetheless be strikingly thoughtful and original. And I try to bring this out for the class. After discussing these samples, I randomly distribute the commentaries (ungraded) from the previous week and ask the students to grade them, this time in pairs, with the stipulation that their grades will be the grades the authors of the papers actually receive.

Students are not used to looking at their own or others' writing from an evaluative point of view, and by doing so, they begin to understand some of the problems in the grading process, and also some of the weaknesses in their own work. They also draw conclusions: the old complaint that "grading is subjective" is true, in a way, but there may be more to this story. What we ought to seek is not an impossible objectivity, but rather an awareness of how important the grader's own attitudes are to the grading process. This may call for rather different kinds of reform than a search for "objectivity."

At the beginning of week 5, my "law-school" colleague returns and conducts the class using the law-school method but in a much more supportive manner (helping students out with answers, for example). (By way of preparation, he visits the class briefly the previous session, stresses that the law-school method works only when students have read the readings in advance, and offers some suggestions about what to read for.) He again calls off names at random from the class list, and he directs his questions toward some very specific points in (and in criticism of) the week's reading, E. D. Hirsch's main argument in *Cultural Literacy*.[3]

The law-school method has a number of advantages. First, student participation is required, not merely invited; anyone may be called upon at any time, and everyone will be called upon eventually. Second, the format precludes a few students from dominating the class. Third, the instructor gets a good sense of how prepared the students are and what they do and do not understand. Disadvantages include a high level of tension and a concentration upon specific facts, positions, and arguments to the neglect of other dimensions of a subject or a reading, such as its rhetorical and emotional dimensions, its suggestiveness, and the possibility of more charitable or imaginative but less literal readings.

In some ways the law-school method is the most active of the teacher-centered styles I use. Although only one student is actually on the spot at any one time, everyone knows that he or she might be next called upon, so students come to think "as if" they have to answer, even when they do not. Still, however, this method is highly teacher dominated (although my students do not think so at first). Apparently, since students participate a lot and since the teacher's role is limited to asking questions, this method seems to students to be more egalitarian.

Week 6 opens with a talk show. I set up five desks facing the class and place the rest in a semicircle with an aisle down the middle. I ask for five volunteers who have definite opinions about the Hirsch debate. Two people represent Hirsch, one plays a critic, one speaks for the students, and one plays our school's president. We outfit the president with a tie, the student with shades. The Hirsches spruce up; all panelists make posters with their "names" and a slogan or symbol. Then I hit the music, introduce the panel, pose a question, and away it goes. Later, I begin calling on members of the "audience" to join the discussion as well.

Students all watch talk shows and know how to behave on them. I am always amazed at how readily they take up the roles, challenge each other, and keep up the pace of the discussion. (In the past I have had a student who played the president immediately find a stereotypical "administrator" voice, talking a lot while saying very little. The class roared. But he and the "student" soon found areas of agreement in resistance to Hirsch's argument, a fact that proved very interesting.) The "Hirsches" typically turn out to have read the book carefully and to be excellent at drawing out its more subtle points. All I have to do is underline a point here and there and steer the discussion a little.

One message of the talk show, then, is that students are entirely capable of intelligently presenting and discussing the course materials. Another message is that there are many ways to come to terms with the readings. Trying to act out the controversies involved is one such way. It is both an effective way to "get inside" an author's argument for the person playing the role and an effective way to introduce a controversy to a class. Notice that the controversy is not introduced by being reported, but rather by being *reproduced*. "Knowledge," once again, becomes an active construction.

Near the beginning of the term, I ask students to list any skills that they would be willing to teach to five or ten of their classmates in about half an hour. At the end of week 6, I make up and hand out a schedule of three sessions of about ten "minicourses" each. Students who are to teach thus have a few days to prepare. At the beginning of week 7, we break up into groups around each student-teacher for half an hour, then switch to the next "minicourse," and then on to the last.

I "take" the minicourses with the students, but they get the point without this bit of symbolism: all of them are knowledgeable; all have something to offer. This is in direct contrast to the usual setting in which students are treated, at best, as if they have a small grasp on something that the teacher can perhaps slowly nurture along. Student-teachers also learn the invaluable lesson that teaching is hard. Some find it extremely provocative and enjoyable.

In week 8, we view a documentary film, "A Class Divided." In this film, Jane Eliot, a third-grade teacher in an all-white Iowa town, tries to convey the depth and the senselessness of racial prejudice with a provocative class exercise. One day her brown-eyed children are told that they are superior and get special approval from the teacher and special privileges at lunch and on the playground. Blue-eyes get disparagement from the teacher, must wear neckbands to identify them from a distance, and are restricted on the playground and at lunch. By early afternoon you see the class deeply split; blue-eyes fight brown-eyes on the playground because the latter use "blue-eyed" as an epithet. The blue-eyes are upset and can barely function in the classroom. The next day the roles are reversed, with identical results. At the end the class discusses the experiment, with special attention given both to how the students felt in their subordinate and superior roles and to how readily a previously irrelevant difference came to play a central role in their lives.

Eliot actually created in her pupils the experiences she wanted them to understand. "What would I feel if this were being done to me?" may be a question that one must ask in order to understand the depth of the effect of racism or of other kinds of prejudice. Eliot enables students to answer this question for themselves.

From class discussion of this film, I learned that students are ambivalent about Eliot's use of enactment as a pedagogical device. Some argue that the pedagogical advantage of learning this lesson—the hurtfulness of racism—should somehow be conveyed without actually inflicting hurt. My students disagree, therefore, on the appropriateness of Eliot's method.

Weeks 9-11: Self-Consciousness

This segment of the course takes up basic questions about "ways of knowing," using as a background text *Women's Ways of Knowing*.[4] In week 9, I ask students to make a texture collage on the general theme of their education in college. The instructions read in part: "You should try to represent how your education *feels*, not describe it in words or even draw it in pictures. You are working primarily for the hand rather than the eyes or ears. Of course it is true that you will also see the collage, so you do not want to ignore color, shape, and the like. But texture should be primary."

The following class we view the collages. The range is usually astonishing, and the care with which some are done defies short description. Some are rambunctious collections of meaningful materials, often on clever backgrounds (as, for example, on Domino's Pizza boxes, representing life and especially late nights in the dorms). Others divide the student's education into stages and offer a set of dominant textures or feelings for each stage. And some are profoundly disturbing—including broken glass or nails or rubber bands stretched to nearly breaking.

The discussion of collage making is revealing. Some students argue that textures are inevitably more ambiguous than words. Others argue that the sense of touch is undervalued and marginalized, especially in institutions of learning, and so is left untrained. Some say that this exercise favors students who are "artistic" or "creative"; others agree, but point out that the academy usually favors those who are verbal, creating an imbalance that is usually invisible. This exercise brings it into focus.

Week 10 is an interview. Students pair up, one male and one female, and the male interviews the female, filling out a three-page questionnaire. The questions fall into two categories: a range of questions about learning styles, using some of Belenky's questions ("what has been your most powerful learning experience?" and "how do we know what is true?" and the like),[5] and a set of questions about the women's experience of sexism in the classroom and on campus.

Male students report enjoying the interviews, feel they listened well, and like the chance to meet and talk with the women. Female students report much more ambivalence—a fact that itself surprises the men. Typically, about half the women feel that their interviewer more or less misunderstood them. Some say that they were just beginning to answer a question, perhaps taking an exploratory attitude toward the issue involved, when their interviewer wrote down a few phrases and moved on to the next question. Others feel that their interviewers recorded their answers inaccurately or ignored the answer entirely. However, almost none of these complaints was voiced during the interview itself. This fact—that many women who knew they were being misheard did not resist, or correct the interviewer—is very striking to the class, and appears to confirm Belenky's claim that certain "female" ways of speaking and thinking are devalued in our educational institutions, especially in higher education, and that this devaluation and even exclusion is usually invisible, at least to many men.

In the following week, we take the class's discussion of miscommunication in the interviews as itself a topic for discussion. As students enter the first class of week 11, they see a videotape of themselves entering class the previous day (it was unobtrusively videotaped by my teaching assistant). I then proceed to show selections from the videotape, stopping for discussion in between and showing some segments several times.

One especially effective segment shows four or five students, all but one male, interacting in a tentative way. Several began their remarks with the supposedly classically female "I don't know if this is true, but. . . ." Others ask questions, rather than making statements, and interact primarily with each other rather than involve the instructor. In short, they seem to follow what Belenky calls a "collaborative" pattern that is supposed to be more characteristic of females in all-female groups. We discuss why this interaction among the males does not fit the "classical" patterns that Belenky identifies. Some of the men reported feeling especially tentative that day, given the topic; other students argued that the patterns discussed by Belenky have to be understood as tendencies not exclusively characteristic of just one gender.

The effect of analyzing the videotape is a little uncomfortable, but also riveting. Students do not usually see themselves as instructors see them, and never with the challenge of analyzing their own interaction patterns. This session proves to be crucial in students' selfreflection on their own behaviors. It is not easy to deny a pattern when you see yourself acting it out.

Much of the videotape also shows students who are *not* participating. Another theme that therefore arises in discussion is the variation in class participation between those who speak a lot in class and others who do not speak at all. Some students argue strongly for the necessity of speaking in class: they resent students who "take" from the class discussions but do not "give" to them. Others want to credit different kinds of participation, or even nonparticipation. In one class, a student who had previously been quite vocal reported that his experience in the interview persuaded him that there were many students, often silent, with real contributions to make, so that he decided to keep quiet for a while to make room for others. On seeing the videotape, he felt that this strategy hadn't worked: the other vocal students just got more time. (I asked this student to lead the next class discussion, which he did, calling on students who had not spoken and did not have their hands up. This not only led to further discussion of the participation question but also to significantly changed and broader participation in the weeks that followed.)

Conclusion

For the last week of the course I ask the students to analyze the implicit messages of the course itself, viewed as a whole. The idea is both to help students begin to sum up the course for themselves and to have them make detailed course evaluations. I have already included many of the students' specific responses in this essay. The most general response is, in effect, an application of what Ira Shor calls "re-experiencing the ordinary."[6] The common theme is the nicely philosophical "I learned to question what I had previously taken for granted": the unchallenged authority of the teacher, the necessity of lecturing, the lack of a "voice" of one's own, student passivity, and indeed the monopoly of school itself over learning.

I do not need to emphasize that many different styles could equally well be used in a course of this sort. In more recent versions of this course, I have had classes learn madrigals, walk silently and as slowly as possible across the quad for an hour, devise together in ever-enlarging groups their own cognitive-developmental theory, and analyze the hidden messages of the ubiquitous classroom desk. I no longer necessarily alternate a variety of teaching methods with "normal" discussion days: sometimes there are two or three "style" days in a row. Every class calls for a different pattern. The main thing, anyway, is to offer a wide variety of styles, for it is the contrast of different styles that "silhouette" the familiar, that lead us to question what was previously taken for granted. Thus, I believe, this course is truly a philosophical laboratory.[7]

NOTES

1. Robert Paul Wolff, *The Ideal of the University* (Boston: Beacon, 1969).

2. Ibid., pt. 2, chap. 1.

3. E. D. Hirsch, *Cultural Literacy* (New York: Vintage, 1988).

4. Mary Field Belenky et al., *Women's Ways of Knowing: The Development of Self, Voice, and Mind* (New York: Basic Books, 1986).

5. Ibid., appen. A.

6. Ira Shor, *Critical Teaching and Everyday Life* (Boston: South End, 1980).

7. What I describe here are mostly early versions of the course; it has varied considerably over the years. Each iteration has its own coherence, though, so it has proved impossible to amalgamate them into a single narrative. It is with regret that I leave out some of the newer and wilder styles. Another paper, perhaps. Peter Williams, Sharon Hartline, and Mike Blackburn stand out for special mention among the many students and colleagues who have inspired, provoked, and supported this course in its various incarnations.

Chapter 26

A Graduate Seminar on Teaching Philosophy

Martin Benjamin

I first began teaching a course on how to teach philosophy when a number of graduate students, in 1986, expressed an interest in learning more about teaching. As we spoke I recalled a passage from Kenneth E. Eble's *The Craft of Teaching*:

> Teaching as a subject, among graduate students who have teaching responsibilities, meets most of the general specifications for a good seminar—a place for exchanging information, for examining research critically, for discussing experiences in teaching, and for fostering continuing study. Students will have common experiences and interests and can examine in common the knowledge useful to the topic at hand. The professor cannot so easily slip into the role of expert and become the lecturer, nor need many of the topics useful to teaching be put off until the students have prepared seminar papers. The very conduct of the seminar—how students learn in this setting—is in itself part of the substance of the course. In addition, the faculty needs this kind of exposure. The teaching seminars are not the property of the 'teaching' specialist; rather they are the common enterprise of faculty and students in a relationship as colleagues. Seminars in teaching should be a routine part of graduate study for all students planning to teach. They should carry credit and be as demanding as any graduate work.[1]

Eble's sentiments had always made intuitive sense to me. So together with the head of the graduate student association, I proposed a 3-credit graduate seminar on teaching to our department. With the commitment of a number of graduate students to enroll in such a seminar if offered, the chair listed it for the next academic year. The seminar ran for ten weeks (at the time, the University was on the quarter system). I offered the seminar again six years later and a compressed, non-credit, version four years after that. When the Department revised the graduate program a year or so later, it added two new required seminars one of which was a 3-credit seminar on teaching, offered in the spring of even-numbered years for all students in the PhD program. (The other required seminar was a 3-credit 'proseminar' to be offered every year to orient entering students to graduate study.)

The seminar has four principal objectives:

1. To enable participants to develop a better understanding of teaching in general and the special nature and problems of teaching philosophy;
2. To enable participants to develop their identities as philosophy teachers (effective teaching, I believe, is highly personalized);
3. To acquaint participants with some of the rich literature on teaching and teaching philosophy; and
4. (As with any graduate seminar) to enable participants to learn more about philosophy and to improve their skills in philosophical understanding and professional writing.

The description of the course on teaching philosophy that is now required of all PhD students in our department follows.[2]

Content of Seminar

The seminar begins with a general overview of college teaching and, for legitimacy as well as inspiration, a discussion of John Ladd's account of Kant as a teacher.[3] Most people do not know that Kant received tenure for his fine teaching rather than for his publications. Ladd emphasizes that "for Kant philosophy and teaching were intimately bound up with each other as they were for Socrates," and that "Kant's teaching was based on a carefully considered theory of what philosophy is good for as well as a theory of how philosophy fits into higher education."[4] I stress that one's teaching should be based on a carefully considered conception of philosophy. Hence, participants are urged, in shaping their identities as philosophy teachers, to reflect on their conception of philosophy and on their understanding, in the context of the college curriculum, of its aims and nature. Thus, a good part of the philosophical substance of my seminar consists of metaphilosophy.

The Syllabus for the Seminar on Teaching

The seminar meets twice weekly for 15 weeks. Each meeting is identified below by a separate heading. Individual reading selections and articles are noted below.

Texts:
(1) Kenneth Eble, *The Craft of Teaching: A Guide to Mastering the Pro fessor's Art*, 2nd ed., (San Franciso, CA: Jossey-Bass, 1988).
(2) Tziporah Kasachkoff, ed., *In the Socratic Tradition: Essays on Teaching Philosophy* (Lanham, MD: Rowman & Littlefield, 1998).
(3) Anthony Weston, *A Rulebook for Arguments*, 3rd ed. (Indianapolis, IN: Hackett, 2001).
(4) Course Pack ('CP': selection of articles noted below)

Schedule of Topics and Readings

Week 1:

Introduction

Teaching and Teaching Philosophy: An Overview

John Ladd, "Kant as a Teacher," *Teaching Philosophy* 5, no. 1 (1982): 1-9.
Tziporah Kasachkoff, "Introduction," *In the Socratic Tradition*: xv-xxiii.
Martin Benjamin, "A Seminar on Teaching Philosophy," *In the Socratic Tradition*: 259-68.
Eble, *The Craft of Teaching*: 1-41.

Week 2:

The Classroom: Getting off on the Right Foot

Jeffrey Wolcowitz, "The First Day of Class," in Margaret Morganroth
Gullette, ed., *The Art and Craft of Teaching* (Cambridge, MA: Harvard

Lecturing; Conducting Discussions; Leading Seminars; and Advising Students

Eble: 68-122.

Week 3:

Assigning Texts, Giving Tests, Determining Grades, and other Important Stuff

Eble: 125-94.
Robert Paul Wolff, "A Discourse on Grading," in *The Ideal of the University* (Boston: Beacon Press, 1969): 58-68.

Learning to Teach

Eble: 197-226

Week 4:

Philosophy Teaching and the Nature of Philosophy

Patrick McKee, "Philosophy and Wisdom," *Teaching Philosophy* 13, no.
4 (1990): 325-30.
Kai Nielsen, "Philosophy and the Search for Wisdom," *Teaching
Philosophy* 16, no. 1 (1993): 5-20.
Joel Marks, "Teaching Philosophy, Being a Philosopher," *Teaching
Philosophy* 16, no. 2 (1993): 99-104.
Konstantin Kolenda, "Rethinking the Teaching of Philosophy," *Teaching Philosophy* 15, no. 2 (1992): 121-32.
Sidney Gendin, "Am I Wicked?" *Teaching Philosophy* 18, no. 2 (1995):
167-68.
Dôna Warren, "Those Who Can, Do: A Response to Gendin," *Teaching
Philosophy* 19, no. 3 (1996): 275-79.

Week 5:

Varieties of The Introductory Course in Philosophy (I)

Steven M. Cahn, "Teaching Introductory Philosophy," *In the Socratic
Tradition*: 3-5.

Douglas P. Lackey, "The Historical vs. The Problems Approach to the Introduction to Philosophy," *Metaphilosophy* 5, no. 2 (1974): 169-72.

Martin Benjamin, "Syllabus, Paper Assignments, Final for PHL 200H" *(handout)*.

Newton Garver, "Introducing Philosophy," *In the Socratic Tradition*: 7-20.

V. Alan White and Jo A. Chern, "Teaching Introductory Philosophy—A Restricted Topical Approach," *In the Socratic Tradition*: 21-28.

Varieties of The Introductory Course in Philosophy (II)

William B. Irvine, "Teaching Without Books," *Teaching Philosophy* 16, no. 1 (1993): 41-52

Jeremiah Patrick Conway, "Presupposing Self-Reflection," *Teaching Philosophy* 22, no. 1 (1999): 41-52.

Julie Eflin, "Improving Student Papers in Introduction to Philosophy Courses," *In the Socratic Tradition*: 47-53.

Jane Freimiller, "The One Page Philosopher: Short Writing Assignments for Introductory Classes," *Teaching Philosophy* 20, no. 3 (1997): 269-76.

Jeffrey K. McDonough, "Rough Drafts without Tears: A Guide to a Manageable Procedure for Improving Student Writing," *Teaching Philosophy* 23, no. 2 (2000): 127-37.

Helping Our Students Improve

Steven M. Cahn, "How to Improve Your Teaching," *In the Socratic Tradition*: 31-5.

Jonathan E. Adler, "Reading and Interpretation: A Heuristic for Improving Students' Comprehension of Philosophy Texts," *In the Socratic Tradition*: 37-46.

Dôna Warren, "How Many Angels can Dance on the Head of a Pin?: The Many Kinds of Questions in Philosophy," *Teaching Philosophy*, 21, no. 3 (1998): 257-73.

Anne-Marie Bowery and Michael Beaty, "The Use of Reading Questions As a Pedagogical Tool: Fostering an Interrogative, Narrative Approach to Philosophy," *Teaching Philosophy* 22, no.1 (1999): 17-40.

Week 6:

Debate and Discussion

James E. Roper and Timothy W. Sommers, "Debate as a Tool in Teaching Business Ethics," *In the Socratic Tradition*: 91-103.

Janice Moulton, "Duelism in Philosophy," *Teaching Philosophy* 3, no. 4 (1980): 419-33.

Susan Peterson, "Are You Teaching Philosophy or Playing the Dozens?" *Teaching Philosophy* 3, no. 4 (1980): 435-42.

Charles Taliaferro and Thomas Chance, "Philosophers, Red Tooth and Claw," *Teaching Philosophy* 18, no. 1 (1995): 15-30.

Neil Thomason, "Philosophy Discussions With Less B.S.," *Teaching Philosophy* 18, no. 1 (1995): 15-30.

Dealing with Student Relativism

Roger Paden, "The Student Relativist as a Philosopher," *Teaching Philosophy* 10, no. 2 (1987): 97-101.

Richard W. Momeyer, "Teaching Ethics to Student Relativists," *Teaching Philosophy* 18, no. 4 (1995): 301-11.

Week 7:

Teaching Ethics

James B. Gould, "Drunk Driving in Introductory Ethics," *Teaching Philosophy* 21, no. 4 (1998): 339-60.

Deborah R. Barnbaum, "Teaching Empathy in Medical Ethics: The Use of Lottery Assignments," *Teaching Philosophy* 24, no. 1 (2001): 63-75.

Heather J. Gert, "Two Ways to Teach Premedical Students the Ethical Value of Discussion and Information Gathering," *Teaching Philosophy* 24, no. 3 (2001): 233-40.

James D. Shumaker, "Moral Reasoning and Story Telling," *Teaching Philosophy* 23, no. 1 (2000): 15-21.

Joan C. Callahan, "From the Applied to the Practical: Teaching Ethics for Use," *In the Socratic Tradition*: 57-69.

John Kleinig, "Teaching Police Ethics as Professional Ethics," *In the Socratic Tradition*: 71-80.

Marshall Missner, "A Social Dilemma Game for an Ethics Class," *In the Socratic Tradition*: 81-89.

The Ethics of Teaching: Advocacy or Neutrality?

Michael Goldman, "On Moral Relativism, Advocacy, and Teaching Normative Ethics," *Teaching Philosophy* 4, no. 1 (1981): 1-11.

Linda Bomstad, "Advocating Procedural Neutrality," *Teaching Philosophy*, 18, no. 3 (1995): 197-210.

Mike W. Martin, "Advocating Values: Professionalism in Teaching Ethics," *Teaching Philosophy*, 20, no. 1 (March 1997): 19-34.

Week 8:

Teaching Logic and Critical Thinking

Robert Ennis, "Critical Thinking: A Streamlined Conception," *Teaching Philosophy* 14, no. 1 (1991): 5-24.

Kathleen Dean Moore, "Using Psuedoscience in a Critical Thinking Class," *In the Socratic Tradition*: 145-52.

Theodore A. Gracyk, "A Critical Thinking Portfolio," *In the Socratic Tradition*: 153-59.

Rory J. Conces, "A Participatory Approach to Teaching Critical Reasoning," *In the Socratic Tradition*: 161-65.

Kerry Walters, "The Case of the Slain President," *Teaching Philosophy* 20, no. 1 (1997): 35-47.

Robert Ennis, "Is Critical Thinking Culturally Biased," *Teaching Philosophy* 21, no. 1 (1998): 15-33.

Teaching History of Philosophy (I)

John McDermott, "The Teaching of Philosophy-Historically," *In the Socratic Tradition*: 169-80.

Michael Goldman, "Dead White Guys," *Teaching Philosophy* 14, no. 2 (1991): 155-64.

Norman Freund, "If It's Tuesday, This Must be Bentham," *Teaching Philosophy* 16, no. 4 (1993): 315-25.

Jonathan Bennett, "Translating Locke, Berkeley, and Hume into English," *Teaching Philosophy*, 17, no. 3 (1994): 262-69.

Week 9:

History of Philosophy (II)

Anne Marie Bowery, "Drawing Shadows on the Wall: Teaching Plato's Allegory of the Cave," *Teaching Philosophy* 24, no. 2 (2001): 121-33.

Mark O. Gilbertson, "A Meeting-of-Minds' Discussion as a Final Exam in History of Philosophy," *In the Socratic Tradition*: 181-84.

Merold Westphal, "A User-Friendly Copernican Revolution," *In the Socratic Tradition*: 187-91.

James P. Cadello, "Charting Kant," *In the Socratic Tradition*: 193-96.

John McCumber, "On Teaching Hegel: Problems and Possibilities," *In the Socratic Tradition*: 197-207.

Merold Westphal, "Hegel and Family Values," *In the Socratic Tradition*: 209-13.

Richard Hogan, "Teaching Nietzsche," *In the Socratic Tradition*: 215-23.

Aesthetics; Philosophy of Religion; Other Areas of Philosophy

Ronald Moore, "The Case Method Approach to the Teaching of Aesthetics," *In the Socratic Tradition*: 107-18.

Louis Pojman, "Teaching Philosophy of Religion," *In the Socratic Tradition*: 121-32.

Michael Martin, "Three Courses in Philosophy of Religion," *In the Socratic Tradition*: 133-42.

Week 10:

Issues of Race, Gender, Culture, and Diversity

Martin Benjamin, "Diversity and Pluralism in the Curriculum," *Teaching Philosophy* 14, no. 2 (1991): 123-26.

Lawrence Blum, "Philosophy and the Values of a Multicultural Community," *Teaching Philosophy* 14, no. 2 (1991): 127-34.

Valerie E. Broin, "Integrating Critical Analysis: Philosophy with a Multicultural and Gender Focus," *Teaching Philosophy*, 16, no. 4 (1993): 301-14.

Charles Mills, "Non-Cartesian Sums: Philosophy and the African-American Experience," *Teaching Philosophy*, 17, no. 3 (1994): 223-43.

Kayley Vernallis, "Pearls of Wisdom: An Exercise in Promoting Multicultural Understanding and Philosophical Engagement," *Teaching Philosophy* 23:1 (2000): 43-51.

Evaluation

Kenneth R. Howe, "An Evaluation Primer for Philosophy Teachers," *Teaching Philosophy*, 11, no. 4 (1988): 315-28.

Kenneth R. Howe, "Evaluating Philosophy Teaching: Assessing Student Mastery of Philosophical Objectives in Nursing Ethics," *Teaching Philosophy* 5, no. 1 (1982): 11-22.

Week 11:

Service Learning

Patrick Fitzgerald, "Service-Learning and the Socially Responsible Ethics Class," *Teaching Philosophy* 20, no. 3 (1997): 251-67.

Stephen L. Esquith, "War, Political Violence, and Service Learning," *Teaching Philosophy* 23, no. 3 (2000): 241-54.

Teachers-Student Relationships: May They Include Friendship and Love?

Peter J. Markie, "Professors, Students, and Friendship," in Steven M. Cahn, ed., *Morality, Responsibility, and the University: Studies in Academic Ethics* (Philadelphia: Temple University Press, 1990): 134-49.

Rodger Jackson and Peter L. Hagen, "The Ethics of Faculty-Student Friendships," *Teaching Philosophy* 24, no. 1 (2001): 1-18.

Rosemary Putnam Tong, "Consensual Sex: Close Encounters of a Dangerous Kind," *Teaching Philosophy* 22, no. 2 (1999): 123-33.

Week 12:

Syllabi and Sample Assignments for Introductory and Specialized Courses Prepared by Participants in the Seminar (I) and (II)

Weeks 13-15:

Work-in-Progress: Discussion of Students' Abstracts/Outlines and Drafts of Term Papers

Written Requirements for the Seminar

1. *Short Papers*: Seminar Participants will review two books as if they had been invited to do so by the book review editor of *Teaching Philosophy*. The instructor will provide the guidelines that the journal distributes to book reviewers. All participants will first review the most recent edition of Anthony Weston's (very short) *A Rulebook for Arguments*. This review is due during the sixth week of class. The second review may be on a comparatively recent book of the seminar participant's choosing (possibly from a list of books awaiting review by *Teaching Philosophy*). This review is due in class seven weeks after the first review.

2. *Term Paper*: A term paper in the form of a possible article for *Teaching Philosophy* will be due on the second day of exam week. The paper may be entirely free-standing or it may continue a dialogue or develop a theme that has already been initiated in the pages of this journal. Participants are strongly encouraged to peruse past volumes of the journal in the library to get the feel of

nearly 25 years of dialogical publication in the area. Seminar participants are encouraged to meet with the instructor to explore possible topics and the structure of the paper.

Thirteen copies of a one-page Prospectus for the term papers should be submitted five weeks before the term paper is due. The prospectus should include: (a) a clear, brief statement of the problem or issue to be addressed; (b) indication of how the author proposes to address the problem or issue; and (c) a preliminary bibliography.

Copies of each participant's prospectus will be distributed to the other seminar participants; the instructor will make comments on each student's prospectus and return it to its author in class four days after it is due.

3. *Sample Syllabi*: Seminar participants will prepare syllabi and sample assignments for both an introductory course in philosophy and a more advanced course related to the participant's area of specialization or special interest in philosophy. These syllabi will be due in class in week 11 and will provide the focus of discussion for week 12. We will discuss each participant's syllabi.

4. *Reflections Papers*: Eight very short papers (no more than one double-spaced page) will be due in class once a week beginning with week two. In these papers students will respond to two different questions: (1) What, to your mind, is the most interesting or important unanswered question (that is, a question that is important but to which there is, at this point, no clear or obvious answer) raised in or by the class meeting prior to the day the paper is due, and why? And (2) What, to your mind, is the most interesting or important point raised in or by the reading assigned for the day the paper is due, and why?

These papers are due at the beginning of class. They will be read, evaluated, and returned at the following class meeting. Late papers will be accepted only in very unusual circumstances and only if cleared with the instructor in advance. Late papers not arranged in advance will receive a grade of 0.0. To do well on these papers, students must answer the question being asked.

Students in the first half of the alphabet will submit their Reflections papers on Tuesdays for the first five weeks in which they are due and on Thursdays after this. Students in the second half of the alphabet will submit Reflections papers on Thursdays for the first five weeks in which they are due and on Tuesdays after this.

Since each student will have eight opportunities to write the ten papers, there will be no makeups except in cases of extended serious illness or family emergency. Students may, if they wish, write up to ten reflections papers, in which case only the best eight will be considered for purposes of the final grade.

Final Grades

The first book review will count 10 percent, the second 24 percent, for a total of 34 percent of the final grade. The Reflection papers count 2 percent each, for a total of 16 percent; and the term paper counts 50 percent. Improvement in written work and informed, thoughtful, and fairly regular participation in seminar meetings will also be considered in determining the final grade.

Commentary on the Requirements of the Course

In evaluating the two short papers which take the form of book reviews for *Teaching Philosophy*, and the term paper, which is written as article for *Teaching Philosophy*, I stress professional standards and writing for publication. I encourage students to read and re-read Bennett and Gorovitz's "Improving Academic Writing"[5] and identify, and deduct for, writing that does not come up to professional standards. A seminar on teaching is a good place to do this because the subject matter is, as a rule, not as technical and difficult for students to master as it is in other seminars. In other seminars students may need to spend so much time understanding the material and finding something useful to say about it that they may have little or no time to bring their writing up to professional standards. A seminar on teaching, however, provides a good opportunity for this sort of development. And, in fact, a number of book reviews written for this seminar have found their way into print in the pages of the journal *Teaching Philosophy* or *AAPT* (American Association of Philosophy Teachers) *News*.

I have found it useful to invite members of my department—logicians, historians of philosophy, and those with experience in using debate in the classroom and in service-learning—to join us when the class is discussing matters in which they have expertise. This is a useful practice, for not only are we joined by faculty who know more about the subject matter than I do, but it also shows that such seminars are not, as Eble puts it, "the property of the teaching specialist; rather they are the common enterprise of faculty and students in a relationship of colleagues."

The last three weeks of the seminar are a work-in-progress seminar where each participant presents an abstract, or outline, or part or all of a draft of his or her term paper, and receives constructive comments on the work from other seminar participants. Not only does each participant receive help with his or her own paper, but he or she also learns from what the others are doing. I try to remain silent during these in-class discussions, but take notes and send authors comments via e-mail later that night. The work-in-progress part of the seminar has great educational value and contributes to better, more polished and professional final papers.

Finally, the Reflections papers, which I use in every course I teach, from introductory courses to graduate seminars, provide practice in finding good, unanswered philosophical questions. Getting the hang of identifying important, unanswered questions is part of being a good philosopher, but it's also vital to good teaching. One of the most important things we do as teachers is writing good paper assignments and exam questions—questions that exercise the student's capacity for independent philosophical reflection, extending their vision and deepening their thought. The Reflections papers give seminar participants practice in finding good questions; and they assure that at each meeting of the seminar at least half of the participants have done the reading carefully and reflected on it.

Though not included in the syllabus, our discussions are often enriched by the students' own past or current experiences as teachers or teaching assistants. Since the seminar is restricted to those in the PhD program, nearly all participants will have had extensive experience in the classroom. Discussions of their past frustrations

as teachers or their daily experiences as teachers are an important
component of the seminar.

NOTES

1. Kenneth E. Eble, *The Craft of Teaching* (San Francisco: Jossey-Bass,
1977): 192.

2. When I offered this required 3-credit semester-long seminar on
teaching for the first time in spring 2000, eight students enrolled. When the
course was repeated two years later, it had an enrollment of thirteen
students.

3. **EDITOR'S NOTE**: The seriousness with which Kant took himself as
a teacher may be found in his account of how he planned his courses in
logic, metaphysics, ethics and geography for the winter semester of
academic year 1765-1766. This account is published in his *Nachricht von der
Hinrichtung seiner Vorlesungen in dem Winterhalbenjahre von 1765-1766*
(*Gesammelte Schriften* II, 305ff, Berlin Academy Edition).

This brief essay—7-8 pages—was called to my attention by Professor
Bert P. Helm. It appeared in English translation, by Eugene Kelly, under
the title *Immanuel Kant: Information Concerning the Organization of His
Lectures for the Winter Semester of 1765-1766* in the *APA Newsletter on
Teaching Philosophy* 89, no. 1 (fall 1989): 24-28.

4. John Ladd, "Kant as a Teacher," *Teaching Philosophy* 5, no. 1 (January
1982): 1.

5. Jonathan Bennett and Samuel Gorovitz, "Improving Academic
Writing," *Teaching Philosophy* 20 (June 1997): 105-20.

ABOUT THE CONTRIBUTORS

Jonathan E. Adler (*Brooklyn College and the Graduate School, The City University of New York*) is president of the Association for Philosophy of Education. He most recently published *Belief's Own Ethics* (MIT Press, 2002).

Martin Benjamin (*Michigan State University*) is a member of the Editorial Board of *Teaching Philosophy*. His most recent book is *Philosophy and This Actual World: An Introduction to Practical Philosophical Inquiry* (Rowman & Littlefield, 2003).

James P. Cadello (*Central Washington University*–Ellensburg) is an advocate of the interactive classroom who uses various methods including charts and other visual aids to engage students in philosophical thinking and learning.

Steven M. Cahn (*The Graduate School and University Center, The City University of New York*) has published numerous books, including *Scamps: Ethics in Academia* and *Puzzles & Perplexities: Collected Essays* (both published by Rowman & Littlefield).

Joan C. Callahan (*University of Kentucky*) is Professor of Philosophy and Director of Women's Studies. She has published four books and numerous articles in ethics, social and political philosophy, and philosophy of law.

Jo A. Chern left teaching several years ago and now runs a successful business in Madison, Wisconsin where she lives with her husband, the director of a private nonprofit agency.

Stephen H. Daniel (*Texas A&M University*–College Station) is author of *Current Continental Philosophy* (Prentice Hall, 2004) and editor of *Current Continental Theory and Modern Philosophy* (Prentice Hall, 2004) Steven H. Daniel has written books on Jonathan Edwards, myth, and John Toland.

Juli Eflin (*Ball State University*) is chair of her department. Her specialty areas are epistemology and philosophy of science. Her most recent publication is "Epistemic Presuppositions and their Consequences," *Metaphilosophy* 34 (January 2003).

Carrie Figdor (*Bernard Baruch College, The City University of New York*) teaches philosophy at a variety of colleges in the New York area. She has been a Writing Fellow at the Graduate School and University Center, CUNY, and is completing her PhD dissertation in philosophy of mind.

Newton Garver (*State University of New York at Buffalo*) has authored *This Complicated Form of Life* (Open Court, 1994); and (with Seung-Chong Lee) *Derrida & Wittgenstein* (Temple University Press, 1994). He is editor (with James B. Brady) of *Justice, Law, and Violence* (Temple University Press, 1991).

Theodore A. Gracyk (*Moorehead State University-Minnesota*) writes on informal logic, history of philosophy, and philosophy of art. Among his publications are *Rhythm and Noise: An Aesthetics of Rock* (Duke University Press, 1996) and "Listening to Music: Performances and Recordings," *Journal of Aesthetics and Art Criticism* 55, no. 2 (spring 1997).

Lawrence M. Hinman (*University of Sandiego*) is Professor of Philosophy and Director of the Values Institute at the University of San Diego. He is editor of Ethics Updates, a World Wide Web site devoted to ethical theory and applied ethics, and is the author of *Ethics: A Pluralistic Approach to Moral Theory*, 3rd ed. (Wadsworth, 2002) and *Contemporary Moral Issues*, 2nd ed. (Prentice Hall, 2003).

Eugene Kelly (*New York Institute of Technology*) has written extensively on Max Scheler, most recently, *Structure and Diversity: Studies in the Phenomenological Philosophy of Max Scheler* (Dordrecht: Kluwer, 1997). He has published several textbooks and anthologies, and has written for *Journal of Value Inquiry*, the *Journal of Aesthetic Education*, and *Aletheia*.

David B. Martens (*Auburn University*) has research and teaching interests in epistemology, metaphysics, logic, and ethics. He has served as a member of the editorial board of the *APA Newsletter on Teaching Philosophy* since 1992.

Michael Martin (Professor Emeritus, *Boston University*) has authored several books including: *Legal Realism* (Peter Lang, 1997); *The Legal Philosophy of H. L. A. Hart; Atheism: A Philosophical Justification;* and *The Case Against Christianity* (all with Temple University Press, 1987, 1990 and 1991 respectively).

John J. McDermott (*Texas A&M University*-College Station) is General Editor of the twelve-volume Critical Edition of *The Correspondence of William James* (University Press of Virginia). He is the recipient of the Danforth Foundation's E. Harris Harbison National Award for Gifted Teaching.

John McCumber (*Northwestern University*) is currently professor of Germanic Studies at UCLA. Among his publications are: *Metaphysics and Oppression: Heidegger's Challenge to Western Philosophy* (Indiana University Press, 2000) and *Time in the Ditch: American Philosophy and the McCarthy Era* (Northwestern University Press, 2001).

Marshall Missner (*University of Wisconsin-Oshkosh*) has published works in the areas of ethics, the history of philosophy, and the history of science. He is author of "The Skeptical Basis of Hobbes' Political Philosophy, *"Journal of the History of Ideas* 44, no. 3 (1983) and "Why Einstein Became Famous in America," *Social Studies in Science* 15 (1985).

Kathleen Dean Moore (*Oregon State University*) is a Master Teacher and Director of the Spring Creek Project for Ideas, Nature, and the Written Word. Among other books, she has authored: *Pardons: Justice, Mercy, and the Public Interest* (Oxford University Press, 1989) and *Riverwalking: Reflections on Moving Water* (The Lyons Press, 1995).

Ronald Moore (*University of Washington*) is the author of *Legal Norms and Legal Science* (University Press of Hawaii, 1978) and *Aesthetics for Young People* (National Art Education Association, 1995) as well as co-author of *Puzzles about Art* (St. Martin's Press, 1989). He has published numerous articles and is the recipient of a Distinguished Teaching Award from his university, a Donald Petersen fellowship for Excellence in Teaching, and a Charles Odegaard award for contributions to minority education.

Louis P. Pojman (*United States Military Academy, West Point*) received the Burlington Northern Award for Outstanding Teaching and Scholarship, as well as the Outstanding Humanities Teacher Award at University of Mississippi. His many books include *Religious Belief and the Will* (Routledge & Kegan Paul, 1986), *Philosophy of Religion: An Anthology, 4th ed.* (Wadsworth, 2001), and *Global Political Philosophy* (McGraw Hill, 2002).

Merold Westphal (*Fordham University*) has authored books on Hegel, Kierkegaard, and philosophy of religion, among which are: *Hegel, Freedom and Modernity* (State University of New York Press, 1992); *Becoming a Self: A Reading of Kierkegaard's Concluding Unscientific Postscript* (Purdue University Press, 1996); *Suspicion and Faith: The Religious Uses of Modern Atheism* (Fordham University Press, 1998); and *Overcoming Onto-Theology* (Fordham University Press, 2001).

Anthony Weston (*Elon University*) is author of *A Rulebook for Arguments* (Hackett, 1987, 1992, 2000); *Toward Better Problems* (Temple University Press, 1992); *Back to Earth: Tomorrow's Environmentalism* (Temple University Press, 1994); *A Practical Companion to Ethics* (Oxford University Press, 1997); and *A 21st Century Ethical Toolbox* (Oxford University Press, 2001).

V. Alan White (*University of Wisconsin-*Manitowoc) has published in *Teaching Philosophy, Analysis, Philosophy* and other journals. Professor White is a former Carnegie—CASE Wisconsin Professor of the Year.

Celia Wolf-Devine (*Stonehill College*) is the author of *Descartes on Seeing: Epistemology and Visual Perception* (Southern Illinois University Press, 1993) and *Diversity and Community in the Academy: Affirmative Action in Faculty Appointments* (Rowman & Littlefield, 1997). She is co-author of *Sex and Gender: A Spectrum of Views* (Wadsworth, 2002).

ABOUT THE EDITOR

Tziporah Kasachkoff (*Ben Gurion University of the Negev* and *The City University of New York*) has been editor of the *APA Newsletter on Teaching Philosophy* since 1986 and joint editor (with Eugene Kelly) of the *Newsletter* since 1994. In 2000 she received the American Association of Philosophy Teachers' Award of Merit for Outstanding Leadership and Achievements in the Teaching of Philosophy.

For most of Professor Kasachkoff's teaching career, she has taught simultaneously at both ends of the educational spectrum—at a community college where students first encounter philosophy as an academic discipline and at a graduate center whose students are studying for their masters and doctoral degrees in philosophy. In addition to her interest in the teaching of philosophy, her professional interests are in political, social, and legal philosophy, with special emphasis on issues that arise in the context of health care and, more recently, morally justified self-defense.

Professor Kasachkoff's articles have appeared as chapters in philosophy anthologies, as well as in such journals as *Canadian Journal of Philosophy, International Journal of Applied Philosophy, Informal Logic, The Mount Sinai Journal of Medicine, Law and Philosophy, Social Theory and Practice, Substance Use and Misuse, Philosophical Studies, The Philosophical Forum,* and *Journal of Philosophy and Medicine.*

Kasachkoff edited the first edition of this volume under the title *In the Socratic Tradition: Essays on Teaching Philosophy* (Rowman & Littlefield, 1998). She is also the editor, with Steven Cahn, of *Morality and Public Policy* (Prentice Hall, 2002).